CENTRAL PLACES
IN SOUTHERN GERMANY

CENTRAL PLACES IN SOUTHERN GERMANY

Walter Christaller

Translated from
DIE ZENTRALEN ORTE IN SÜDDEUTSCHLAND
by
Carlisle W. Baskin
Randolph-Macon College

PRENTICE-HALL, INC. Englewood Cliffs, New Jersey

Current printing (last digit):

10   9   8   7   6   5   4   3   2   1

Library of Congress Catalog Card No. 66-14747

Preface

With the increasing interest in the study of the spatial dispersion of economic and social activity by geographers, sociologists, economists, and others, it was almost inevitable that a translation of Professor Walter Christaller's *Die zentralen Orte in Süddeutschland* should be made. Some investigators have employed a reading knowledge of German to incorporate the contents of this work in their own studies. However, such "translations" were from the somewhat specialized needs and interest of the individual geographer or other researcher. The present translation was undertaken to provide a more general and comprehensive treatment of Christaller's concepts and scheme. My belief in the importance of such a translation has been confirmed by numerous requests for copies from researchers in the United States, South Africa, the United Kingdom, and Australia, and from such disciplines as sociology, geography, demography, and economics.

Die zentralen Orte in Süddeutschland reveals Christaller's dedication to the study of settlement-geography. His academic training shows depth and breadth, and, in a day of specialization, it is encouraging to discover a writer who is versed in so many social science fields. He did much of his work at the University of Erlangen, where he studied under Robert Gradmann. The high scholarship of his work represents meticulous care in research, and his copious bibliography contained in the notes of the translation is probably the best that could have been compiled during the period in which he wrote.

Christaller brought a comprehensive view and concrete approach to the study of the spatial structure of a social system. Whereas von Thünen studied the relation of the location of the various types of agriculture to a population center, and Alfred Weber studied the location of industry to the factors of transportation, labor, and agglomeration, Christaller attempted to study an entire economic system, which was spatially-oriented, -coordinated, and -located. He incorporated political, social, economic, and geographic factors into his investigation.

The main contributions of the book were not the particular spatial pattern and measurements derived, but the systematic attempt to designate certain attributes of the spatial strucure of a large, highly populated area. The methods discussed and selected, and the measurements made and compiled, show deliberateness and thoughtful comprehension of some basic economic relationships. Although conditions have changed and the specific results of Christaller's study are now somewhat out of date, his contribution to the method and procedures for investigating the organized relationships and functions of an economic system from its spatial point of view has not diminished. His work has served as a model and point of departure to present-day researchers in social science. Their works have filled in certain veiled areas of knowledge in this field. Contemporaries have referred to the work of Christaller because they saw in his efforts and formulation the means of improving the results of their own research. The spatial aspects of human life and such matters as distance, population density, and values of goods and their markets are of increasing interest to industry and commerce.

The Table of Contents indicates something about his technique of research. Propositions are set forth, terms are defined and made explicit, a method of measurement is developed, appropriate data are collected and analyzed, and the results are compared with his theoretical scheme and explanations of incongruity are made. These explanations are somewhat unsatisfactory in that too much rationalization and arbitrary decision-making were used to fit the places of southern Germany into the theoretical scheme.

Acknowledgments are due certain organizations and individuals who played significant roles in the project of the translation. It originally was suggested by Dr. Rutledge Vining and was sponsored by the Bureau of Population and Economic Research at the University of Virginia. Adolph Presber and Owe Peters, exchange students from Germany, aided in the translation and offered many helpful facts about the geography and economy of southern Germany. Carl H. Madden and Jere W. Clark, fellow researchers, read and criticized all of the translation, thereby increasing its usefulness. Miss Mary Bersch, whose interest was exceeded only by the writer and his family, performed the arduous task of typing the original draft. I would be remiss if I did not state that the author, Walter Christaller, was cooperative, interested, and enthusiastic about the prospect of bringing out the translation. If there is any dedication to be made, it should be to him for his original conception and scholarly research. I hope this translation will bring him the recognition he so justly deserves.

Carlisle W. Baskin

Table of Contents

Introduction   1

Are there laws which determine the number, sizes, and distribution of towns? 1   Some remarks about the plan and sources of the study under investigation, 4

I. THE THEORETICAL PART:
ECONOMIC-THEORETICAL FOUNDATIONS OF TOWN GEOGRAPHY   13

A. Fundamental Meanings   14

Centralization as a principle of order, 15   Central places, 16 Importance and centrality, 17   Central goods and services, 19 The complementary region, 21   The economic distance and the range of a good, 22

B. Static Relations   27

Introduction: The consumption of central goods and the development of central places, 27   The distribution of the population of central places, 28   The density and structure of the population, 33   The central goods, 35   The region, 43   The traffic, 47   The range of central goods, 49   The system of central places, 58

C. Dynamic Processes   84

Introduction: The dynamic point of view, 84   The population, 85   The central goods, 90   Production costs and technical progress, 95   The region, 101   The traffic, 104   The range of central goods, 107   The dynamic aspects of a system of central places, 111   Business cycle, 126

D. Results   133

General and Special Economic Theory, 133

II. THE CONNECTING PART: APPLICATION OF THE THEORY OF LOCATION TO THE ACTUAL GEOGRAPHY OF SETTLEMENTS   137

A. The Method of Determination of Central Places   139
The importance of a place, 139   The centrality of a place, 147

B. Preliminary Results   152
*The central places, 152   The other elements of the system, 159
The systems, 164*

III. THE REGIONAL PART: THE NUMBER, SIZES, AND DISTRIBUTION OF THE CENTRAL PLACES IN SOUTHERN GERMANY   169

A. The *L*-System of Munich   170
The Basic Facts, 170
*The L-center, 170   The L-directions lines, 171   The P-places,
172   The G-places, 173*

An Analysis of the Individual G-Systems, 175
*The P-system of Munich, 175   The P-system of Augsburg, 180
The alpine system, 182   The eastern G-systems, 184*
Results, 307

IV. CONCLUSION   189

A. Verification of the Theory   190
*Laws of distribution, 190   Tertiary deviations explainable by
economics, 192   Deviations not explainable by economics, 195*

B. Methodological Results for the Geography of Settlements   198
*The economic method in the geography of settlements, 198
Other methods of the geography of settlements, 199   National
economy or economic geography, 201*

APPENDIX   203
Frequency Distributions of the *L*-Systems of Munich, Nuremberg,
Stuttgart, Strassburg, Frankfurt, and Southern Germany, 203
The *L*-System of Munich, 204

BIBLIOGRAPHY   228
Books, 228
Articles, 229

CENTRAL PLACES
IN SOUTHERN GERMANY

Introduction

1. Are There Laws Which Determine
the Number, Sizes, and Distribution of Towns?

In recent literature on geographical settlements, following the example of Gradmann, rural and urban settlements have been sharply distinguished from one another.[1] Gradmann speaks very correctly of "two things as different at the root as the village and the town."[2] The root of the village is distinct: it is typically agriculture and other land uses. The connection between the number of people living in villages and on farms, and the size of land area is stated in this manner: There are as many people in a given area as can live from the cultivation of the land with given agricultural technology and organization. Whether these people live in large settlements, i.e., large closed villages, or in smaller villages, hamlets, or on individual farms is not clear *a priori*. However, the investigations of Gradmann and others have clarified the issue, for they say that a particular type of settlement is usually predominant within a certain region.

The situation with towns is somewhat different. In the same region we see large and small towns of all categories, one category beside another. Sometimes they agglomerate in certain regions in an improbable and apparently senseless manner. Sometimes there are large regions in which not a single place deserves the designation of town, or even of market. It is usually asserted that the connection between the town and the professional activity of its inhabitants is not accidental, but rather is based upon the nature of both. But why are there, then, large and small towns, and why are they distributed so irregularly?

We seek answers to these questions. We seek the causes of towns being large or small, because we believe that there is some ordering principle heretofore unrecognized that governs their distribution.

These questions are dealt with not only by geographers,[3] but also by historians, sociologists, economists,[4] and statisticians. But only once was there a significant attempt to find the real laws determining the distribution and sizes of towns. It was made almost 100 years ago by Kohl.[5] The conclusions of this attempt have been oddly contradictory, and Kohl has been strongly criticized for straying too far from nature. For example, Ratzel said that one cannot deviate so far from the "truth" (he meant reality) if one is to still have something scientifically useful.[6] Hassert said that because nature is so diverse, one should refrain from trying to order it into a scheme easily constructed on the basis of statistical figures.[7] Hettner, on the other hand, acknowledged the value of the work by stating that Kohl arrived at rules, "most of which may still claim validity today." [8] Schlüter stated that the task of tracing the traffic net back to theoretically fundamental laws had been solved, "once and for all," [9] by Kohl. And Sax constructed his own theory on the basis of the "laws of traffic routes" formulated by Kohl.[10] Kohl's ingenious attempt to discover laws governing the sizes and distribution of towns failed, not because he proceeded too abstractly, but because he started with suppositions which were basically wrong. Evidence for this conclusion will be provided later.

But how can we find a general explanation for the sizes, number, and distribution of towns? How can we discover the laws?

Can purely geographical inquiry produce them? It begins, as a rule, with topographical and geographical conditions and then explains simply that here a town "had to originate," [11] and, if the location is favorable, that here especially a town "had to develop favorably." But there are innumerable locations, where no town is found, that are equally or even more favorable. In fact, towns may be found in very unfavorable spots, and those towns, circumstances permitting, may even be fairly large. Neither the number, nor the distribution, nor the sizes of towns can be explained by their location in respect to the geographical conditions of nature.[12] Hettner demonstrated in 1902 the importance of an investigation into the number of settlements and the average distances between settlements of the same economic character.[13] Since that time, such factors are seldom missing from monographs on the geography of settlements. Nonetheless, up to now, no one has obtained clear, generally valid laws in this manner.

Could, perhaps, a historical investigation divulge a general answer? If the development of all towns from their earliest beginnings up to their present state were investigated in detail, one could discern laws from this material which have a definite distinction, regionally and in point of time. One can find a certain order in diversity, but the principle of order itself can never be found through historical investigation alone. This concept was recognized by the historical school of economics, which brought to light abundant factual material, but which could never obtain valid economic laws with its historical method.[14]

Finally, can the statistical method help us? One can compute the town-density of a region and the average distance between towns; one can establish size-classes and record the number of towns belonging to each class; and one can find, in this manner, frequencies and averages, perhaps certain regularities, and frequently existing combinations of particular phenomena. The logical proof that these are genuine laws, however, can never be furnished by statistics alone.[15]

If the geography of settlements* were a discipline of the natural sciences, or at least predominantly such a discipline, as some authors almost appear to consider it, there would be no question but that the laws of natural science would apply, for every natural phenomenon is governed by such laws. But we believe that the geography of settlements is a discipline of the social sciences. It is quite obvious that for the creation, development, and decline of towns to occur, a demand must exist for the things which the town can offer. Thus, economic factors are decisive for the existence of towns. For the existence of rural settlements, the houses of which are all simultaneously places of production, economic factors are manifestly decisive. Therefore, the geography of settlements is a part of economic geography. Like economic geography, it must draw upon economic theory if it is to explain the character of towns. If there are now laws of economic theory, then there must be also laws of the geography of settlements, economic laws of a special character, which we shall call *special economic-geographical laws*. The question of whether there really are economic laws cannot be dealt with here; we believe that there are such laws, and so agree with the great majority of economists.[16] These laws, to be sure, are of a different type from natural laws, but no less "valid" on that account. They should, perhaps, be designated not as *laws*, but, more conveniently, as *tendencies*, because they are not so inexorable as natural laws. But the terminology is not so important when one is not dealing with abstract theoretical research. It will suffice

---

* The term "*Siedlungsgeographie*," or *settlement-geography*, does not mean simply the study of a particular settlement or community, nor even that of a few settlements. It is instead understood by this translator to mean the study of how a given large area of the world's surface is colonized or settled. Christaller here wants to find the order or regularity with which any large land area is settled. He asks the question: Are there laws which determine the number, distribution, and sizes of settlements? and strives to find an answer. His investigation is thus one of the geographical and economic developments of a given land area.

for us to keep in mind the fact that there are economic laws which determine the life of the economy, and that there are also, consequently, special economic-geographical laws, such as those which determine the sizes, distribution, and number of towns.[17] Therefore, it does not seem senseless to search for such laws.

A second question is still open: What is to be understood by the term *town?* The answer to this question will be given in Part I.*

2. Some Remarks About the Plan and Sources of the Study Under Investigation

Following are the reasons why the usual method of those engaged in geographical investigations will be discarded in the construction of the study under consideration. The procedure employed here is more synthetic in Part I and more analytical in Part III.† The plan of the work is to be concrete throughout. The facts of sizes, number, and distribution of the towns in southern Germany will be established and clarified. The work will begin, however, not with a descriptive statement of reality, but with a general and purely deductive theory. It is unfortunately necessary to go that far back because up to now there has been no really coherent theory concerning the economic foundations of towns; such a theory is indispensable, however, if we are to seek conformity to law (*Gesetzmäßigkeiten*).

Hence, we have a practical reason for beginning with the theory. This theory, which will be indispensable in the later demonstration and analysis of economics, will be developed, and an introduction to the economic presentation will be given. Then the fundamental classifications of previous studies will be considered. The theory, from a disciplinary point of view, cannot be derived inductively, but only deductively. It is, therefore, unnecessary to begin with a description of reality.[18] Hence, the theory has a validity completely independent of what reality looks like, but only by virtue of its logic and "the sense of adequacy" [19] (*Sinnadäquanz*).‡ When this *eo ipso* theory is confronted with reality,

---

* See Part I, "The Theoretical Part: Economic-Theoretical Foundations of Town Geography."

† See Part III: A, "The *L*-System of Munich."

‡ *Sinnadäquanz* is formed by the word *Sinn* (in the sense of, sense) and *adäquat* (adequate), the word being a special one for Max Weber. It is extremely difficult to translate into English the meaning intended by Weber, or Christaller for that matter. A. M. Henderson and Talcott Parsons, in their translation of *Grundriss der Sozialökonomik*, have preferred "adequacy on the level of meaning," as the translation of *"Sinnhafte adäquat."* *Sinnadäquanz* is presumably a shortening of this phrase. It will be translated in the present study as "the satisfying level of knowledge," which Henderson and Parsons insisted is what Weber meant. It may be here understood simply to mean "the current attainments of economic knowledge."

it becomes clear to what extent reality corresponds to theory, to what extent it is explained by it, and in what respects reality does not correspond with the theory and is therefore not explained by it. The unexplained facts must then be clarified by historical and geographical methods, because they involve personal, historical, and naturally conditioned resistances—factors which cause deviations from theory. They have nothing to do with the theory itself, and above all cannot be cited directly as proof against the validity of the theory.[20] Alfred Weber, who followed the same method with great success in his location theory,[21] has termed this method *verification of the theory*.

It should be stressed that the theory offered here is not complete. We set forth only such relationships and developments as are of considerable importance for the clarification of the concrete questions asked here. Therefore, the theory is not developed strictly systematically, but rather pragmatically.

Between the theoretical and the regional parts of this book a connecting part will be inserted,* in which methods and principles will be developed to aid in determining which places currently and concretely have the function of towns, how their size can be demonstrated statistically, and how far their influence extends.

Thus the four parts of the study will be: Part I, the presentation of a theory; Part II, the development of a method in order to comprehend reality more exactly; Part III, the description and clear individual demonstrations of reality; and finally, Part IV, the conclusion and the verification of the general geography of settlement theory.

Concerning the origin of the theoretical foundations, which was discussed in the first part of this Introduction, something may be added: The theory of the newer theoretical economics largely came from a combination of the classical theory (Adam Smith, Ricardo, and Thünen); the work of the marginal utility school (Menger and von Wieser); and the sociological approach of the younger historical school (especially Sombart and Max Weber).

Unfortunately, theoretical economics concerns itself far too little with the spatial relationships and the influence of space,[22] and far too much with the time element, as shown by Böhm-Bawerk,[23] and, more recently, by Cassel,[24] as well as by studies of the business cycles.[25] The Harms School strove to investigate the spatial aspects and to incorporate them into economic theory.[26] Harms had already drawn attention[27] to the theoretical foundations then existing, as well as to the dissimilarities between national economics and world economics resulting from differences in spatial extension. One can also derive, with equal correctness, a theory of small economies,[28] which would include above all the local

---

* See Part II, "The Connecting Part."

market relationships, the sociological neighboring community relationships, and the home relationships in their peculiar structure. The terms introduced by this group—*"spatial economy"* and even *"spatial structure"* [29] (which have not been accepted)—are, incidentally, indistinct and therefore not to be recommended. What is meant is the economic-theoretical treatment of spatial relationships and developments, for example, the consideration that all economic activity takes place in spatial relationships and that the theoretical analysis of concrete economic phenomena (*Gebilde*) includes all of its concrete spatial and temporal connections. Developing the ideas and challenges of Harms further, Weigmann has more recently published the promising "Ideas of a Theory of Spatial Economics," [30] in which, for example, the term *economic regions* would take its position in the structure of economic theory. Of the older authors, Eugen Dühring has examined spatial questions theoretically,[31] while Albert Schäffle mentions such questions, but does not treat them from the theoretical point of view.[32] On the treatment of general geographical problems by representative economists, P. H. Schmidt gives an excellent survey.[33]

That each economic relationship and each economic event are, without exception, related to space and that the spatial relation is also a constituent element of these relationships are facts of which only a few economists are fully aware. But when these spatial relationships are illuminated by economic theory, and their special laws are exposed, they prove very fruitful, not only for economics, but also for geography. Therefore, the economist, as well as the geographer, must return to the fundamental and guiding work of von Thünen, *The Isolated State*,[34] if he wishes to solve economic-geographical problems. Thünen deals primarily with agricultural aspects. He seeks to find according to what economic laws the spatial distribution of different agricultural production is established. His method of isolating and mathematically treating the isolated elements has become indispensable for all investigations into economic theory. It is surprising that reference is made so rarely in geographical literature to this important economic-geographical work, with the praiseworthy exception of von Sapper, who applies the teachings of Thünen in his *General Economic and Traffic Geography*,[35] and of Lautensach, who refers to it in his *General Geography*.[36] In an essay by Pfeifer,[37] which is intended to survey the use of spatial economic terms and conceptions, we find Thünen referred to only briefly and almost insignificantly. In Hermann Wagner's widely read textbook, there are no references to Thünen. On the other hand, P. H. Schmidt[38] gives a detailed evaluation of the importance of this classic in economic-geographical theory.

Alfred Weber continued to build on Thünen, adding a theory of location of industries, which finally reintroduced spatial relationships into economic theory.[39] On this newly created foundation, economists as well as economic geographers continue to build. But only Engländer went so far as to connect all parts of economic theory with spatial relationships. He examines, especially, the dependence of prices—the keystone of economic theory—on the distance from markets and other spatial factors.[40]

Besides the works of these three authors, there are no extensive works which are concerned with the importance of space in economic theory, although there are some smaller works which should be mentioned: von Furlan on the hinterland of seaports,[41] and some important contributions on more specialized problems by Schilling, P. Krebs, von Dobbeler, and Schneider,[42] published by the periodical *Technik und Wirtschaft* under the general heading of "Transportation and Economic Geography." In some respects, "Means of Communication in Political Economies" by Sax[43] is also relevant.

Finally, the *System der Soziologie* by Oppenheimer,[44] which is strongly determined by spatial relationships, should be mentioned. (Terms such as *"market," "cooperatives,"* etc., as used by Oppenheimer, are to be taken as spatially concrete.) Even though this work is very stimulating, there are numerous laws, such as the "law of market sizes," the "law of flows," the "law of transport obstacles," and the "fundamental geocentric law," which are too broad and therefore too inexact to be used in our inquiry.

For the purposes of this work, we must make new paths in order to demonstrate the spatial effects of economic laws and rules on the geography of settlements. The way was prepared by Thünen, Alfred Weber, and Engländer. It should suffice to refer to the works of these authors only once, because reference to special citations must be frequently repeated. The theory developed in Part I* could also be called *the theory of location of the urban trades and institutions,* to correspond with Thünen's theory of location of agricultural production and Alfred Weber's theory of location of industries, for which Engländer had worked out the common framework.

The division of the theory into static and dynamic parts derives mainly from Stucken.[45]

NOTES

1. Robert Gradmann, "Das ländliche Siedlungswesen des Königreichs Württemberg," in *Forschungen zur deutschen Landes- und Volkskunde,* 21, Part I (Stuttgart: 1926).

---

* See Part I, "The Theoretical Part."

Robert Gradmann, "Die städtischen Siedlungen des Königreichs Württemberg," in *ibid.*, Part II.

2. Robert Gradmann, *Süddeutschland* (Stuttgart: 1931), Vol. I, p. 162.

3. The task of answering these questions may have been determined for him since the "science of distance" helped him to explain the "spatial arrangement of the earth's surface." (Friedrich Ratzel, *Anthropogeographie oder Grundzüge der Anwendung der Geographie auf die Geschichte* (Stuttgart: 1882), Part I, p. 177.) Ratzel himself refers to Part I of Ritter's formulation of a "theory of geographic relations." (Carl Ritter, *Einleitung zur allgemeinen vergleichenden Geographie und Abhandlungen zur Begründung einer mehr wissenschaftlichen Behandlung der Erdkunde* (Berlin: 1852), p. 137.) The attempt of Götz to develop a science of distance certainly failed completely. (Wilhelm Götz, *Die Verkehrswege im Dienste des Welthandels: Eine historisch-geographische Untersuchung, samt einer Einleitung für eine "Wissenschaft von den geographischen Entfernungen"* (Stuttgart: 1888), pp. 1-28.)

4. Bücher: A medieval German town was about 4.3 square miles in size, and served, perhaps, thirty to forty farms, villages, and hamlets. "This organization of the settlements illustrates a social order," in which the little town plays a determining role. However, in their functional relations, the town and countryside stand dependent on one another. (Karl Bücher, "Die Großstädte in Gegenwart und Vergangenheit," in "Die Großstadt," *Jahrbuch der Gabestiftung* (Dresden: 1927), 21f.)

Economists have altogether ignored the more geographical question of the distribution of towns; there is still no theory of the location of towns, although the dependencies on the size of the town are frequently considered. Thus, Werner Sombart states, "The size of a town is conditioned by the amount of the products of their supporting regions and the extent of their dividend, which we may call the surplus product." (*Der moderne Kapitalismus* (Munich and Leipzig: 1916), Vol. I, p. 130.) Adam Smith had already stated (Book III, Chap. I, citing Sombart): "It is the surplus produce of the country only . . . that constitutes the subsistence of this surplus produce." This sentence is valid only under conditions of very little traffic development; in modern economic organization of the European-American culture sphere, it applies only in a figurative sense.

Hans Bobek, in his excellent discussion, understands by the expression, "basic questions of town geography," that which has been covered in the current investigations of the expression. To a great extent, it is the "additional product" (surplus output and extra demand, creating a sort of "traffic tension") which determines the practical and actual size of the town (in *Geographischer Anzeiger,* 28th year (Gotha: 1927), 213ff., 221.)

5. Johann Georg Kohl, *Der Verkehr und die Ansiedelungen der Menschen in ihrer Abhängigkeit von der Gestaltung der Erdoberfläche,* 2nd ed. (Leipzig: 1850).

6. Friedrich Ratzel, in *op. cit.,* "Die geographische Verbreitung des Menschen," Part II, p. 466.

7. Kurt Hassert, *Die Städte geographisch betrachtet* (Leipzig: 1907), p. 13.

8. Alfred Hettner, "Der gegenwärtige Stand der Verkehrsgeographie," in *Geographische Zeitschrift,* 3rd year (Leipzig: 1895), 628.

9. Otto Schlüter, "Über die Aufgaben der Verkehrsgeographie im Rahmen der 'Reinen' Geographie," in *Hermann Wagner, Gedächtnisschrift,* Supplement No. 209 of *Petermanns Mitteilungen* (Gotha: 1930), 298-309, cit. 307. Similarly treated: "Die Stellung der Geographie des Menschen in der erdkundlichen Wis-

senschaft," *Die Geographie als Wissenschaft und Lehrfach* (Berlin: 1919), pp. 25ff.

10. Emil Sax, "Die Verkehrsmittel in Volks- und Staatswirtschaft," *Allgemeine Verkehrslehre,* 2nd ed. (Berlin: 1918), Vol. I, pp. 71ff.

11. As Goethe said of Regensburg.

12. Representative of the geographical method are Friedrich Ratzel in his *Anthropogeographie oder Grundzüge der Anwendung der Geographie auf die Geschichte* and Kurt Hassert in his *Die Städte geographisch betrachtet.*

13. Alfred Hettner, "Die wirtschaftlichen Typen der Ansiedelungen," in *Geographische Zeitschrift,* 8th year (Leipzig: 1902), 98.

14. See the extensive literature on the methodological disputes included in "Volkswirtschaft und Volkswirtschaftslehre," in *Die Handwörterbücher der Staatswissenschaften,* 4th ed. (Jena: 1928), Vol. VIII, and recently from all the critical discussion of Werner Sombart, *Die drei Nationalökonomien, Geschichte und System der Lehre von der Wirtschaft* (Munich and Leipzig: 1930).

15. See Hans Jürgen Seraphim, "Statistik und Sozialökonomie," in *Jahrbücher für Nationalökonomie und Statistik,* 3rd series, 76 (1929), 321ff.

16. See Franz Eulenberg, "Sind 'historische Gesetze' möglich?" in *Hauptprobleme der Soziologie, Erinnerungsgabe für Max Weber* (Munich and Leipzig: 1923), Vol. I, pp. 23ff.

Above all, see Werner Sombart, *Die drei Nationalökonomien . . . ,* esp. pp. 248ff., which contain a fundamental and exhaustive discussion of all the comprehensive theoretical and methodical hypotheses of economics.

17. Franz Eulenberg, who investigated economic methods by making an exhaustive study, guided by the "fact that all social cooperating conditions require enlargement in space," found a special group of social laws. He gives, therefore, the "laws of settling . . . , a valid law of the organization of transportation." ("Gesellschaft und Natur." Commencement address in *Archiv für Sozialwissenschaft und Sozialpolitik,* 21 (Tübingen: 1905), 537.)

18. See Werner Sombart, *Die drei Nationalökonomien . . . ,* p. 319: "The 'laws' stand for us, not as an end, but as the beginning of our investigation."

19. The terminology and the whole interpretation in general is taken from Max Weber, as we find it for example in "Wirtschaft und Gesellschaft," in *Grundriß der Sozialökonomie,* 2nd ed. (Tübingen: 1925), Vol. III, Part II.

20. This "system or formulation of the question" corresponds approximately to the "rational scheme" of Sombart and to the "ideal types" of Max Weber. (Otto Schlüter, "Die Stellung der Geographie des Menschen . . . , p. 267.)

21. Alfred Weber, "Über den Standort der Industrien," *Reine Theorie des Standorts,* 2nd ed. (Tübingen: 1922), Part I.

22. See Gerhard Menz, *Irrationales in der Rationalisierung, Mensch und Maschine* (Breslau: 1928). Menz also thinks that the problem of the "rational economic regions" is little known in contrast to the rationalization of the time element in economic life. What is lacking here is the determination of the fundamental facts and relationships.

23. Eugen von Böhm-Bawerk, *Positive Theorie des Kapitals* (Jena: 1921), Vol. I.

24. Gustav Cassel, *Theoretische Sozialökonomie* (Leipzig: 1927), esp. pp. 568ff.

25. For example, Rudolf Stucken, *Die Konjunkturen des Wirtschaftslebens* (Jena: 1932).

26. Mostly published in *Weltwirtschaftliches Archiv* (Jena: about 1913), as well as in the series, *Probleme der Weltwirtschaft* (Jena: n.d.).

27. Bernhard Harms, *Volkswirtschaft und Weltwirtschaft, Versuch der Begründung einer Weltwirtschaftslehre* (Jena: 1912).

28. Hermann Lautensach gives in his *Allgemeine Geographie zur Einführung in die Länderkunde* (Gotha: 1926), p. 290, written with great anthropogeographical understanding, the following independent spatial "Steps of the Distance of Trade-Traffic": (1) individual economy, (2) neighborhood economy, (3) national economy, and (4) world economy.

29. Bernhard Harms, "Strukturwandlungen in der Weltwirtschaft," in *Weltwirtschaftliches Archiv*, 25 (Jena: 1927), 4.

30. Hans Weigmann, "Ideen zu einer Theorie der Raumwirtschaft. Ein Versuch zur Begründung einer realistischen Wirtschaftstheorie," in *Weltwirtschaftliches Archiv*, 34 (Jena: 1931), 1-40.

31. Eugen Dühring, *Kursus der National- und Sozialökonomie*, 2nd ed. (Leipzig: 1876), esp. pp. 81ff.

32. Albert Schäffle, *Das gesellschaftliche System der menschlichen Wirtschaft*, 3rd ed. (Tübingen: 1873), Vol. II.

33. Peter Heinrich Schmidt, *Wirtschaftsforschung und Geographie* (Jena: 1925).

34. Johann Heinrich von Thünen, *Der isolierte Staat in Beziehung auf Landwirtschaft und Nationalökonomie*, 2nd ed. (Jena: 1910).

35. Karl Sapper, *Allgemeine Wirtschafts- und Verkehrsgeographie* (Berlin: 1925), pp. 159f.

36. Hermann Lautensach, *op. cit.*, pp. 317f.

37. Gottfried Pfeifer, "Über raumwirtschaftliche Begriffe und Vorstellungen und ihre bisherige Anwendung in der Geographie und Wirtschaftswissenschaft," in *Geographische Zeitschrift*, 34th year (Leipzig, and Berlin: 1928), 321.

38. Peter Heinrich Schmidt, *op. cit.*, pp. 68ff.

39. See note 21 above. Also: Alfred Weber, "Die industrielle Standortlehre (allgemeine und Kapitalistische Theorie des Standortes)," *Grundriß der Socialökonomie* (Tübingen: 1914), Part VI, pp. 54ff.

40. Oskar Engländer, "Preisbildung und Preisaufbau," *Theorie der Volkswirtschaft* (Vienna: 1929), Part I.

Oskar Engländer, *Theorie des Güterverkehrs und der Frachtsätze* (Jena: 1924).

Oskar Engländer, "Volkswirtschaftliche Theorie des Personenverkehrs," in *Archiv für Sozialwissenschaften und Sozialpolitik*, 50 (Tübingen: 1923), 653ff.

41. V. Furlan, "Die Standortsprobleme in der Volks- und Weltwirtschaftslehre," in *Weltwirtschaftliches Archiv*, 2 (Jena: 1913), 1ff.

42. A. Schilling, "Die wirtschaftsgeographischen Grundgesetze des Wettbewerbes in mathematischer Form," in *Technik und Wirtschaft*, 17th year, 7 (Berlin: 1924), 145ff.

P. Krebs, "Die frachtgrenze der deutschen Braunkohle," in *Technik und Wirtschaft*, 17th year, 9 (Berlin: 1924), 213ff.

C. von Dobbeler, "Mathematische Beiträge zur Wirtschaftsgeographie," in *Technik und Wirtschaft*, 17th year, 9 (Berlin: 1924), 201ff.

Erich Schneider, "Mathematische Betrachtungen über den nationalen Gütertransport," in *Technik und Wirtschaft*, 17th year, 9 (Berlin: 1924), 204ff.

43. Emil Sax, *op. cit.*, esp. Vol. I.

44. Franz Oppenheimer, esp. "Theorie der reinen und politischen Ökono-

mie," *System der Soziologie* (Jena: 1923), Vol. III, pp. 272ff., as well as the earlier one, *Theorie der reinen und politischen Ökonomie* (Berlin: 1910).

45. Rudolf Stucken, "Zur Lehre von den Bewegungsvorgängen des Wirtschaftslebens," in *Zeitschrift für die gesamten Staatswissenschaften,* 89 (Tübingen: 1932), in addition to the previously mentioned theory in note 25.

I

THE THEORETICAL PART

**Economic-Theoretical Foundations
of Town Geography**

A
Fundamental Meanings

1. Centralization as a Principle of Order

The crystallization of mass around a nucleus is, in inorganic as well as organic nature, an elementary form of order of things which belong together—a centralistic order. This order is not only a human mode of thinking, existing in the human world of imagination and developed because people demand order; it in fact exists out of the inherent pattern of matter.

The same centralistic principle is also found in some forms of human community life, predominantly in certain organizational structures and expressed in an invisible objective form. We therefore think of single buildings: the church, the city hall, the forum, the school—these are the outward signs of a centralistic order in various types of communities. These buildings, because of their location in the center of scattered individual residences (the usual mode of expression of noncentralistic family organizations), their special type of construction, their towers, their porches, and above all, their size and height, have a special rank among the buildings of the settlement. The stronger and more purely the location, form, and size express the centralistic character of such community buildings, the greater is our aesthetic pleasure, because we acknowledge that the congruence of purpose and sense with the outer form is logically correct and therefore can be recognized as clear.

Hence, we take great pleasure in looking at a picture of a medieval town. At the market place, which usually lies in the middle of the settlement, stand the more important representative houses—the apothecary shop, the inns, the warehouses, the doctor's house, the rent and tax office (with the most distinguished front), and perhaps in the middle of the market place, the city hall. A short distance from the noise of the stores stands the bulky mass of the church over which towers its magnificent steeple. Toward the periphery, the houses become fewer and fewer, with gardens lying at the edge, and also the simple hospital, or monasteries, and the sprawling warehouses with their great courtyards. All this is a clearly visible symbol of the centralistic order of a community. And if we look further, we find that this whole entity is enclosed by a wall which suggests once more that this entity is something distinct, important, and unique, and in its essence the center of a regional community. On the outside, in the country, there are many shapes of farms, hamlets, and villages looking like the pawns in a chess game,* which are settlements (places not part of the town—*Unabgesondert*†), still more attached to the soil, although not so clearly in the higher sphere of noble human life as in the vegetative.[1] ‡

If we enter a young, modern town, however, we regret the lack of order; such a town frequently appears chaotic to us, and therefore unattractive. Does the centralistic order of communities no longer exist? Has it been replaced by pure atomism and the occasional accidental composition of heterogeneous elements? The order still prevails; the orientation to the center is in part stronger and in part weaker. Frequently the type of community life has changed—new aspects have been added, others have declined in importance. But the town's organization has remained centralistic. Yet in important modern towns, this centralistic order no longer has the clear, almost simple, visible expression of the medieval town; the order has become nearly imperceptible from the outside. Certainly the crowd on the streets, the lights, and the city stores in a large modern town show us that here, too, is a centralistic order; also, the smaller town shows that it has another task in the life of the population of the country. But the outward signs of the center of a town, as well as of a region, are today missing or very difficult to recognize.

It is not for us to consider in this book the outward forms of centralistic order, for, the town with a medieval nucleus is on the same level with a modern town or any settlement which appears as a village, in that

---

* Although they appear small and insignificant, they each have an important role in the life of the countryside.

† *Unabgesondert* has a special meaning in German. It has to do with the political (sociopolitical) organization of a number of people into a community organization within limits, i.e., an organization which separates itself into an entity from the rest of the land and its inhabitants. Outside the walls (which separate the medieval town from the rest of the land) are those farms, hamlets, and small villages which are unseparated, i.e., not organized or protected.

‡ Here the cultivation of crops is meant rather than the rural life of a nobleman.

both are central organs of centralistic orders. We look not at the appearance of a town, but at its function in human community life.[2]

2. Central Places

We do not look at the entire appearance of a town, but only at those definite characteristics which are decidedly important to the meaning of the town and the geography of settlements. It is that meaning which Gradmann has called the *chief profession* of a town, namely, "to be center of its rural surroundings and mediator of local commerce with the outside world." [3]

As one might think, this chief profession affects the small country towns which are really exceptions, being nothing more than the centers of their rural surroundings. But it also affects in the same way the larger towns, not only in respect to their immediate vicinities, but also in respect to their places in systems of many smaller regions. All regions have some centers which are closer, yet their centers of a higher order are found in larger towns which satisfy those demands of the country and of the smaller towns which the little towns are not able to satisfy. Thus we can broaden and generalize Gradmann's statement in this manner: The chief profession—or characteristic—of a town is to be the center of a region.

Because this chief characteristic does not apply only to those settlements which we usually call towns—it applies also, for example, to most market spots—and because there are, on the other hand, towns which do not, or only in a very small measure, show this characteristic, we shall call those settlements which are mainly centers of regions, *central settlements*.[4] *Central* is relative in meaning. It refers to regions, but more correctly, it refers to the settlements dispersed over a region.[5]

In contrast to these central places are the dispersed places, i.e., all those places which are not centers.[6] They include: (1) areally-bound ones —those settlements the inhabitants of which live on their agricultural activities, which are conditioned by the land area surrounding them; and (2) point-bound ones—those settlements the inhabitants of which make their living from resources found at specific locations. The latter are: first, the mining settlements which are very limited in space as compared to the agricultural possibilities of the land, and generally are more point-like in their location in the country; and second, all those settlements which are bound to certain points of the surface of the earth, i.e., bound at absolute points (not at relative ones as in the case of central places)—for instance, bridges and fords, border or custom places, and especially harbors. Very often, harbors simultaneously become central settlements, whereas mining settlements and health resorts are seldom central places. Finally, (3) we have settlements which are not bound to a central point, an area, or an absolute point. Monastery settlements (but not shrines, which are usually bound by the place of the miracle) are examples. Other examples are settlements of workers who perform work in the home, and large industrial settlements, the locations of which are seldom determined according to any economic advantages such as transportation facilities or the labor supply.[7] Purely residential settlements lying on outstanding sites near great towns do not belong to this group because they are absolutely determined by the beauty of the landscape (and therefore are point-bound), or are relatively determined by the nearness of the large town.

Henceforth, when we speak of central settlements, we shall have to avoid introducing a new meaning of *town*,[8] for that would cause considerable confusion. We should go even further and substitute another term for *settlement,* in order to have greater precision of expression. The word *settlement* has many meanings, but it especially evokes a detailed picture of streets, houses, towers, and so on, which could veil the individual meaning of the facts important to us. We do not mean the multifold meaning of *settlement,* but rather only the localization of the functions of a center at the geometrical location of the settlement. We shall therefore speak of *central places.*[9] *Place* is also more correct in a concrete sense, because in our consideration we deal neither with settlement units, nor political communities, nor economic units. Thus *place* includes as far into the surrounding settlements as the inhabitants of those settlements exercise urban or, as we should now say, central professions.[10] The place may be larger or smaller than the settlement unit or community.[11]

Those places which have central functions that extend over a larger region, in which other central places of less .importance exist, are called *central places of a higher order.* Those which have only local central importance for the immediate vicinity are called, correspondingly, *central places of a lower* and *of the lowest order.* Smaller places which usually have no central importance and which exercise fewer central functions are called *auxiliary central places.*

3. Importance and Centrality

Every place has a certain importance which is usually defined, rather inexactly, as the *size* of the place. The size of a town is determined by its spatial dimensions in area and height. Following statistical conceptions, we are far more accustomed to using the number of the inhabitants as a measurement of the size of the town. Neither area nor population very precisely expresses the meaning of the *importance of the town.* Hermann Wagner correctly disagrees with the frequently held opinion that "places of equal population are equal." [12] *Importance* is not a numerical value, a sum of people, or what is little better, the sum of the *weighted population,* which means that every person is given a value according to the importance of his economic activity and has a definite number assigned him as a weight. The size of his income, for instance, could be used as a basis of evaluation. The *importance* is no sum at all, but is rather the combined economic efforts of the inhabitants. This effort involves degrees of intensity, and is something quite different from the mere sum of the single economic results. This combined effort, which we shall call *importance,* is what is referred to when one calls a town "flourishing," "blossoming," or "significant."

This life of a town, that is, its importance, is not necessarily parallel to the number of inhabitants, for it is possible that a surplus of importance exists and that most central places possess such a surplus. (The dispersed places correspondingly show a deficit of importance.) What causes this surplus? The answer becomes clear, for instance, in the large town where there are many workers' housing projects nearby. Perhaps the town has a very small population and yet has a higher importance as a central place, for the workers' housing projects with a large population have almost no importance in our sense of the word. The location of the cooperating activities is the town, not the village. If we conceive of the importance as determined by size, then part of the importance must be ascribed to the town itself as an agglomeration of the population, and another part of the town as a central place. In simple mathematics—illustration only and not exactness is intended—one can say that if the town has an aggregate importance of B, of which Bz represents the town's population, then $B - Bz =$ the surplus of importance for the surrounding region.* We shall call the aggregate importance *the absolute importance,* and the surplus of importance *the relative importance*—relative in regard to the region that has a deficit of importance. The surplus of importance shows us the degree to which the town is central. Thus, a conclusion may be drawn as to the size of the region which is supplied from the town (the greater the surplus importance of the central place, the larger the size of its complementary region). Let us in this sense speak simply of the *centrality* of a place, and understand *centrality* to mean the relative importance of a place with regard to the region surrounding it, or the degree to which the town exercises central functions. Thus we are able to speak of a higher, lesser, increasing, or decreasing centrality of a place.

---

* These symbols are derived from the German word *Bedeutung,* which means importance. Bz is the importance of the central place and B is the importance of the town plus the immediate surroundings; therefore the surplus of importance ($B - Bz$) represents the town's importance as a central place for a region.

4. Central Goods and Services

But in an exact sense, it is not the place, or even the settlement, which is central. Centrality refers less to the merely spatial central location than to the central function in a more abstract sense. Within a region, it is possible for the geometric center to be a very simple, dispersed place. Because the population is unequally distributed over this region, the population center is, as a rule, the central place. This means that the sum of the distances which the inhabitants travel to and from this central place is the smallest conceivable sum. But in our sense, a place deserves the designation *center* only when it actually performs the function of a center. It performs this function if the inhabitants have professions which are bound by necessity to a central location. These professions will be called *central professions*. The goods being produced at the central place, just because it is central, and the services offered at the central place, will be called *central goods* and *central services*. Similarly, we shall speak of *dispersed goods* and *dispersed services* in reference to goods which are necessarily produced or offered at dispersed places, and of *indifferent goods* and *indifferent services* in reference to goods which are not necessarily produced or offered centrally or dispersedly. Engländer, together with numerous economic and geographic authors, uses the term *urban goods* in contrast to *rural goods*.[13] We shall avoid these definitions because they are neither all-inclusive nor exact.

It is possible to define the meaning of *central goods*. Central goods and services are produced and offered at a few necessarily central points in order to be consumed at many scattered points. Dispersed goods and services are necessarily produced and offered at many scattered points (or at few points, but not at central points), preferably in order to be consumed at few points. Moreover, it is frequently the case that a good which is not centrally produced will nevertheless be centrally offered (e.g., at the most industrialized points), or that a good will be centrally produced and dispersedly offered (e.g., the newspaper, which is necessarily centrally produced, but is usually offered at every suitable place). In the first case, the offering is central, and in the latter case, the production is central.

Furthermore, we may distinguish between central goods of a higher order which are produced and offered at central places of a higher order, and central goods of a lower order which are produced and offered at central places of a lower order (but also at all places of a higher order). *Goods of a higher order* has already been used to designate means of production and raw materials,[14] but because we use the term only in connection with central goods, there will be no occasion for confusion.

Central goods in respect to production, i.e., those which are produced at central places with the greatest advantages, seldom exist, because the advantages of central production (above all, the most economical freight costs to the individual dispersed and centrally-located consumers) are more often balanced by such disadvantages as more expensive production in consequence of higher wages and higher prices for real estate. Above all, those manufacturers which, according to Alfred Weber's terminology, are *consumer-oriented* (excluding those which can be found at almost any village), belong in central places; and, indeed, production is ascribed to a confined location—namely the center—within one of the scattered settlements composing a consumer place (which can also be a larger region). Center-oriented production occurs when the collection and further manufacture of dispersedly produced unfinished goods or raw materials occur at the center. Typical illustrations of center-oriented production are the many handicraft industries, frequently the food industries, breweries, dairies, sugar refineries, and container industries. Breweries are consumer-oriented and dairies, sugar refineries, and container industries are raw material-oriented. The locations of newspaper businesses, which are not necessarily consumer-oriented, are determined organizationally.*

But chiefly, it is not the production of goods, but the offering of goods and the rendering of services which are bound to the central place. In economics, the offering of services is considered together with the offering of goods. That is why, in economic theory, one speaks frequently not of goods and services, but simply of goods, which includes the rendering of services.[15] To these central services belong, first of all, trade, which is center-oriented almost exclusively (an exception is the huckstering of the peddler), then banking, many handicraft industries (repair shops), state administration, cultural and spiritual offerings (church, school, theater), professional and business organizations, transportation, and sanitation.[16]

Under our present economic system, these goods and services are, as a rule, offered centrally in towns, or at other central places, because it is most advantageous from an economic standpoint. This rule, however, does not hold for all times and societies. Even today we find that these services are frequently still not offered centrally.[17] There are two main methods by which one can distribute goods to the consumer: one can offer them at the central place to which the consumer must come, or one can travel with the goods and offer them to the consumer at his residence. The former method leads necessarily to the development of central places or market places; the latter method, however, does not

---

* That is, by their need of extensive but centralized organization, and of large, heavy pieces of equipment.

require central places. In earlier times, the traveling salesman was far more prevalent than he is today. The peddler, the knife-sharpener, the wandering minstrel of the Middle Ages, and the traveling priest all brought goods to the consumer. Even the administration of the medieval state frequently was not center-oriented, but rather was handled by means of messengers. At present, it seems that the noncentral offering of central goods is again increasing. The increase in mail-order business is one clear sign. But one must always decide which of the two methods offers the greatest economic advantage. One cannot state *a priori* that one form is higher or more developed than the other.

Hence, today's central goods are more often offered centrally, i.e., on the market and not by peddlers, because with the sale of far larger quantities of wares, complicated accounting and organization, etc., not only the production but also the offering makes necessary an increased capital investment which, consisting frequently of fixed capital, demands a fixed location. This increase in capital investment is made possible only through the transfer of production from customer-oriented production* to production for the anonymous market, that is, through the free intercourse of economic activity.

5. The Complementary Region†

The region for which a central place is the center will be called *the complementary region*.[18] We avoid such usual terms as *market region, radiating region,* and *market outlet,* because they are used mostly to describe trade, and thus would cause confusion here. Besides, the term *complementary region* includes both the relationship of town to country and the relationship of country to town. It therefore expresses the mutual relationship better.[19]

We shall call the complementary region of a central place of a higher order the *complementary region of a higher order,* and the complementary region of a central place of a lower order the *complementary region of a lower order.* Frequently, we shall refer, for short, to *the region of a central place,* by which we mean the complementary region. The complementary region of a central place is difficult to determine, mainly because its size is different for different types of goods and it undergoes periodic and seasonal variations. Besides that, it consistently overlaps the neighboring complementary regions at its periphery. Even so, its size is

---

* Production for specific, known customers.

† *"Ergänsungsgebiet"* may be translated as: supplementary, complementary, or supplying. Of the alternatives, complementary seems to convey the meaning intended by Christaller, which is the idea of the mutual dependence of the central place on its supporting region and the surrounding region on its center.

relatively constant, although not quite unchangeable, because it is determined to a great extent by the distance from a neighboring central place of equal or higher order.[20] Remembering the meaning of *centrality,* we find that the complementary region is that region in which an importance-deficit exists. This importance-deficit is counterbalanced by the importance-surplus of the central place. Thus the region and the central place together make an entity.

6. The Economic Distance and the Range of a Good

Among the economic processes and circumstances which lead to the formation of the special spatial organs—the central places—distance plays a very important role. The more developed an economic system is, and the more it operates by free enterprise, the more decisive is the factor of distance. In this regard, the mathematical expression of distance, in meters or kilometers, is quite unimportant. Only the economic expression of distance corresponds with the economic importance of the distance. This *economic distance*[21] is determined by the costs of freight, insurance, and storage; time and loss of weight or space in transit; and, as regards passenger travel, the cost of transportation, the time required, and the discomfort of travel.[22] Let us quote Zopfl's definition: "The economic distance is equal to the geographical distance converted into freight and other economically important transportation advantages or disadvantages," [23] by which we mean to say *in money value* instead of *numbers.*

This economic distance is a very important element for determining *the range of a good,*[24] by which we mean the farthest distance the dispersed population is willing to go in order to buy a good offered at a place—a central place. If the distance is too great, the population will not buy this good because it becomes too expensive for them; or they will buy it at another central place from which they can obtain it more cheaply. Furthermore, the range of a good is influenced quite strongly by the good's price at a central place, especially if the good is sold at a somewhat higher or lower price at another central place. Moreover, the range is determined by the number of inhabitants concentrated at a central place, the density and the distribution of the population scattered outside, the income conditions and the social structure of the population,[25] the nearness or remoteness of other central places, and numerous other elements. Hence, every good has a special characteristic range; and this range may be different in each concrete case, at every central place, and also at every point in time.

Because we obviously deal here with very complicated processes which do not lend themselves to simple solutions or fixed formulas, we shall leave further development of the meanings to our later investigations.

NOTES

1. It is remarkable that Otto Maull in his *Politische Geographie* (Berlin: 1925) does not consider these quite different positions of the town and the village in the body of the state. He counts as "cultural spatial organs" (p. 593): settlements, traffic thoroughfares, areas from which the population derives its sustenance; and as "spatial organs" of the state (p. 112): prisons, sustaining organs, protective organs (borders), besides the thoroughfares. The nucleus, the center, the town is surely one of the most important "spatial organs" of the state, and in its function, quite different from the rural settlement.

2. M. Aurousseau ("Recent Contributions to Urban Geography," in *Geographical Review*, 14 (New York: 1924), 444) says, "The city has to be interpreted as an organic part of the social group, as well as described as a mass of material." This investigation is limited to the first of these considerations.

Carlberg's narrow conception, which was influenced by Schlüter, is that the "proper" task of the geographer is "to study the physical appearance of the town." This approach is to be avoided. (Berthold Carlberg, "Stadtgeographie," in *Geographischer Anzeiger*, 27th year (Gotha: 1926), 153.)

3. Robert Gradmann, "Schwäbische Städte," in *Zeitschrift der Gesellschaft für Erdkunde* (Berlin: 1916), 427.

4. This expression refers to what Paul Vidal de la Blache more generally and extensively calls the *organe directeur*, which directs the supplying of, e.g., raw materials for mining regions and also the collection of the mine products. This *organe directeur* should be in the center of, e.g., an industrial region (*groupement*). (Paul Vidal de la Blache, *La France de l'Est* (*Lorraine-Alsace*) (Paris:1920).)

Our meaning of central settlement is still more precisely conveyed by *citta completi*, as Marinelli calls the great centers. Quite in accordance with our point of view he says: Considering the professions of the inhabitants, one doubts whether agricultural, fishing, mining, or industrial towns can be called towns at all. Rather, commercial and administrative towns are to be individually considered as towns. "Complete towns," for Marinelli, are not the specialized towns. We, as geographers, prefer a meaning which stresses the spatial aspects rather than the makeup of a town. (Olinto Marinelli, "Dei tipi economici dei centri abitati, a proposito di alcune citta italiane ed americane," in *Rivista Geografica Italiana*, 22, 23 (Florence: 1916), 413ff., cit. 430.)

5. Passarge classifies settlements according to their locations with respect to other settlements. His classification, however, is based wholly on outward characteristics such as individual locations, group locations, linear locations, and suburban locations. The most important location in respect to the recognition of valid relations, the central location, is not cited at all. (Siegfried Passarge, "Beschreibende Landschaftskunde," *Die Grundlagen der Landschaftskunde* (Hamburg: 1919), Vol. I, p. 15.) His classification of the "structure of the settlements" [the pattern of distribution of the settlements] is similarly without meaning. Passarge (*Die Erde und ihr Wirtschaftsleben* (Hamburg and Berlin: 1926), Part II, p. 164) suggests: Central structure (mono- and polycentral); and

the starry structure. Beside the diffused and cloud-like order of the former, the latter is ordered in the form of strips radiating outward.

6. The distinction between central and dispersed places refers to an entire region. It is different from the distinction between centripetal settlements (towns in which the economic interests of the inhabitants are mainly directed to the center of these settlements) and centrifugal settlements (villages in which the area of economic activity of the inhabitants lies at the periphery), as Hassinger construes it. (Hugo Hassinger, "Über Aufgaben der Stadtkunde," in *Petermanns Mitteilungen,* 56th year, 2 (Gotha: 1910), 292.)

7. See the following, which are fundamental:

Alfred Weber, "Die industrielle Standortlehre (allgemeine und kapitalistische theorie des Standortes)," *Grundriß der Sozialökonomie* (Tübingen: 1914), Part VI.

Werner Sombart, *Der moderne Kapitalismus* (Munich and Leipzig: 1917), Vol. II, Part II, pp. 800ff., 901ff.

Andreas Predöhl, "Das Standortproblem in der Wirtschaftstheorie," in *Weltwirtschaftliches Archiv,* 21 (Jena: 1925), 294ff.

Nikolaus Creutzburg, "Das Lokalisationsphänomen der Industrien. Am Beispiel des nordwestlichen Thüringer Waldes," in *Forschungen zur deutschen Landes- und Volkskunde,* 23, Part IV (Stuttgart: 1925).

8. See the abundant literature on the meaning of *town,* which is cited in the review of Hans Dörries, "Der gegenwärtige Stand der Stadtgeographie," in *Hermann Wagner Gedächtnisschrift* (Gotha: 1930), 314ff.

See also the compilation of the nongeographical meanings of town by Werner Sombart, "Städtische Siedlungen, Stadt," in *Handwörter der Soziologie,* ed. Alfred Vierkandt (Stuttgart: 1931), pp. 527ff.; and "Der Begriff der Stadt und das Wesen der Städtebildung," in *Archiv für Sozialwissenschaften und Sozialpolitik,* 25 (Berlin: 1907), 4ff. Ratzel's meaning of town is useless for our purposes because it refers in no way to the specific character, and the genesis, or function of a town. For him, the geographical meaning of town is "a permanent agglomeration of human beings and residences which covers a considerable area and lies in the center of greater traffic routes." (Friedrich Ratzel, "Die geographische Lage der grossen Städte," in "Die Großstadt," *Jahrbuch der Gabestiftung,* 9 (Dresden: 1903), 37.)

9. According to Grimm's *Wörterbuch,* Vol. VII: *Ort* means "a firm point in a space, a position, a place." Under Sec. 4: "A place that people seek and utilize, a place of public intercourse."

See also Peter Heinrich Schmidt, "Raum und Ort als geographische Grundbegriffe," in *Geographische Zeitschrift,* 36th year (Leipzig and Berlin: 1930), 357ff.

10. This corresponds in principle with Hugo Hassinger, "Beiträge zur Siedlungs- und Verkehrsgeographie von Wien," in *Mitteilungen der geographischen Gesellschaft,* 53 (Vienna: 1910); and with E. Hanslik, *Biala—eine deutsche Stadt in Galizien* (Leipzig: 1909); and with numerous other authors.

11. *Place* means approximately what Ernst Hasse means when he combines the political community (first circle) and the "suburban population—which together form a living and settling unit" (second circle)—with the traffic region (the result of the "exchange between the residing and laboring populations"). Therefore, circles one and two together form, according to the Belgian example, the "agglomeration." ("Die Intensität großstädtischer Menschenanhäufungen," in *Allgemeines staatlisches Archiv,* 2nd year (Tübingen: 1892), 615f.)

Sigmund Schott, relying on this meaning, introduces the ten-km. circle, thoroughly acknowledging the mistakes of this method. ("Die großstädtischen Agglomerationen des Deutschen Reichs, 1871-1910," in *Die Schriften des Verbands deutscher Städtestatistiker,* Part I (Breslau: 1912).)

12. Hermann Wagner, in "Allgemeine Erdkunde," *Lehrbuch der Geographie,* 9th ed. (Hannover and Leipzig: 1912), Vol. I, p. 885.

13. Oskar Engländer, "Preisbildung und Preisaufbau," *Theorie der Volkswirtschaft* (Vienna: 1929), Part I, pp. 114ff.

14. This term is to be found in the system of the order among goods as it was introduced by the marginal utility school following the example of Carl Menger, *Grundsätze der Volkswirtschaftslehre,* 2nd ed. (Vienna and Leipzig: 1923).

15. See Hans Mayer, "Gut," in *Handwörterbuch der Staatswissenschaften,* 4 (Jena: 1927), 1277ff.

16. This list makes it clear that we should understand central goods to include not only economic goods and services but also noneconomic, cultural, sanitary, etc. Their offering and consumption occur according to economic laws because their acquisition causes burdens and costs and their offering requires expenditures of money and labor. Although the goal is the satisfaction of cultural, sanitary, and political demands, it is nevertheless important that costs are necessary in order to attain this goal. A lesser expenditure will always be preferred to a higher expenditure in the acquisition of goods.

17. Maunier wrote an interesting composition on the distribution of industries, from which we may learn something for our special theme. (René Maunier, "La distribution géographique des industries," in *Revue internationale de Sociologie,* 16 (Paris: 1908), 481ff.) He states that dispersing and centralizing industries always brought about changes in one another in the historical economic epochs: village economy—centralized; large-estate economy *(seigneurie)*—dispersed; medieval-town economy—centralized; period of home industry—dispersed; period of national economies—concentrated. Today we are viewing a period of dispersion. Maunier thus speaks (p. 433) of a *"rhythme de concentration et de dispersion,"* so that either the migration of industry towards the most advantageous location of production and markets, or the migration of industry towards the most favorable labor market *(distribution selon l'habitat)* is found. He concludes (p. 511) that *"grosso-modo, les conditions géographiques agissent de plus en plus,"* and that it is wrong to say that the industry of the more primitive stages of economic development depends strongly on geophysical factors. On the contrary, these factors play a greater role in modern industry because the sharper competition demands the utilization of the smallest advantage obtainable from geographical nature.

18. This corresponds with the definition which Bobek gives: "The regional influence of a town (i.e., the typically urban types of labor) extends generally, if not artificially fixed (by political or administrative borders), so long as the expenditures for transportation (in trading with the town) do not exceed the advantages which are offered by this urban center." (Hans Bobek, "Innsbruck. Eine Gebirgsstadt, ihr Lebensraum und ihre Erscheinung," in *Forschungen zur deutschen Landes- und Volkskunde,* 25 (Stuttgart: 1928), 222.)

19. In the publications of the Committee for the Investigation of the Production and Sales Conditions of the German Economy *(Enquete-Ausschuss),* see *Das Wirtschaftsleben der Städte, Landkreise und Landgemeinden* (Berlin: 1930), Vol. I, p. 1, the "active and passive relations" of towns with surrounding country (a strikingly expressed statement) are referred to.

20. Gradmann *(op. cit.,* 456) speaks of an "unchangeable size of the market

regions." That is correct for many regions, especially remote ones which are limited in a forceful manner by the conditions of nature. For most, however, the conditions are of "short duration" that is only relative. On the other hand, the great consistency of the rural market regions is a striking fact for the economist. This fact apparently does not stand in harmony with the effects of economic laws in an economic organization which rests upon freedom of enterprise.

21. See Kurt Hassert, *Allgemeine Verkehrsgeographie,* 2nd ed. (Berlin and Leipzig: 1931), Vol. I, p. 63.

22. Ferdinand von Richthofen subsumes these factors under the collective phrase, "time and labor" (*Vorlesungen über allgemeine Siedlungs- und Verkehrsgeographie,* version and edition of Otto Schlüter (Berlin: 1908), p. 210); economic theory simply speaks of "costs," which do not necessarily consist of money values nor which must be expressed in money values.

23. Cited in Kurt Hassert, *loc. cit.*

24. Oskar Engländer uses the expression, "selling extent," as it is bad to speak of a sale in connection with a central service such as the administrative activity of a state which we refer to with the more general expression, "range" (Oskar Engländer, *Theorie des Güterverkehrs und der Frachtsätze* (Jena: 1924), p. 3). Engländer's expression is not complete enough for our purposes.

25. Engländer includes all of this under the term, "price-willingness of the buyer." This short expression is very striking; it means approximately that a certain population or a certain stratum of the population, with regard to its structure and composition, is willing to pay a certain higher price for particular goods it desires. (Oskar Engländer, *Theorie der Volkswirtschaft,* pp. 29ff.)

B
Static Relations

1. Introduction: The Consumption of Central Goods and the Development of Central Places

There is a definite connection between the consumption of central goods and the development of central places. The development of those central places the inhabitants of which live by the sale of central goods becomes more pronounced if many central goods are consumed than it does if few central goods are consumed. *Development of central places* is to be here understood quite generally. This expression says nothing about where this development occurs. A second question, then, is whether the demand for central goods exists in one or in several places.

The consumption of central goods depends upon the distribution of population, and especially on the degree of agglomeration in the central place itself. Furthermore, the consumption of central goods depends primarily upon the demand for goods, which is determined by the professional and social structure, as well as by the wealth or income structure of the population. The consumption of the different types of central goods is determined by the available quantity, the law of supply and demand, and, above all, the price of the goods at the central place. That price is itself determined by such factors as rent, interest, wages, and taxes. Moreover, the demand depends upon the size and geographical formation of the complementary region. These factors determine the range of the good; the particular conditions of transportation also play an important role.

When we have determined the amount of consumption and the location of the offering of central goods, according to the factors just mentioned, the question of the sizes, location, and number of central places can, at least generally, be answered.

But to correct what has been said, the most decisive factor in the development of central places is not the consumption of central goods, but the receipts from the sale of the central goods, i.e., the net income (equal to the gross income minus the production and other costs) which the inhabitants of the central places earn. If this sum is high, then many individuals can live on it, for everyone is economically well off, and the central place flourishes. If it is small, however, then only a few individuals find a modest living, and the central place is badly developed or is declining.

2. The Distribution of the Population of Central Places

Next, we seek insight into the relationship between the distribution of population and the consumption of central goods.

Let us suppose a region of about 80 sq. km. which has 4000 inhabitants uniformly distributed over the entire region, except for one small place at which the population tends to agglomerate. We shall refer to this region as Case 1. Suppose that a doctor, in order to offer his central service in this region, establishes himself in the center of the region. The demand for medical services is basically the same for the entire population, i.e., each inhabitant has about the same number of illnesses or complaints. Further, suppose that all persons in this region have equal incomes which permit six marks per person per year for medical costs after the other pressing demands, such as food, clothing, and shelter, are provided for. Let the cost of a medical consultation be three marks.

It is incorrect to say that every inhabitant consults the doctor on the average of twice a year and that 4000×6 marks, or 24,000 marks, is the doctor's income. Those who live farther away must add to the doctor's fee because they have two trips of one or two hours, which means they lose working time and have the expense and inconvenience of a long trip. Yet they can spend only six marks for illnesses altogether. Thus it appears that only those living in the neighborhood of the doctor—let us say less than one-quarter of an hour away—actually consult the doctor twice a year. Those living in Ring I—one-quarter of an hour to one-half of an hour away from the doctor—lose an average of one working hour because of the long trip, which they value at 70 pfennigs. The cost of the doctor for them is thus 3.70 marks. Besides the doctor's fees, the costs and inconveniences already mentioned must be added, and the "transportation-obstacles" [1] must also be taken into account. Thus, they can afford out of their six marks per year only one and a half consulta-

tions per year, i.e., three every two years. Those living farther away, in
Ring II, lose two working hours in traveling to and from the doctor.
Besides that, they must go to an inn for breakfast, at a cost of about 60
pfennigs, because of the longer absence from home. Thus a consultation
costs them 3 + 1.40 + .60 marks, or a total of 5 marks. When we add to
that the increased obstacles, we find that they can afford only one consultation per year. And those living still farther away can afford correspondingly only one-half of a consultation per year (one every two years).

Within the neighborhood of the doctor (a region of about 5 sq. km.,
less than one-quarter of an hour away), there live 250 persons (assuming
a population density of fifty per sq. km.). In Ring I, within the half-hour
ring minus the quarter-hour nucleus (about 15 sq. km.), there live 750
people. And in Ring II, one-half of an hour to one hour away from the
doctor (60 sq. km.), there live 3000 people. We can imagine, however,
that the region does not describe a perfect circle (this is the rule in
reality), and that there are only fifty people per sq. km. within the one-
hour ring, ten per sq. km. lie outside, i.e., 2500 people live within Ring
II and 500 outside of Ring II and within Ring III. Hence, the number
of consultations will be as follows:

	Population	Consultations per capita	Number of Consultations
Nucleus	250	2	500
Ring I	750	$1\frac{1}{2}$	1125
Ring II	2500	1	2500
Ring III	500	$\frac{1}{2}$	250
Total	4000		4375

The consultation cost of 3 marks times the appropriate number of consultations gives the doctor 13,125 marks in gross annual receipts—and
not 24,000 marks, as one might superficially think.

We can state generally, then, that the consumption of goods, despite
equal demands and equal incomes, varies in different places of the region.
It is higher near where the central good is offered, and it becomes less
with increasing distance until finally, at the periphery, the consumption
might cease entirely.

But we shall dwell no longer on this case which is merely construed.
Let us rather consider immediately the present reality and assume that
a certain net of central places already exists.

Let us suppose that the population is distributed unequally in the
region, but that the total population is the same as in Case 1. In the
center of the region there is a town of 1000 inhabitants; Ring I (half-
hour ring) has a population of 750 (density: 50 inhabitants per sq. km.);

Ring II (one-hour ring) has a population of 2000 (density: 40); and Ring III has a population of 250 persons (density: 25)—this is Case 2, a region with a small central place. For this case, the computations would be:

	Population	Consultations per capita	Number of Consultations
Nucleus	1000	2	2000
Ring I	750	$1\frac{1}{2}$	1125
Ring II	2000	1	2000
Ring III	250	$\frac{1}{2}$	125
Total	4000		5250

Consequently, the doctor in Case 2, even though he has the same number of inhabitants in his working region as the doctor in Case 1, has an annual income of 15,750 marks, instead of 13,125 marks.

Let us now assume a town of 2000 inhabitants, with 500 in Ring I (density: $33\frac{1}{3}$), 1250 in Ring II (density: 25), and 250 in Ring III (density: 25)—this is Case 3, a region with a large central place. In this instance, the computation is as follows:

	Population	Consultations per capita	Number of Consultations
Nucleus	2000	2	4000
Ring I	500	$1\frac{1}{2}$	750
Ring II	1250	1	1250
Ring III	250	$\frac{1}{2}$	125
Total	4000		6125

Thus there are 6125 consultations in Case 3 in contrast to 5250 in Case 2 and 4375 in Case 1.

If there are two central places in a region of 80 sq. km., and if the region is divided into two halves, each with a central place of 1000 inhabitants in its center and with the other inhabitants distributed as in Case 3, then the computation is as follows:

	Population	Consultations per capita	Number of Consultations
Two Nuclei (1000)	2000	2	4000
Two Rings I (500)	1000	$1\frac{1}{2}$	1500
Ring II	1000	1	1000
Total	4000		6500

There are 6500 consultations in contrast to 6125 in Case 3. A region with two central places has, consequently, despite an equal population and an equal number of center-living persons, a higher consumption of central goods than a region with only one center.

We must notice, however, that which is valid for all other eventual situations. It might seem that a region with two centers would be most favorable, because more central goods would be consumed in that case. Because the more favorable aspects of a situation at any given time influence the economic activity of the individual acting economically, one can say that there is a tendency to build numerous central places. Such a tendency can indeed be observed. There exists, however, a counter-tendency of more weight, which is that the seller of central goods must be able to live on the income of his sales. We shall now explain this by means of a special example. The most favorable situation, i.e., the one with the greatest number of consultations, exists in the following case. There is a doctor in every village and consequently, every one of the 4000 inhabitants in the region can afford two consultations because no inhabitant has to pay other incidental expenses. Accordingly, there will be 8000 consultations and incomes of 24,000 marks for the doctors. If the region has ten settlements, then there should be ten doctors, each of whom has an average annual income of 2400 marks, on which no one of them could live. In reality, two doctors at best could practice in this region, perhaps at two different central places. Then each of them would receive one-half of 6500×3 marks (according to Case 4), or 9750 marks. We presume that a doctor has to have at least 8000 marks annual gross income in order to have enough to live on, to cover his expenses, to receive interest on, and to amortize the capital he has invested in his practice for training, instruments, apparatus, and furniture. Consequently, the most favorable situation must lie somewhere between where all demands are satisfied and where no demands are satisfied. It must lie where as many demands as possible are satisfied, and where, simultaneously, the service results in an income as high as possible for the one who offers the central good.

If the central place where the doctor practices does not lie at the center of the region and its dispersed population, but rather lies eccentrically, then the consumption of central goods and, accordingly, the income of the doctor are again not maximized. In this instance, relatively more people live a greater distance from his office and therefore, relatively more people are, to a lesser degree, in the market for the purchase of central goods.*

We may state the following as a result of our discussion: The total consumption of central goods is less in regions with weakly developed

---

* That is, more people must now spend more money out of their available income for traveling and incidental expenses in connection with consulting a doctor.

centers than in regions with strongly developed centers, but higher than in regions without any center at all but with an equal population. If the center-living population is distributed between two central places, then the consumption of central goods is higher under certain assumptions than if the center-living population lived at only one central place. Eccentric location of central places produces the consumption of central goods.

In discussing the distribution of population in a region, we should not consider only whether the population is central or dispersed. The dispersed population might live either in larger settlements—larger villages—or in smaller settlements—hamlets—or on single dispersed farms.[2] Every type results in special conditions with respect to the consumption of central goods.

Let us set one extreme possibility against the other: a region with only segregated farms, and a region with larger villages. The number of inhabitants of the regions, the number of inhabitants of the central places, and the sizes of the two regions are assumed to be equal respectively. Then we can state that the dispersed population of the region of segregated farms does not have satisfactory access to central goods of the lowest order. Bakers, butchers, and grocers are seldom found in such a region,[3] for they do not find purchasers for their goods, because of the distance between them and their potential customers of 2 or 3 kms. This distance does not allow for the purchase of more than rolls or one-quarter of a pound of sausage. Such a situation would result in a comparatively better development of the higher ranking central places because of the costs at the places which otherwise would offer the central goods of a lower order (also the costs of nonexistent places as indicated by the fact that they do not even exist). In a region with predominantly villages, the large villages, accordingly, deprive the town of a part of its central function, namely, its offering of central goods of lower and even of the lowest orders. This tendency surely exists, but it might be of more importance in this sort of a region than in regions of segregated farm units where many goods which are produced and consumed centrally in the predominantly village regions are produced in the individual workshops of the consumers. Consequently, the central place of a higher order does not function in this case either. The bread-baking, butchering, spinning, and even repairing of wagons might be done at home. The individual inhabitant in a region of single dispersed farms must rely on himself more at all times, for he has less possibility of reliance on or desire for social intercourse. Therefore, he has less demand for it. Because central goods are frequently of such a social nature, the consumption of these particular goods will be diminished. It is different in predominantly village regions, where the time-consuming and inconvenient baking of bread is more expensive for the individual household than buying the bread at the baker's, and where the interdependence is stronger; here, the demand for central goods is greater than in regions of segregated farms.

But there is still a third point which must be included: The journey from the individual dispersed farm to the central place regularly includes a considerable distance over bad roads from the farm to the first good road. These bad roads from many farms merge into good roads which later merge into a highway. In the predominantly village region, however, there is usually a good road from the village to the town. Consequently, the inconvenience, the loss of time, and perhaps the direct transportation costs of a trip from an individual dispersed farm to town are greater than for a trip of equal distance from the village to the town. Therefore, the central good is more expensive, on the average, for the inhabitant of a region of single farms. This means that he can afford a smaller quantity of this good with his income. Thus, the development of central places in regions of single farms is generally less than in regions of villages, especially with regard to central places of a lower order. Central places of a higher order might be better developed for the reasons already mentioned, but also for another reason to be discussed later on, namely that the income conditions of regions of single farms are more advantageously developed.

3. The Density and Structure of the Population

Densely populated regions generally have a higher consumption of central goods. The fact that the people live closely together causes more frequent social contacts. Subjectively, these contacts result in higher estimation of central goods and greater consumption of them—frequently of a collectivist nature. Objectively, this greater consumption enables the denser population to establish a greater degree of labor specialization, by which many goods, otherwise produced dispersedly,* are now centrally produced. And finally, the dense population enables a greater use of the capital necessary for the production of central goods. Thus the product itself becomes cheaper, and an increased consumption of the cheaper good results. Hence, whether this dense population is equally distributed over the region or is concentrated at single places with thin distribution in the country affects the amount of consumption of central goods.

---

* Dispersedly produced simply means not produced at a central place. Even production in certain villages and hamlets is dispersed because such places cannot be classified as central places.

As to the real structure of the population, it is very obvious that individuals of a higher cultural standing have a higher consumption of central goods, because a large number of central goods are of a cultural nature. Likewise the independent professional has a higher consumption than the nonindependent worker—no doubt because of his enterprise. Finally, the professional population, like the industrial worker in the country, has a higher consumption of central goods than the farmer, i.e., the worker buys most of his food in the shops, thus demanding central services; while the farmer grows his own food and therefore does not need such central services.

The sizes and spatial distribution of incomes have special but not so obvious importance. Engländer's theory emphasizes it particularly, and therefore it is not necessary to discuss it in detail at this time. First, in regard to the size of incomes: generally, if the incomes in a region A are all of 2000 marks and in region B of 2400 marks, it would be incorrect to conclude that (assuming equal prices) only 20 per cent more of all goods will be consumed in B than in A. Rather, with 2000 marks, the most urgent demands of food, shelter, and clothing are first covered, and then social and cultural goods are covered to a lesser degree. Among these most urgent demands of centrally offered goods, the dispersed goods—again those of the lowest order (goods demanded daily)—usually play a greater role than central goods of a higher order. The additional 400 marks of income in region B, no longer needed for the most urgent demands, are available for the less urgent ones, among which the central goods of a higher order are strongly represented. One may therefore conclude that in regions with generally greater incomes, the consumption of central goods is considerably higher, and the development of central places is therefore more likely than in regions with generally smaller incomes (assuming that prices are the same in both cases).

This relationship is somewhat different if the incomes of one region vary greatly and are unequally distributed. In region A, there are ten persons with incomes of 42,000 marks each and 990 persons with incomes of 2000 marks each. The 1000 persons have a total income of 2,400,000 marks. In region B, on the other hand, there are 1000 persons with individual incomes of 2400 marks, again a total income of 2,400,000 marks. In both regions, the total number of people receiving incomes and the sums of their incomes are the same, which means that the average incomes are also the same. Nevertheless, the consumption of central goods in region B is considerably higher than in region A, because each of the 1000 persons in region B generally spends 400 marks on central goods, for a total of 400,000 marks. In region A, the 990 persons with individual incomes of 2000 marks enter only into the consumption of central goods. The ten persons with higher incomes probably spend no more than

40,000 marks for central goods.* The rest of their income might be spent for other purposes, such as traveling, lodging, and savings. A great number of medium-sized incomes is apparently important for the consumption of central goods and the development of central places, for these incomes are what one refers to when one speaks of the "general wealth of the people." In regard to the spatial distribution, it should be noticed that higher incomes in the central place itself lead to more consumption of its central goods than do higher incomes in outlying places; for with the latter, the costs of transportation must be deducted, and only the balance can be spent at the central place.

4. The Central Goods

We began with the statement that the consumption of central goods is decisive in the development of central places. The consumption of goods is in no way identical with the demand for these goods. The demand is, as a rule, much greater than the actual consumption; it is, in fact, practically unlimited. The first restriction on the demand is that its satisfaction costs money and that the potential consumer has a limited income instead of unlimited funds in order to satisfy unlimited wants. We have just considered the significance of limited income.

The second limitation is imposed by the amount of existing goods: the quantity of a good may be limited and not increasable at a given place, or the quantity offered (or produced) may be unlimited, and increasable as desired. Accordingly, economic theory differentiates between goods of a given quantity and goods the production of which can be increased as desired. The prices of these two categories of goods are determined differently. For goods of a given quantity, prices are determined mainly by the fact that these goods are scarce; whereas for goods the production of which can be increased as desired, prices are determined mainly by the costs of production of these goods, which is why they are also called *cost-goods*.

The third limitation on the consumption of a good is the price of the good, which is directly related to the amount of the existing good—

---

* In a systematic form it would look like this:

Incomes: Region *A*:   Region *B*:

       990 × \$ 2000 = \$1,980,000   1000 × \$2400 = \$2,400,000
         10 ×   42,000 =   420,000
                     \$2,400,000

Expenditures: (assuming each individual spends one-eighth of his income)
       990 × \$ 250   =   247,500
         10 ×   5400   =   54,000
                 \$301,500   1000 × \$400 = \$400,000

the supply; the desire for the good—the demand; and some other factors. Consumption, therefore, shows relatively independent development. With respect to prices, it is important to know whether or not the price was firmly established from the beginning, as monopoly prices and railway rates are fixed by law, or if it was a variable one (i.e., with an oscillating market price).

Combining the relationships of the amounts and prices of goods, we have four main kinds of goods:

1. Goods of a given quantity with a fixed price
2. Goods of a given quantity with a market price
3. Goods the production of which can be increased as desired with a fixed price
4. Goods the production of which can be increased as desired with a market price

Because the mechanism according to which the consumption of goods takes place is different for each of these four main kinds of goods, each must be dealt with individually. Otherwise, the significance of a central place cannot be fully understood.

Central goods of given quantity with a fixed price include the services of a physician, because the amount of those services is limited by the working capacity of the physician—at least as long as a second doctor does not increase the amount of offered services—and because they are, in general, subject to a fixed price according to a list of fees for physicians. Also, there is the hospital, the supply (receiving capacity) of which is limited by the available number of beds, at least until an increased demand brings about the construction of an additional building. Matters are comparatively simple here. Is the demand for central goods of this type larger than the supply? If so, part of the demand cannot be satisfied. Those whose demands could not be considered must either forego the satisfaction of their want or satisfy it at the central place of a neighboring area, where, perhaps, there is an excess of supply over demand for those goods desired. In that case, however, they have to consider the higher secondary costs for the journey or transportation. Because the journey is now longer, they cannot afford, with their limited income, the central good as frequently or in such quantity as before.

Therefore, in areas where the demand is greater than the supply, relatively fewer central goods will be consumed than in areas where the whole demand can be satisfied. The central place, accordingly, is relatively unfavorably developed. The same applies if the whole supply of central goods cannot be disposed of because the demand is too low. Therefore, that central place has the most favorable position in which the total existing amount of goods is just equal to the total demand. For example, if there are too few doctors in one area (too low a supply) or there are too many doctors (too high a supply and, therefore, not enough income), then the central places are not so well developed as when the number of doctors corresponds to the demand. This will perhaps become even clearer in the hospital example: if the hospital is too small, then the patients who cannot be received will be transported to the hospital of the neighboring town or will be treated at home; if the hospital is too large for the town which owns the hospital, the costs of interest and administration are too high to be covered by the fees. In both cases, this means the importance of the central place will diminish —in the first case, the neighboring town correspondingly gains in importance, and in the second case, the deficit of the hospital must be covered by excessive community taxes, by which the trades of the community are damaged.

The problem of emigration to the central places of neighboring regions because of unsatisfied demands is important here. Since the price is assumed to be fixed and equal in both central places, the possibility of emigration can be easily reckoned with. To the extent that the increased costs for the journey do not consume the whole amount which one intends to spend for the satisfaction of a want, it is assumed that the emigration of demand brings a more favorable development of central places of the neighboring regions. The development of the central places in the whole of a larger region, however, is damaged because more is spent on travel.

The result in the case of goods of a given amount with a market price or a variable price is similar, although the mechanism is different. An example of this type of good is the cinema: the supply is limited by the available number of seats, but the admission can be increased or decreased. Or, regarding the agricultural products offered on the market, the supply is determined by the extent of importation (which may possibly be diminished by continued frost), and the price is (generally) variable according to the bargaining. We shall explain these relationships, using the example of the cinema.

If every night a number of visitors is turned away because all seats are sold out, the owner of a cinema with 300 seats will increase the admission, for example, from one mark to 1.20 marks. If the visitor designates 12 marks per year out of his disposable income for cinema attendance, then he who formerly was able to attend twelve performances can now attend only ten performances. The demand has diminished by 20 per cent as a result of a price rise of 20 per cent. The income of the owner of the cinema was formerly 300 × 1 mark, or 300 marks per night; after the increase in price, it is 300 × 1.20 marks, or 360 marks. Hence, the development of the central place increases following the price increase, because the central goods are now sold for 360 marks instead of 300 marks. Thus, the owner with costs of 280 marks per night will receive a profit of 80 instead of 20 marks. Emigration of theater-goers to a central place of a neighboring area enters the consideration only when the price rise of 20 pfennigs is greater than the additional cost of the longer journey to the neighboring place. A price decrease in the case of inadequate attendance at the theater works the same as a price increase: out of 12 marks of disposable income, the visitor could afford ten shows at 1.20 marks each, so that with a given number of people who are interested, perhaps only 180 seats are occupied, which gives the owner an income of 216 marks. With a reduction of the price to 80 pfennigs, the people already attending can go to fifteen instead of to ten shows; therefore, 270 seats will be occupied every evening. Also, new people will become interested, especially those from the periphery of the area who thus far, because of the excessive travel costs, preferred a dispersed good, e.g., a book; now, perhaps, all 300 seats will be occupied. With an admission of 80 pfennigs, the owner's income is 240 marks, which is more than he would receive with an admission of 1.20 marks. The consumption of and earnings from central goods will have increased at the expense of the consumption of dispersed goods. As a consequence, the central place will be better developed despite the lower price for one piece of the central good. If the price of a good with a given quantity is such that the whole amount can just be disposed of and the whole demand can be satisfied, then, as a rule, the central place is most favorably developed. If the price is too high or too low, either a part of the demand cannot be met or the whole amount cannot be disposed of, with a result disadvantageous to the development of the central place.

The problem of emigration in this connection is of a different nature from the case of goods of a given amount with fixed prices. A rush of unsatisfied demands from area A to area C can lead to a price rise in area C, with the result that a part of the rush returns to area A. Furthermore, the emigration is not necessary, because with an increase of prices in area A, all wants which were not urgent will have been already sifted out and, therefore, the whole demand can be satisfied.

In the case of the third group—goods which can be increased as desired with a fixed price—matters are simple. As for the transportation facilities, the number of seats offered is increasable according to the demand: coaches kept in reserve can be used, with the fare being fixed by law. Similar conditions exist for the post office where, with greater demand, additional labor can easily be hired, unlike in the case of the doctor. The apothecary with prices fixed by a schedule of prices is another example. We take as another example the selling of brand articles with monopoly prices, that is, fixed and prescribed selling prices, as, for example, the drugs sold by the apothecary. If there is a greater demand in a certain area for these drugs, it can always be satisfied by corresponding farsighted planning by the druggist. Because the supply can be increased as desired, higher consumption results in a higher income for the druggist. Lower consumption in another area results in correspondingly lower incomes. In the former area, the central place is better developed than in the area with the lower consumption. An emigration of demand to neighboring areas does not enter the consideration. Therefore, the amount of consumption clearly determines the development of the central place.

State administration activities and the cultural institutions, especially schools, belong to the category of goods with fixed prices which can be increased as desired. Towns, which are national, provincial, or county government seats are, to an especially high degree, subject to the relationships described above. They do not have to fear competition (emigration of consumption to neighboring central places) because their importance is determined by the size and number of inhabitants of the administrative district as well as by the extent of state administration in general.

Finally, it remains for us to look at the fourth case: goods the production of which can be increased as desired with a variable price (cost-goods). These include especially the central services of the trades, insofar as they are not subject to price-fixing and are supported by large inventories. The amount of goods offered can be increased as desired; the cost to the merchant is determined essentially by the buying price of the goods; and the selling price can be set freely. If the turnover is great, the merchant can still obtain the same or higher return with low selling prices. The mechanism is fairly complicated here. We choose the following example for explanation:

In the central place of area A, there is a shoeshop which buys shoes for 9 marks and sells them again for 12 marks, so that it earns 3 marks on each pair. If the turnover in this area is 2000 pairs per year, the shoeshop's gross income will be 6000 marks. In the neighboring area B, there may be a shoeshop at the central place, which can also sell 2000 pairs in its area. With the same buying and selling prices, it would also have, accordingly, an income of 6000 marks. If it is assumed that this shoeshop B with a selling price of 11.50 marks per pair for shoes, in an area which has thus far spent an annual total of 24,000 marks, sells 2100 pairs for 24,000 marks altogether, it follows that some of the people in area A, especially those who live close to the neighboring area B, are buying perhaps 400 pairs in area B, because of the lower price for shoes. If so the total turnover in A will be only 1600 pairs with a gross income of 4800 marks for the owner of the shoeshop; but in B, there will be a turnover of 2500 pairs at a profit of 2.50 marks each, or 6250 marks income. Hence, a central place, at which a certain cost-good of a certain quality is offered more cheaply than at neighboring central places, increases its selling area at the expense of the areas of the neighboring central places. Whether or not the central place itself improves its position is not fully dependent upon this. In our example, the shoeshop in area B has improved its position, because it now earns 6250 marks, as compared with the 6000 marks it could earn at the higher selling price. If, however, after the reduction of prices, only 200 pairs have been demanded from area A, and, as a consequence, only 2300 pairs with a profit of 2.50 marks per pair are sold in area B, then shoeshop B would have an income of only 5750 marks,—less than 6000 marks. The owner, therefore, would have done better to adhere to the old price and be satisfied with the customers of his own area. With variable prices, therefore, the central place at which the highest net revenue is obtained with a certain level of prices and corresponding turnover, and *not* the central place at which there is merely the greatest turnover, will be the central place with the most favorable position.

Because most merchandise belongs to that group of goods having fixed prices and supplies which are increasable as desired, the typical market towns are naturally subject to the influence of the relationships described above to an especially high degree. Because a large turnover of merchandise is the most important condition contributing to low prices, there is a profit margin from sales; and this profit margin at the same time determines whether or not the one town remains superior to the other in competition. Therefore, the town with a high turnover, perhaps as a consequence of dense population with a large disposable income in the town and its close vicinity, outstrips those neighboring towns which do not have such a population. There are, however, other determining factors. The principle of competition comes fully into play in the case of typical market towns.

More must be said of the influence of prices on the consumption of central goods. The factors which determine prices are immaterial here. A high price does not necessarily mean a correspondingly high profit for the seller of central goods, because less will be bought at a high price; and at a still higher price, nothing at all will be bought. However, if the acquisition of a good is urgent, that is, necessary, then the good will be bought despite the high price. These relationships must be examined more closely.

In our earlier examples, the doctor's fee was 3 marks. In Case 2, the doctor thus has a yearly income of 15,750 marks. In another area B, of equal size and with equal number and distribution of population, the doctor's fee is 4 marks. For the 6 marks which each inhabitant in area *B* allots for doctor's services, the inhabitant of the center can afford one and one-half consultations. The inhabitant of the first ring must evaluate the visit to the doctor at 5 marks (one mark more than in the earlier example), the inhabitant of the second ring at 6 + 1, or 7 marks, and the inhabitant of the third ring at 12 + 1, or 13 marks. We thus obtain the following total number of consultations:

	Population	Consultations per Capita	Number of Consultations
Center	1000	$1\frac{1}{2}$	1500
Ring I	750	$\frac{6}{5}$	900
Ring II	2000	$\frac{6}{7}$	1714
Ring III	250	$\frac{6}{13}$	116
Total	4000		4230

The 4000 consultations at 4 marks give each doctor an income of 16,920 marks. We may thus conclude that if in cases of an important central need, to the satisfaction of which 6 marks are allotted under all circumstances (or 24,000 marks in an entire region of 4000 inhabitants), then with the central good at a higher price, the part of the 6 marks (or 24,000 marks) expended (which serves as an enumeration of the good itself) is comparatively higher than that part which is expended for the cost of travel to the central place. This is because, with fewer consultations, less travel is required. Therefore, the seller of the central good receives a larger portion of the 6 marks allotted to the central need. As a result, more persons can live from the profits in the central place; and these profits will be larger than those where the central goods are cheaper. (Later on we shall discuss counterreactions, but, for the time being, the above applies fundamentally.)

But we should remark that this conclusion applies only to important central goods, which are produced and offered centrally. If a less important good is involved, one will forego its acquisition as soon as it becomes too expensive, because one can now buy, with greater satisfaction and enjoyment, a greater amount of a similar and perhaps dispersed good for the 6 marks. If, for example, the cinema is so expensive that one can afford only six shows at 2 marks each instead of twelve shows at one mark each, then one will perhaps be satisfied with two shows at 2 marks each and use the remaining 8 marks to acquire books (which are here considered as a noncentral good). Results: urban development is weaker if the prices of central goods are too high, or if one transfers the production of the same good from the central to the dispersed place. If dairy butter is too expensive, it is worthwhile to churn your own butter (as was done, for example, during the War); if this occurs, the central place with its dairy will be eliminated or will become less developed.

Now let us describe how the prices of a central good affect the development of central places. If there is an urgent, inelastic, and non-substitutable demand for central goods, with no possibility for an emigration of demand to another place with lower prices, then a high price yields favorable results for the central place. But if there is a less urgent, elastic, and easily substitutable demand—which is more frequently the case—too high a price will unfavorably affect the consumption of central goods and thereby, the income situation of the inhabitants of the central place. Too low a price, however, will hardly cover the cost. What is important here is the competition between the prices of central goods and dispersed goods, the substitution of an expensive central good by a cheaper dispersed good, or, in the present and more frequent case, the substitution of an expensive dispersed good by a cheaper central good of a similar kind.

So far, we have examined in isolation one kind of good. We shall now deal with the supply of several kinds of central goods at a central place. For example: At the central place of an area, A, there are a doctor and a druggist. At the central place of another area, B, there is only a doctor. It is assumed that each inhabitant allots 3 marks of his income for drugs. The demand for the doctor as well as for the druggist may be assumed to be equal everywhere. In area B, the demand for the druggist is satisfied by having the drug delivered by messenger from an apothecary situated outside the area, for a fee of 50 pfennigs. The total consumption by area A (corresponding to Case 2 of our earlier example) for the central service of the doctor amounts to 5250 consultations, which yield a gross income of 15,750 marks for the doctor. The drug is now acquired from the apothecary on the way to the doctor, so that special travel costs are eliminated. The amount of 3 marks, or 12,000 marks for the whole area, can be spent for drugs, so that in area A, central goods are sold for 27,750 marks. In area B, 15,750 marks are also spent for drugs; however, only 3 marks minus 50 pfennigs, or 2.50 marks, are spent by each inhabitant, or altogether, $4000 \times 2.50 = 10,000$ marks. The consumption of central goods in area B is therefore only 25,750 marks. This means that in an area the central places of which offer several kinds of central goods, the total consumption of central goods is higher than in an area which offers only one or a few kinds of central goods. As a central place at which several kinds of central goods are offered is an important central place, one can also say that in an area with an important central place, relatively more central goods are consumed than in an area with a less important central place.

If the demand for drugs in area B is supplied by the apothecary in area A, then the central place of area A receives an additional income of 10,000 marks, which causes the place to grow in importance. The central place of a higher order or situated at a great distance from its neighbors has, therefore, a higher significance or importance, because the consumption of central goods is higher in its own area, and the demand of the neighboring area has to be covered. A third intensifying element should be added: Someone who would buy something from the apothecary will, on the same trip (that is, with the travel costs already expended) consult the doctor at the place of the apothecary rather than the doctor who lives at a nearer place, but who could be reached only at the cost of another special trip. Therefore, the central place of a higher order directly draws customers away from the central place of a lower order. All of this proves the superiority of the central place of a higher order and can be looked upon as an explanation of the favorable development shown by larger towns over that of smaller towns and an explanation of why central places of a lower order are so often missing from the vicinities of larger towns.

In the case of most cost-goods the prices of the goods are especially dependent upon the production costs. These are mainly determined by the rate of interest on the capital; the amounts of rent, wages, and taxes; the economic organizations; and finally, the existing money supply. These relationships, however, will be dealt with later within the framework of the dynamic theory.

5. The Region

What is the connection between the importance of a central place and the characteristics of its complementary region?* These characteristics are understood to be: the size of the area, the landscape† and means of transportation, its natural endowment—the fertility of the soil and minerals, and, finally, whether the whole region or only a part of the region belongs to a central place.

Let us consider first the size of a region. To begin with, a higher consumption of central goods is equivalent to a greater importance of the central place. It is obvious that in a larger region, more central goods are sold than in a smaller one, even though both have the same population density and structure in respect to incomes, etc., and that consequently, the larger region will have a larger central place than the smaller region. But it should be remembered that a double-sized region with twice as many inhabitants does not accordingly have twice as large a central place, but perhaps only one-and-a-half times as large a central place as the smaller region. This is because a proportionately higher share of the income available for purchase of central goods must

---

* See text and editor's footnote, p. 21.
† The topography and visible material landscape.

be spent for travel, etc., in the larger region. Besides, the inconveniences in purchasing central goods are greater because of the long trips. Consequently, more dispersed goods are consumed at the periphery. Let us make this clear in quantitative terms.

Region A is 80 sq. km., with a population density of 50 inhabitants and a population of 4000 quite evenly distributed over the region. This was our Case 1, which resulted in 4375 consultations. Region B is 160 sq. km. and has, with an equal population density, a population of 8000, evenly distributed over the region. The nucleus is designated by a quarter-hour isochrone,* Ring I by a half-hour isochrone, Ring II by a one-hour isochrone, and Ring III by a one-and-one-half-hour isochrone. The computation is as follows:

	Area (sq. km.)	Population	Consultations per capita	Number of Consultations
Nucleus	5	250	2	500
Ring I	15	750	$1\frac{1}{2}$	1125
Ring II	60	3000	1	3000
Ring III	80	4000	$\frac{1}{2}$	2000
Total	160	8000		6625

Thus, in a double-sized region with twice as large a population, only one-and-one-half times as many central goods are sold. Consequently, the central place must have developed only one-and-one-half times, not twice as strongly as the central place in the region half as large.

If, however, the larger region B has the same population as the smaller region A; i.e., if the two have different population densities, then we must also consider what we said earlier about the influence of the population density on the development of central places: In thinly populated regions, the consumption of central goods is relatively less than in more densely populated regions. That means that two circumstances—the small population density and the size of the region—simultaneously bring about a smaller development in the central place. In quantitative terms, region B would accordingly have only 3000 consultations in contrast to 4375 in region A, assuming equal populations.

Therefore, one cannot determine, merely from the size of the region or from the population of the region, the size of the central place belonging to it. One has to combine these two factors, for there is a functional relationship between the size of a central place, and the size of the complementary region and its population. We find, using our old example, that there is a total of 4375 consultations when the following conditions exist:

---

* Isochrones: These are unbroken lines drawn around a central place, all points of which are an equal time-distance from the center.

Area (sq. km.)	Population	Density
80	4000	50.0
100	4270	42.7
120	4668	38.9
160	5312	33.2

The formula for the importance of the central place (Z) is:

$$Z = D(2a + 1 - 1/2b + 1c + 1/2d),$$

where Z stands for the sum of the central goods consumed, i.e., *cum grano salis* the importance of the central place; D for the density of the population; $a, b, c,$ and $d,$ for the areas in square kilometers of each ring; and the numbers for the quantity of central goods consumed per capita within each ring. Hence, either a small region with a high population density or a larger region with a lower population density belongs to each central place; and the sum of the inhabitants must be greater in the larger region than in the smaller region. If the population is unequally distributed, the preceding formula must be changed accordingly.

The influence of an almost impassable region on the development of central places should now be discussed. For our purposes, it is sufficient to reduce the different landscapes of the region to the terms of their *Wegsamkeit*.* In light of our previous discussion, the relationship is clear. Central places of equal population density show relatively less development in regions of poor transportation than in regions of good transportation, because relatively more of the income devoted to the purchase of central goods must be spent on travel costs.

The natural endowment of a region—the availability of fertile soil and minerals—has no immediate effect on the development of central places. Only when it decisively determines the density, the distribution, and the income conditions of the population will its influence be noticeable. These connections are discussed in the chapters on the distribution of the population† and the density of the population and the population structure.‡ It should be noted, however, that the fertility of the soil and the density of population (or the wealth of the population) are not parallel concepts. The type of soil cultivation, the crops planted, the customs inherited, the historical developments, the cultural level of the peo-

---

* Wegsamkeit is a word invented by Christaller to represent the communication potentialities of a region, i.e., whether the region can have (or already has) a good transportation system which will permit low freight costs or passenger fares. Good navigable rivers, passable plains, or mountain passes serve as good *Wegsamkeit* and swamps, shallow rivers, impassable mountains serve as poor *Wegsamkeit*.

† See Chapter B.2.
‡ See Chapter B.3.

ple, the market conditions, etc., play important roles in determining the density and the income conditions of the rural population. As for minerals, their extraction usually occurs at definite points; therefore, the concentration of population occurs at definite points. These places of concentrated population have, purely because of this agglomeration, a higher demand for central goods and services; and they frequently develop into central places. That is why the number of central places is usually greater in mining regions than in nonmining regions.[4] A good example of these places are the mountain towns, and better still, the mountain mining towns which often exist without hinterland, i.e., without a complementary region.

Central places such as customs, trade places, and harbors, are very frequently located at the borders of a nation. As a consequence of the difficulties and costs of transporting goods across the border, the region, which as a rule lies beyond the border (that is, in regard to a great many types of central goods), no longer serves as the complementary region to the central place in question. Ideally, the complementary region takes the form of a semi-circle. Thus, for instance, most similar types of goods on which duties are levied and which might be purchased beyond the border do not cross the border. For other central goods, e.g., theater performances, the border plays no role at all. In this case, the complementary region has the ideal form of a circle. Even if a strong cultural difference exists between two countries, i.e., if the quality and price-dignity* of the central goods are considerably higher in one country and the types are more numerous than in the neighboring country, then the complementary region for such more cultural central goods might extend far into the neighboring country. All such connections of the border place with the foreign country, together with the development of trading activity at the border, the storage of goods, the collection of duties on goods, and the earnings derived from them, strengthen the importance of the border place, even though it has no, or almost no, complementary region. Procedures and activities of international economics play a role here, but these will not be considered in the present investigation. It should be sufficient here just to give this hint of the exceptional situation of border places.[5]

Frequently, the central function is shared by two central places which lie close together. It is difficult to divide the region between these two central places. They have a common complementary region and may be called *sister cities*. What are the effects of this fact? Would they, united at one spot, have a higher importance? First, a greater number of central places in a region means, as we know, a greater consumption of central goods, i.e., more favorable development for everyone. But this

---

* Price-dignity is nothing more than the prestige-value related to a high price.

is only in regard to central goods of a lower order. In regard to central goods of a higher order, the contrary is true. If their offering is simultaneously located at both places, the production or offering becomes too expensive because purchasers are too few. If their offering is located at one place only, then the inhabitants of this location buy the maximum number of pieces that can be bought in a place of this size. The inhabitants of the neighboring place, because of the additional travel costs, buy less than the maximum number. If only one, yet double-sized, central place existed, then all inhabitants would buy the maximum number. The division of the central importance of a higher order between two neighboring central places consequently means a diminution of their aggregate importance.

6. The Traffic

We turn now to the importance of the means of transportation to the development of central places. It may indeed be astonishing to learn that up to the present there is still no well-articulated rule that explains this relationship, even though the importance of transportation facilities is the most significant factor determining the size and distribution of towns. What is more, we have been led to the understanding that the traffic first evokes the town (Kohl,[6] Ratzel,[7] Schrader,[8] and von Richthofen[9]). This understanding is in sharp opposition to Gradmann[10] and the younger school of the geography of settlements.[11]

Traffic in a limited way is an independent economic factor; and, in the main, is no longer a visible expression of the economic relations and events. These are the fundamentals and determinants; by preference they form the net of settlements and production places. Traffic plays the role of mediator; it usually brings about exchange,[12] insofar as exchange-demands exist. The volume of traffic and the distribution and line forming of the traffic routes with respect to quantity and direction correspond to exchange-demands (in the market), whereby, as a rule, the demand for transportation gives precedence to a successful line of transportation because of traffic locations, and the demand for it follows. Cases in which the traffic locations evoke the demand are rare. They come to light, however, very obviously, especially when associated with a modern enterprising workshop economy. The customary medieval economy created the first arrangement, and the demand then followed. On the contrary, an intensification of the demand for and offering of goods is generally to be expected when a new transportation line is created. In the framework of our consideration of the essentials, traffic has the immediate importance of determining, in an excellent way, the range of the transportation costs and the transportation central goods obstacles.

Of the least similarity, if not of greater importance, however, is the traffic mediator, for it influences the degree of division of labor. With limited traffic possibilities (*Verkehrsmöglichkeiten*), the division of labor is possible only to a limited degree; with a higher development, it is possible to a greater degree. In any case, the division of labor increases, and, as many more central goods are produced—moderately mixed according to the number of types, the central places of exchanges will be fewer and their development will be stronger.

Better traffic conditions mean a reduction in the economic distance —reduction not only of the effective costs, but also of the loss of time and of the psychological restraints by which the inconvenient, dangerous, and, at times, almost impassable routes with wretched traffic conditions repeatedly offset the gains of the central goods. In our earlier examples, we have perhaps made good headway by putting, as the foundation, the valuation of the journey on foot (Fußmarsch) from the place of the dispersed residence to the central place, which is simply a basic relationship. Indeed, in the small region of the neighborhood of the central place, we may prefer to deal with the existing mode of personal transportation instead of well-developed roads (i.e., for the bicycle) or railway traffic, which first obtains essential importance with an increased division of labor.

Case A: There are fewer traffic possibilities; the walking distance corresponds to the previously mentioned Case 2; the region is 80 sq. km.; the central place has 1000 inhabitants; and the dispersed residents number 3000. Thus, the importance of the central place corresponds to the 5250 consultations. Case B: Through the use of bicycles, there are better traffic possibilities; otherwise, everything is the same as in Case A. Walking to and from Ring I took less than one hour; but now, by bicycle, it takes only twenty minutes; and the loss of wages would be only 25 pfennigs. The wear and tear on the bicycle, the depreciation per kilometer, is to be reckoned at perhaps 2 pfennigs, and for the distance traveled 10 pfennigs. Thus, the time lost from work and the cost of the 5 km. journey is 35 pfennigs, half as much as it would cost going on foot. The inconveniences of stopping, etc., along with the walking were valued at 30 pfennigs; we could, perhaps, set it here at two-thirds, so that the doctor's consultation for a Ring I resident would be valued at 3 + 0.29 + 0.35 marks, or about 3.60 marks. With his disposable income of 6 marks, a Ring I resident would pay 3.60 marks (per consultation), or have 1.67 consultations in a year. One living in Ring II, with valuations of a consultation of 3 + 0.70 + 0.70 marks (breakfast can now be omitted), or 4.40 marks, which he would have to pay, has 1.35 consultations. One living in Ring III, with valuations of a consultation of 8 marks (formerly, 12 marks), would have to pay 8 marks and thus would have .75 consultations a year. The record of the total number of consultations is:

	Population	Consultations per capita	Number of Consultations
Nucleus	1000	2.00	2000
Ring I	750	1.67	1250
Ring II	2000	1.35	2700
Ring III	250	.75	188
Total	4000		6138

Results: In a region with better traffic conditions, i.e., in the sense of a reduction of the *real* distance, the central place will be larger than in a region with wretched traffic conditions.

This result was indeed foreseen. Furthermore, it appears that the relationship between the importance of a central place and good traffic conditions is still necessary, and demonstrates that better traffic conditions lead to a strengthening of this importance.

It is fundamental that we observe the same proceedings in the transportation of goods. We should continue to note especially that following a reduction in price and time of transportation, many goods became immediately transportable in the economic sense. The transportation of bulky goods, such as coal, ore, and grain, was profitable only if the cost was cheap; and the transportation of light perishable goods, such as fruit, fresh fish, and milk, was profitable only if it was quick. The same is true for central goods: With cheaper and quicker transportation, more types of goods, which formerly were offered only dispersedly or locally, will be centrally offered in all regions. In the larger towns, that means a strengthening of the importance of the central places. To be sure, the simultaneous occurrence of reductions in price and time of transportation would cause many goods, formerly produced only centrally, to be now produced and offered centrally at indifferent places with favorable production conditions, along with individual central goods which were dispersedly offered (mail-order houses). The former tendency is again the prevailing one.[13]

7. The Range of Central Goods

The range of the central goods represents simultaneous spatial effects* of all the factors considered up to this point. *The range* is the

---

* Simultaneous spatial effects cover such factors as the demand (taken by the size of the population), the income distribution, transportation facilities, and other well-known market conditions which work interdependently to establish the range of any central good or service.

distance up to which the dispersed population will still be willing to purchase a good offered at a central place.

First of all, the range is influenced by the distribution of the population. If, according to our former assumption, a doctor must have at least 2667 consultations a year in order to make a living, and can make no more than 8000 consultations a year, then the range of the central service in a town of 4000 inhabitants in which every inhabitant has two consultations is obviously limited to this town. In a very small central place, the range must extend far enough so that 2667 consultations can be made, and on further until 8000 desires for consultations are satisfied. This, however, holds only in the cases of goods with a fixed supply. Goods with elastic supplies have the reverse effect, depending upon the distribution of population. Central goods offered at a larger central place generally have a larger range than do the same goods offered at a smaller central place because the determination of prices in the larger place is different from the smaller place. But this will be discussed later in connection with the influence of prices on the range. Similar to the effect of the distribution of population is the effect of the density of population, which will also be discussed later.

The fact that a central place is larger or smaller has an immediate influence on the range of a central good, because more types of central goods are offered at a central place of a higher order than at a central place of a lower order. This means that, on the basis of a single trip (round-trip costs), one may simultaneously obtain several types of central goods. This has an effect similar to that of a general price decline of the central goods offered in the larger towns. It will be shown in the following discussion of prices that the range of a good is greater when it is offered in a larger central place than when it is offered in a smaller central place.

The structure of the population, which is understood to include the income conditions, the social, professional, and cultural structures, and the customs and special demands of the population, determines what part of its income the population is willing to spend for the purchase of a certain central good, i.e., *the price-willingness* of the consumer. If, in a region of predominantly industrial workers, one is willing to spend 10 marks a year for the cinema, and in another region with the same income but with a predominantly agricultural population one spends only 2 marks a year for the cinema, then, with an admission price of one mark and a population of 4000 in each region, the demand for tickets in the industrial region is 40,000, and in the agricultural region only 8000. If a round trip of 3 km. requires the expenditure (in money and time) of one mark, then the range of the cinema as a central good is 3 km. in the agricultural region (one mark for admission plus one mark for the trip) and in the industrial region perhaps 20 km. (one mark for the cinema plus 9 marks for the travel). But the industrial worker might prefer to spend his money for another central or dispersed good which is obtainable with a smaller expenditure on travel; he will at most spend 5 marks for a performance, including travel, so that the range is actually no more than 10 km. Were the admission to the cinema 2 marks, then perhaps only 16,000 tickets would be demanded in the industrial region and only 2000 in the agricultural region, because the total spent is less for an expensive central good than for a cheaper one.[14]

At this point the following should be considered: The industrial worker might value a journey of 3 km., in order to attend the cinema, at perhaps 50 pfennigs, while the farmer might value it at one mark. If this were the case, the range in the industrial region would be considerably higher, say 20 or 30 km., as against 3 km. in the agricultural region. These widely varying valuations of the same journeys which involve the same objective, i.e., expenditures of money, the same losses of time, and the same burdens for the worker as well as for the farmer are thus explained: The industrial worker values the time outside of his fixed working hours as almost equal to zero; it is really "free" time to him. For the farmer, however, who has no fixed working day, the time which he consumes in traveling is always alternative working time. He has to decide whether he will use this time for work or for pleasure. Its value is determined by the value of the quantity of work which he could perform in this time. The difference between the price-willingness* of the worker and that of the farmer is consequently determined not only by the central good itself, but also by the travel expenses. The willingness to pay for travel also differs according to whether the journey made to purchase a central good is a trip to the cinema or a trip to the dentist— because the "pleasurable" trip is valued less than the "unpleasurable" trip. Thus, when we consider the influence of distance on the range of a central good, we must calculate by using a thoroughly subjective element.

One of the most important factors which always determine the range of a central good is the distance between those who live dispersedly†

---

* See Chapter A, note 25, for the meaning of this term.

† *Dispersedly* is a term applied by Christaller to goods production or to settlements to signify the opposite of *central,* which he reserves for those places having a central function and those goods which have been produced for fulfilling the central function. In other words, if the good is produced because the surrounding complementary region is demanding it, then the good is a central one; if it is produced for the consumption of the producer or the town itself, then it is a dispersed good. This is particularly obvious in the case of individual farms and very small groups of population. The central aspect of a good or town is derived entirely from the relationship between region and central place; without this center-orientation of the region the place or good is a dispersed one. See page 33, footnote *.

and the place where the central good is offered. The distance in kilo-meters is economically unimportant. Only the time-cost-distance, which we shall call *the economic distance,* can be a determining factor for weighing the advantages and disadvantages. In other words, *the economic distance* means the transportation advantages expressed in money terms —or in values which are conscious decisions with regard to transporta-tion costs, loss of time, security, and convenience. Because such "ad-vantages" comprise not only objective but also subjective elements (a certain actual situation appears, subjectively, more advantageous to one person than to another), we must, in order to be correct, base our con-sideration of the range upon the subjective economic distance, i.e., upon the subjective value of the distance with respect to certain economic or other advantages. Thus, the distance to the central place appears to be of smaller value to the industrial worker because he subjectively values it less. The farmer, however, values distance much more. And one who lives dispersedly is willing, in order to see a certain central good, a movie, to spend a higher sum for the journey than for another central good, e.g., dental work.

Naturally, the primary elements of the economic distance are the objective ones. Most important are the freight and passenger fares, and the costs of insurance, storage, weight-loss, and possible spoilage caused by the delay in transit. These elements were investigated by Engländer in great detail.[15] Only the result is important for us: generally, high fares reduce the range of a central good; low fares increase it; and this phenomenon is not as important with goods which are valuable (in pro-portion to their weight) as with less valuable goods. High fares are espe-cially important where cheap river transportation is available in addi-tion to expensive railroad transportation; where truck transportation exists as a goods-collector for the railroad; or where trucks or streetcars compete with the railroad. The rings of Thünen's system, which show the range in regard to agricultural products of certain kinds, extend along the rivers[16] because river transportation is cheaper than land transportation. Therefore, the line of equal freight costs (*isodapanes*)[17] is pushed farther along the river (and out from the central place).

With respect to passenger transportation, speed and the frequency of traffic connections, in addition to low costs, are important. Quick and frequent suburban trains traveling short time-distances lessen the eco-nomic distances, not only objectively by saving travel and waiting time, but also subjectively by the fact that distances on routes with convenient connections are more easily traveled than the same distances with in-convenient and bothersome connections.

Another factor influencing the range of a central good which is very often neglected or not mentioned at all is highly important: the type of central good. A central good, the demand for which is not urgent (i.e., it has an elastic demand), which may be replaced easily by another similar central or dispersed good, has *a priori* a smaller range than a very necessary and almost irreplaceable good for which there is an urgent demand (i.e., an inelastic demand). We stated previously that within very short distances from the central place, the demand for cinema or theater performances ceases, while the demand for medical consultations ranges very far out even though the travel costs are objectively the same and the prices do not differ too much for those two central services. Furthermore, we have stated that goods with a fixed supply have a different relationship to range than goods with an augmentable supply, and that a price which is the same everywhere has an effect different from a variable market price, which may be different with respect to time and place. With goods of a fixed supply and fixed prices, the range is determined almost exclusively by the available quantity of the good (as we indicated at the beginning of this chapter); however, with goods of a fixed supply and a variable price, it is largely determined by the price of the central place. With augmentable goods which have fixed prices, the range is determined only by the costs of the distance; with augmentable goods which have variable prices, the price at the central place is the prime influence upon the range.

This meaning of *price* will be considered in more detail. In the central place of region *A*, a central good is offered for 2 marks. In the central place of region *B*, it is offered for 2.50 marks. It is assumed that the dispersed population purchases this good only if the costs of the journey and the good itself are together no more than 4 marks. In this case, the range of the good is 7 km. from *A*, if a kilometer is valued at about 30 pfennigs for the round trip. The range from *B* is, however, only 5 km., assuming equal valuations of the kilometer.

As a rule, the same central good can be produced and offered more cheaply in a larger town than in a smaller town, because production in greater quantities is cheaper and the larger amount of sales permits a lower cost per unit. One can say, therefore, that a good which is produced and offered at a larger central place has a greater range than the same good produced and offered at a smaller central place. A higher population density has a similar effect: it makes the production cheaper, and the range of the central good greater than would be the case in a central place with a lower population density.

Let us sum up what we have said: Basically, every single type of good, even though there are only small differences in quality, has its own special range. The same good has a different range at every central place, and its range is not the same in all directions from the same central place. Hence, the range is not shaped like a circle, but rather varies according to the objective economic distance and the subjective economic distance; i.e., it is irregularly shaped like a star. Finally, the range is subject to short-term fluctuations as a consequence of price changes or population migrations. In those cases, the range of a certain central good is mainly determined by: (1) the size and importance of the central place and the distribution of population; (2) the price-willingness of the purchaser; (3) the subjective economic distance; and (4) the type, quantity, and price of the good at the central place.

When we examine this range in detail, we find, in looking at it spatially, that there is not a line, but rather a ring* around the central place. It has an outer (or upper) and an inner (or lower) limit. The upper limit of a particular good is determined by the farthest distance from the central place from which it can be obtained from this central place; and indeed, beyond this limit, it will either not be obtained, or it will be obtained from another central place. In the first case, the absolute limit (ideal range) is reached; and in the latter case the relative limit (real range) is reached. Up to the present, we have called, however inexactly, this upper limit of the range simply *the range*.

The lower limit of the range is of a considerably different nature, and is primarily determined in a different way. Let us suppose that the central good is a theater performance. All of the planning of the construction, establishment, and maintenance of the theater was based on the expectation of 100,000 tickets sold annually (200 performances a year with an average attendance of 500). The upper limit of the range of this central good, a theater performance, amounts to 40 km., i.e., the population beyond a 40 km. ring does not consider attending that theater. The region from which the theater attendance comes is therefore about 5000 sq. km. This region has a population density of 80 inhabitants per sq. km. and a population of 400,000. If this population is so distributed that 20,000 persons live in the capital of the region, and the other 380,000 inhabitants live in smaller towns and in the country, then it obviously will be impossible to sell the minimum number of 100,000 seats; for the town with its 20,000 inhabitants is itself too small and only a considerably smaller part—less and less toward the boundaries of the region—of the balance of the population will attend the theater. The lower limit of the range of the central good is therefore determined by the minimum amount of consumption of this central good needed to pay for the production or offering of the central good. However, the consumption is dependent, as we know, upon the number and distribution of the population in the region; the income positions; the demands, quantity, and price of the central good, etc.

If, in the last example, the inhabitants were distributed so that

---

* See Thünen's rings in his *Isolierte Staat*.

80,000 lived in the capital of the region, and if this place, whether it serves as a national capital or as a university town, for example, had a high demand for theater performances, and also had for this purpose a sufficient income, then matters would be quite different. Perhaps the existing population in the capital is already sufficient to support a theater, and the estimated minimum number of 100,000 tickets of admission would be sold. If we assume, however, that the population is still not sufficient and that the population within a circle of 10 km. around the town must participate in order for 100,000 seats to be sold, then 10 km. is the lower limit of the range.

It is also possible that an industrial town of 60,000 inhabitants exists in addition to the capital of 80,000 inhabitants. In this case, let the lower limit of the range of the central good, a theater performance, for this second town be 30 km. Consequently, the industrial town must depend on the attendance of the rural population to support its theater because of the smaller income of its own population. There are two possibilities: Either the two towns lie so close together that the 30 km. ring of the second town partly covers the 10 km. ring of the first town, so that the second town must attract the inhabitants from distances greater than 30 km. in order to balance its shortage of theater attendance. (If the distance exceeds the upper limit of the range of 40 km., a theater cannot exist in the second town.) Or—the second possibility— if both towns lie so far apart that each receives ample attendance for its theater from within the 40 km. ring, then both theaters can exist, and the central good, a theater performance, can be offered at two central places within a 40 km. radius, provided that the prices and the quality of the performance are equivalent in both theaters. Otherwise, a shift to the better or cheaper theater might occur, with the result that the one which loses out in the competition can no longer exist.

Let us pause for a moment at this point, because it is obviously of great importance to understand the role played by the size of a town. In the case in which a region has but one town, of 80,000 inhabitants, the ring between 10 and 40 km. around the town has a very special importance. It is this ring which, properly speaking, primarily determines if and how much of the earnings of the town or its inhabitants flow (from the theater owner) to the theater employees. If only the population of the town and of the 10 km. circle are attracted to the theater, then the income will just cover expenditures, and there will be no profits. The profits are created only by the inhabitants of the 10 to 40 km. ring. This ring is, in a sense, the spatial projection of the net profits of the owner,* which equal, as we know, the difference between sales and costs.

---

* This ring is analogous to the "economic domain" of the conventional cost and revenue curves.

It is obvious that the social, professional, and income conditions of the population in this important ring, between the upper and the lower limits of the range of a central good, influence to a high degree the size of the profits which are obtained at the central place from the sale of the particular central good. It is just these profits which are decisive for the development and growth of the central place. The high importance of the complementary region in the development of a central place is thus made clear.

The lower limit of the range also partly determines, within a region, whether one or several places of a certain rank may exist. This point will be discussed in connection with the consideration of the dynamic theory. It will suffice here to give a schematic outline in which, by way of example, the upper limit of the range is always 40 km.:

Case 1. An important center for which the lower limit of the range is very low. The central good *may* also be offered at nearby important central places.

Case 2. An important center for which the lower limit is 10 km. It is uncertain whether the central good is offered at other central places. (It depends upon the distribution of the population, and on the location and size of the other central places.)

Case 3. An important center for which the lower limit is 30 km. The central good is offered only at this one central place.

Case 4. An important center for which the lower limit is 50 km. The central good cannot be offered even at this central place.

If the capital of the region is a central place of small importance, the possibility of the existence of other central places where the particular central good might be offered is accordingly greater, as in Cases 1 and 2. But with a lower limit of the range only 20 km., there is no possibility that the central good will also be offered at other places of the region, too.

We have already stated that each type of central good has its own typical range. If its upper, as well as its lower, limit is high, the good will be offered at central places of a higher order and thus be sold within a larger region. Such a good will be called a *central good of a higher order*. If, however, the upper and the lower limits of the range are low, then the central good must be offered at numerous and also smaller places in order to supply the whole country. Therefore, this sort of good will be called a *central good of a lower order*. And if the upper limit is high and the lower limit is low, the central good may be offered at many central places which, in regard to this good, will compete vigorously for the complementary region. These goods are goods of a lower order because they may be offered at central places of a lower order. If the lower limit is high and the upper limit is low, then the central good can only be offered at central places of a higher order, and only when there is a highly developed complementary region, because the critical ring which determines the gain from the sale of the central goods will be very small.

Up to now we have discussed the range of a central good offered at an isolated central place. However, if this central place is adjacent to larger and smaller central places, the outermost limits of the range may only seldom be reached. Furthermore, the economic range is in reality often smaller than the range of the good itself. Consequently, we can distinguish an *ideal range* from a *real range:* the ideal range reaches to the full limit of the range of the central good from an isolated central place, whereas the real range reaches to where the central good can be obtained with greater advantage from a neighboring central place. Segments are everywhere cut away from the ideal circle-forming (*isoline*) complementary regions of the isolated central place, and these segments belong to the complementary regions of the neighboring central places. This also occurs when there are two central places competing with one another. The one which offers the greater advantages in respect to its range widens its complementary region at the expense of the other central place.

Let us discuss two more important cases. Within a larger region, one place lies on a navigable river, and the other lies a short distance away from the river. As a result of the cheaper river transportation, numerous goods can be offered more cheaply at the place next to the river than at another central place away from the river, at least insofar as the goods arrive finished or as raw materials and are not produced at the place. The range of goods offered at the place next to the river is consequently larger than the range of the goods·offered at the other place. Accordingly, the complementary region of the place next to the river is larger, and this place enjoys a more favorable development. Its larger complementary region, however, does not extend equally to all sides; its largest extension is rather vertical to the river, because the neighboring central places also lying on the river enjoy the same advantages of cheaper river transportation. Thus, there will be no extension of the complementary region in the directions of the neighboring river towns. The previously mentioned extension of the complementary region along the river, expounded by Thünen[18] in regard to a river town, is consequently valid only in the case of an isolated central place, but not in a case in which a net of central places actually exists. The complementary region is accordingly not an ellipse the long axis of which is formed by the river, but an ellipse the short axis of which is formed by the river. In fact, the towns generally lie on the rivers, i.e., they are lined up densely like pearls on a string, a situation which is conditioned by the fact that their complementary region has the elliptical form just mentioned. As a result of this the towns on the rivers can develop densely beside one another; and yet every region reaches such a population and size that the production and offering of central goods is worthwhile.

Another important factor of the competition between two central places is price determination. If a central good has an ideal range of 8 km., and if the good is offered for 2 marks both at place A and at place B, which is 10 km. away from place A, then the real range, measured on a line between A and B, is 5 km. for both places; the limit of the complementary regions of both lies midway between the two places. If, however, the good is offered at B for 2.50 marks, and if the travel costs are assumed to be 30 pfennigs per kilometer, then the real range on the line between A and B can be computed by the following formula:

$$(X)\ 0.30 + 2.00 = (10 - X)\ 0.30 + 2.50,$$

in which X is the range for A in kilometers. The result is:

$$X = 5.8 \text{ km.}$$

The real range for A in this example is consequently about 6 km. and for B, 4 km. A has the larger complementary region at the expense of the complementary region of B. Such is often the case for health resorts. The prices there are, as a rule, too high, partly because the production costs resulting from higher taxes and rents are higher, and partly because the price-willingness of the wealthy guests is higher. The range of the goods offered there is, consequently, small; its neighboring central place of the ordinary type can get along with normal prices, and the range of its goods offered is therefore larger, often so much larger that the health resort has no complementary region of its own.

8. The System of Central Places

We come now to the chief problems of our investigation. We are not satisfied with discovering relationships with which we can explain the size, number, and distribution of central places in individual concrete cases. We are going to search for laws that will bring order to the apparently arbitrary distribution, to the apparently accidental number, and to the apparently individually conditioned sizes of the places.

First: We always find great numbers of central places of a lower order, i.e., lesser importance and smaller size. Besides them, we find a considerably smaller number of central places which have a somewhat greater importance, a still smaller number of places of a higher order, and only very seldom, places of the highest order. That is, generally and less exactly speaking, besides a great number of the smaller and smallest towns and market places, there are only a small number of greater towns; and the greater a town is, the smaller is the number falling in its respective category. This fact has already led to the statement of a most incredible law.[19] Is there a possibility of truly explaining this fact? Are there rules governing the relations of the frequency of a given size-class of city to the frequencies of other size-classes?

Second: In some regions, we find many towns of great population; in others there are few such towns. Is the size-distribution of central places arbitrary, can it be explained only in particular cases, or is there a set of laws governing distribution?

Third: There is a great range of sizes among central places, from the smallest market spots up to the largest metropolises. It is not only for statistical purposes, but also for purposes of general investigation of types that it is necessary to formulate size-groups of towns, as is done, for instance, in the *Statistisches Jahrbuch des Deutschen Reichs:*

Size	Population
Country town	2,000-5,000
Small town	5,000-20,000
Medium-sized town	20,000-100,000
City	100,000-1,000,000
Metropolis	1,000,000

Gradmann's classification makes more geographical sense:[20]

Size	Population
Dwarf town	under 2,000
Small town	2,000-20,000

(Gradmann classifies the other towns in the same way as does the *Statistisches Jahrbuch.*)

One can hardly deny that there are certain types of towns which have different characters;* the above groups are not formulated merely for systematic orderliness.[21] The large town has a different character than the small town. The German language makes an important distinction here, and the finely developed (though somewhat stiff) official language of the Chinese distinguishes between the *king-, fou-, tschaou-,* and *hien-*towns. But it is not true that the character of the size-type can be determined only by the number of population. Furthermore, we should not designate the limits between two types merely by a round number

---

* That is, there are genuine types of sizes of towns.

such as 20,000 or 100,000. First, we must formulate a continuum of all towns according to their sizes; then we shall have, where a large number of towns are accumulated within the statistical series—if they are graphically represented—typical size-values; and, where few towns appear in the series, we shall find typical boundaries between the size-groups.[22] Are there such size-types to be recognized? And how is the formation of types to be explained?

Let us recall what was said in section 7 about the range of a central good. Every central good has a range characteristic to itself, which, in every concrete case (because of the distribution and structure of the population and conditions of traffic), deviates more or less from the average specific range of the central good, which is determined above all by the average conditions of the economy of the nation, regarding demand, prices, and public finance. The upper limit of this range—spatially, the outer limit—is determined by the distance from a central place beyond which the particular good cannot be purchased from this central place. Or perhaps it is not purchased at all: if the particular place lies outside the effective range of any central place in respect to this central good, the good can perhaps be obtained with greater advantage from another central place which is nearer or in some way more economical. In the latter case, we speak of a real (relative) limit of the range, whereas in the first case we speak of the ideal (absolute) limit. The lower limit of the range—or, viewed spatially from the central place, the inner limit— is determined by the minimum sales of a central good in order to make the offering pay. This least quantity may be sold inside this limit. The lower limit determines whether the central good can be offered at one or more places within a certain region which is determined by the upper limit. Together the upper limit and the lower limit determine whether a central good can be offered at any central place of the region with any chance of success at all. The lower limit circumscribes the region with the smallest number of sales which must exist in order to offer the central good at a central place in this region, while the upper limit circumscribes that region in which sale of the central good may be possible at all. That means that both limits determine the smallest area and the largest complementary region of a central place in regard to a certain central good. These range-limits run in closed curves, and are more or less circular, i.e., the curves are *isolines*.

Let us suppose that the upper limit of the range of central good Number 21 is, under certain concrete conditions, 21 km. from central place *B*, which may have about 10,000 inhabitants (See Figure 1). That means that a region with a radius of 21 km., or 1400 sq. km. (the shaded area in Figure 1), is supplied with this good solely from *B*. The lower limit of the range, however, again under certain concrete conditions, is

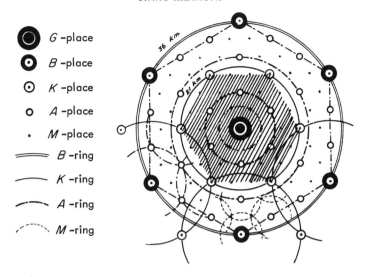

G -place

B -place

K -place

A -place

M -place

B -ring

K -ring

A -ring

M -ring

FIGURE 1

A System of Central Places According to the Market Principle

such that the central good may be offered at only one central place within the region, namely B. If there is now another central good, Number 20, which has a range of only 20 km. under the same conditions, then, obviously, there is a ring 1 km. wide at the edge of the region which cannot be supplied with this central good by B alone. For supplying places within this ring, at least three other central places* are necessary, which must lie equidistant from each other. Aside from that, they can be located at any point we may choose in the region, except in a circle of 1 km. radius around B; thus we assume that the lower limit of the range permits the existence of three more central places.

If instead of an isolated region, we assume that outside of the region there are more central places of a size similar to B, called B_1, B_2, i.e., a total of six central places equally distributed on a 36-km. ring around B (the number and distance assumed here will become understandable later), then it is more reasonable to suppose that the places which should regularly supply the unsupplied ring with central good Number 20 lie in such a way that they are able to supply simultaneously the respective rings around B_1, B_2, and B_3, with central good Number 20. Thus the lower limit of the range will definitely be more elastic, i.e., less restricted, so that more types of goods can be offered in the additional places. Other central places, which we call K, must lie at those points farthest

---

*More central places could be used, but three is the least number which will satisfy the requirement.

distant from the neighboring B-places.[23] That is, they must lie in the center points of those triangles which are determined by each group of three neighboring B-places. These K-places supply the unsupplied parts of the region around B_1, B_2, B_3, etc., with the central good Number 20. If there is now another central good, Number 19, with a range of 19 km., then it is possible for the entire region to be supplied from the K- and B-places with this central good also. The same may also be the case with central goods Numbers 18, 17, 16, 15, 14, 13, and 12, with respective ranges of 18, 17, 16, 15, 14, 13, and 12 km. But with central good Number 11 with a range of 11 km., it may no longer be possible to supply the entire region from the central places B and K. There are again rings 1 km. broad at the edge of the range around the K- and B-places which cannot be wholly supplied. Now, if other central places (which we shall call A-places) are equidistant from the three neighboring K- or B-places, it will again be possible to supply the whole region with central good Number 11. Likewise, the same may hold for central goods Numbers 10, 9, 8, and 7, with respective ranges of 10, 9, 8, and 7 km.

In regard to central good Number 6, with a range of 6 km., the existing central places are no longer enough to supply the entire region. Either some parts of the region (which cannot be supplied with this good at all) must remain unsupplied—distant rural regions or sparsely inhabited forest districts, as they are frequently too far from towns—or there must be still other places from which these parts can be supplied with central good Number 6. The location of these additional central places—called M-places—is likewise equidistant from three neighboring A-, K-, or B-places. The entire region is now supplied with central good Number 6 from the M-, A-, K-, and B-places. The same holds with central goods Numbers 5 and 4, with respective ranges of 5 and 4 km. Central goods with a smaller range—e.g., central good Number 3, with a range of 3 km.—are already of a local nature; and it is not possible to supply the entire region with this central good from the M-, A-, K-, and B-places.

Thus we must add still another set of places as suppliers, which we will call H-places, and which lie in the center of a triangle formed by neighboring central places. These H-places are not characteristic central places, but rather auxiliary central places, according to the definition of the term given in Part I, Chapter A.2. Goods with a smaller range than 3 km., down to 1 km., do exist, but they are of such a local nature that we cannot call them central goods; they are goods which are offered for sale in every village, e.g., the food and home wares demanded daily by households or the services of the elementary schools. Goods with the smallest ranges are significant in wastelands; there, the lower limit of the range is very frequently 2 or even 3 km., so that such goods frequently cannot be offered there at all.

This system of central places just developed, which we shall call, according to its centrally located capital, a *B*-system, can be developed further. Hence, central goods with ranges of 22, 23, or 24 km. will be sold in the *B*-places and from there will satisfy the demand of the whole region—always assuming that the lower limit of the range lies in such a way that the respective central good is offered only at one place of the region (at the *B*-place, which is the most favorably situated one and which consumes most of what it produces). Now, finally, there are central goods of a higher range, which are so large that it is no longer necessary for all *B*-places to be employed in order to provide the land with this central good, i.e., one place alone—the *B*-place which lies most favorably in the center of our figure—may be sufficient (Figure 1). This range is given a value of 36 km. in our example. The places B_1, B_2, B_3, etc., in our figure can be supplied with the central good of this range from *B*. They will have to be supplied from there if the lower limit of the range is so large that only in a single place, namely *B*, can the question of its offer be raised. Hence, *B* has a higher importance as a central place than the ordinary *B*-places such as B_1, and B_2. *B*, therefore, will be called *G*. The entire region exceeding that which is shown in the figure is now supplied with all central goods which have larger ranges, i.e., of 37, 38, and up to 62 km. (always $\sqrt{3}$ or 1.73205 times the next lower range-limit, which permits the transition from one type of central place to the next higher type, e.g., from a *B*- to a *G*-type with a range of 36 km.). For central goods with a range of 62 km., there is a new type of central place, the *P*-place; for central goods with a range of 108 km., there is still another type, the *L*-place, etc.[24]

It seems appropriate at this time to explain just why a total of six *B*-places was assumed to lie on the 36 km. ring around *B*: If the land is to be served by a perfectly uniform net of central places, so that there are neither too many nor too few places of this type, and so that there is no unsupplied part, then the neighboring central places must be equidistant from one another. This is the case, however, only if the places lie at the corners of equilateral triangles six of which together form hexagons. That is,

not this distribution, but this distribution

```
* * * *        * * * *
* * * *        * * * *
* * * *        * * * *
* * * *        * * * *
```

is the most uniform one. If, for instance, at a distance of 36 km. from the central place of a certain type, central places of that same certain type should develop, then obviously they also would be 36 km. apart from each other. That means that a total of six must be distributed on a circle around the first central place. Naturally, there frequently are deviations from normal, but these deviations always have definite causes which can be explained.

In the lowest type, the H-place (which, however, is not properly to be counted as a central place), only those types of goods which have a range of 3 km. (more exactly, of less than 4 km.) will be offered. Let us assume that there are ten types of goods which have such a low range. The noncentral goods offered and sold in every village are not included because they are sold everywhere and do not take part in making a place central. In the M-type of central place, there are offered the first ten types of goods which are offered in H, and also all central goods with a range of 4 to 7 km. (6.9 km. to be exact). If there are 30 types of goods in this group, then a total of 40 types of goods are sold in M. In the A-places, central goods with a range of 7 to 12 km. are added. If we assume that there are 50 types of goods with this range, then 40 plus 50, or 90 types of goods are marketed in A. In the K-places, central goods with a range of 12 to 21 km. (20.7 km. to be exact) are added. If there are 90 types in this group, then 90 plus 90, or 180 types of goods are marketed at the K-places. At the B-places, perhaps 150 types of goods are to be added, so that 330 types of goods are offered here. At the G-places, there are perhaps altogether 600 types that are marketed. It is possible to show empirically how many types of goods are marketed in every single concrete central place and to determine the number of types of goods which are sold in each of the different types of central places, for instance the K-place. This, however, would be an enormous task which would in no case be worthwhile. We wish only to demonstrate that the next higher type of central place offers more types of goods than the lower type, and that the progression is not gradual. The following example of a progression may correspond approximately with reality (southern Germany).

$$H : M : A : K : B : G = 10 : 40 : 90 : 180 : 330 : 600$$

The number of types of central goods which are offered at central places, in addition to other factors such as the quantities sold, the prices set, and the like, is a fundamental influence on the size and the importance of the respective central place. Thus, we can almost equate the number of the types of goods marketed with the importance of the respective central place. Perhaps we can obtain a better idea if we simply, though inexactly, equate every type of good with a profession, e.g., grocer, shoemaker, druggist, innkeeper, doctor, policeman. But, it is obvious that 40 active central professions in the central place do not compare with 90 or 180 working in such professions. It is important for us to show that there are necessarily definite indices of importance for central places according to the number of types of goods offered. If there are 40 types of goods with ranges up to 7 km., then 40 types are offered at the M-places. The types of goods with a range of 8 km., however, are offered only in the higher places. The next higher places are the A-places in which all 50 types of goods with a typical A-range (7 to 12 km.) can be offered simultaneously with hope of success. Intermediate values, that is, central places in which only six types of goods are marketed, are rare —they exist where, because of a thin population, there is a break in the regular supply, or where, because of a dense population, several central places share the regular supply of a region with a central good, i.e., they are determined by the lower limit of the range. Consequently, we find genuinely typical sizes of central places.

On Figure 1 (p. 61), we can count the number of places which belong to every single type of importance. We find in the shaded area of the B-region: one B-place; six K-places on a 21-km. ring around the B-place; six A-places on a 12-km. ring around B; twenty-four M-places around B, six of them on a 7-km. ring, six on a 14-km. ring, and twelve on an 18-km. ring. But if we consider that each K-place belongs simultaneously to the two systems of the respective neighboring places B_1 and B_2, then we can count only two K-places for each B-place. And in the same manner, the twelve M-places on the 18-km. ring belong simultaneously to the respective neighboring systems B_1, B_2, etc. Thus, we can count, mathematically, only half of them for this B-system. We find that two K-places, six A-places, and eighteen M-places are to be counted for one B-place. The numerical order progresses upward in the same manner, so that we find:

$$1L, 2P, 6G, 18B, 54K, 162A, 486M.$$

This would give a total theoretical number of 729 places ordered as to types in an L-system.

Moreover, every central place has its complementary region. The M-place has such a region with a radius of 4 km. The A-place has two regions: one in respect to central goods of M-range (4 to 7 km.) with a radius of 4 km., and another in respect to central goods of A-range (7 to 12 km.) with a radius of 7 km. (6.9 km. to be exact). For the K-place the regions are: (1) an M-region with a radius of 4 km., (2) an A-region with a radius of 7 km., and (3) the typical K-region in regard to central goods with a range of 12 to 21 km. with a radius of 12 km. The B-place has the following regions: (1) its M-region with a radius of 4 km., (2) its A-region with a radius of 7 km., (3) its K-region with a radius of 12 km., and (4) its B-region with a radius of 21 km., in regard to central goods with a range of 21 to 36 km. The G-place has the following regions: (1) its M-region, (2) its A-region, (3) its K-region, (4) its B-region, and (5) its

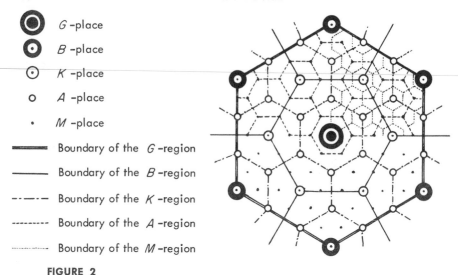

◉	*G* -place
◉	*B* -place
⊙	*K* -place
○	*A* -place
•	*M* -place
▬▬▬	Boundary of the *G* -region
────	Boundary of the *B* -region
─ ∙ ─ ∙ ─	Boundary of the *K* -region
--------	Boundary of the *A* -region
·············	Boundary of the *M* -region

FIGURE 2

The Marketing Regions in a System of Central Places

G-region with a radius of 36 km., in regard to central goods with a range of 36 to 62 km., etc. In Figure 2 these complementary, or market, regions are depicted schematically. These regions are always hexagonal; their areas are therefore equal to the area of the circle minus six segments, and are accordingly computed: the *M*-region, with a radius of 4 km., is equal to about 45 sq. km.; the *A*-region, with a radius of 6.9 km., is equal to about 133 sq. km.; the *K*-region, with a radius of 12 km., is equal to about 400 sq. km.; etc.

The table systematizes these facts and extends the values up to the *L*-type, thus showing a complete normal *L*-system. In the last two columns, the average number of inhabitants are given for southern Germany in order to give a concrete and easily visualized meaning to the size-types; thus they are nothing more than rough estimations for predominantly agricultural regions.

The results of these theoretical considerations are surprising, but clear. First, the central places are distributed over the region according to certain laws. Surrounding a greater place (*B*-type), are a wreath of the smallest places (*M*-type) and a wreath of small places (*A*-type). Toward the periphery there are a second and a third wreath of the smallest places (*M*-type), and on the periphery itself we find the medium-sized places of the *K*-type. The same rules are valid for the development of greater systems. Second, following the laws of economics, there are necessarily quite definite size-types of central places as well as of complementary regions,

Type	Number of Places	Number of Complementary Regions	Range of Region (km.)	Area of Region (sq. km.)	Number of Types of Goods Offered	Typical Population of Places	Typical Population of Region
M	486	729	4.0	44	40	1,000	3,500
A	162	243	6.9	133	90	2,000	11,000
K	54	81	12.0	400	180	4,000	35,000
B	18	27	20.7	1,200	330	10,000	100,000
G	6	9	36.0	3,600	600	30,000	350,000
P	2	3	62.1	10,800	1,000	100,000	1,000,000
L	1	1	108.0	32,400	2,000	500,000	3,500,000
Total	729						

and indeed characteristic types, not order-classes.* Third, the number of central places and their complementary regions which are to be counted for every type form a geometric progression from the highest to the lowest type.

In developing the scheme up to this point, we have spoken simply of the range, and the fixed value of the upper limit of the range was set at this range. That is not quite right. What role does the lower limit of the range play in the system? We have assumed up to now that the good in question in this region, which is determined only through the upper limit of its range, can be offered only at one single central place. This conclusion, however, applies only under special circumstances and to certain central goods. If the lower limit of the range is very low, then there is the probability that, as we have said, the central good will also be offered at other central places in the region. That is the case if there is either strong consumption of the central goods at the central place itself, which alone rewards the offer of the central good, or if it is a central good the production or offering of which demands only a little effort— i.e., little capital investment or little special education of the producer— so that it can be produced and offered with little expenditure. These additional places are no others than those with which we are already acquainted: the central places of the next lower type. If, however, the lower range-limit is high, i.e., higher than the upper limit, then, as we have said before, the certain central good will not be offered in this region at all.

With regard to the lower limit of the range of central goods, there is no new constellation in the net of central places, but only a change in the size of the types. If, in a region, the lower limit of the range for certain central goods is higher than normal, then the central places are generally more weakly developed because the offering of such goods frequently falls off. If the lower limit of the range is low, a central good which is normally offered at one single central place of the region, e.g., the B-place, will also be offered at the K-place. Consequently, the central places in a region with low lower limits of the range are generally so much more strongly developed under such circumstances that B-places become G-places and K-places become B-places, etc. Because, however, the size of the lower limit of the range is usually determined by the number and distribution, and the social, cultural, and professional structure, as well as by the income conditions of the population (and, indeed, in this sense, a concentrated, highly cultural, and wealthy population reduces the lower limit of the range, and vice-versa), we can conclude that in a densely populated, wealthy, and highly cultural industrial region there are more central places of a higher order than in a region with

---

* Order-classes refer to the ordering of places by the letters *M, A, K,* etc.

the opposite characteristics. But this will occur only if the mutual location-relationships corresponding to the system of central places remain the same.

The strict mathematical scheme developed previously is imperfect in some respects; it is even incorrect in its strictness. The scheme should approximate reality; therefore we must study the factors which bring about considerable change. These factors are no other than those already discussed in detail: the distribution and the density of population (both of which vary regularly according to the topography), the industrial location, etc. All these cause an expansion here and a contraction there in the complementary region; that is, they cause variations in the types of systems of central places. The larger central place has larger M- and A-regions than the smaller central place, and the wealthy sector of the system has a tighter (the poorer one, a broader) domination-net of central places. The transportation conditions and the fact that a region is a long or recently settled one play their roles.* The price differences of the central goods (e.g., if goods are cheaper in the B-place than in the K-place) cause the expansion of those regions in which the central good is produced more cheaply, etc. It may be that the importance of the B-place is shared by two smaller places B_a and B_b, or that one A-place is omitted (because of extensive unproductive land areas with thin populations). On the other hand, the neighboring A- and M-places are strongly developed—which, however, are only local developments. In the special case of the H-place (auxiliary place), those places at which the central goods with the smallest range are offered frequently do not exist at all (i.e., are absent). This is especially true in forested border districts with scarcely any population, which, because of the distribution of the land and their locations, are no longer desired, or are deliberately conceived of as protection against unfriendly neighboring regions. We can find such concrete cases everywhere.

Our example of a B-system is based on a definite typical distance for the range of those central goods offered in the M-places, and indeed not quite the arbitrary distance of 4 km., which might be the average radius of the M-regions. It would be difficult to determine the typical distance deductively even after the most careful compilation of facts and consideration of all elements in respect to prices, population, and wealth, although such a determination should be possible in principle. This radius could be determined empirically as the "typical" one, but there will be more detail in Part II. If the 4 km. radius is to be valid for the "normal" region in southern Germany, then a smaller radius should be more valid for densely populated, wealthy, and open regions composed of smaller towns (e.g., Neckarland and Pfalz), than a larger one in regions with the

---

* See Part I, Chapter C.8.

opposite characteristics (e.g., Alpenländer and Oberpfalz). According to this radius, the whole B-system, including the superior systems, is concentrated in the area in the first case and broadened in the second case.

Hence, it should be borne in mind and emphasized again and again in order to avoid misunderstanding that we have only a scheme, a rational scheme of general economic theory,[25] or, in more picturesque but less explicit everyday speech, we have the most favorable state, not in the sense of valuation but in the sense of the highest rationality with the least loss of value. Yet the real values which are most rational change consistently as a consequence of changes in population, customs of life, technology, etc. In former times, only in quite isolated cases, did a town have its own newspaper; until recently, nearly every place of any importance had one. At present, a retarding development may be observed, caused mainly by rationalization or by the radio. There will be more about this in our discussion of dynamic theory.

It seems unnecessary to express in mathematical formulas the results discussed in the previous paragraph. The possibility of mathematical expression is self-evident and is easily realized. But in economics, in anthropogeography, and in all the disciplines combined, only a few factors can be given precise values; and since most of these factors are unmeasurable intensities of desire, action, valuation, and comparison, which can be put into mathematical terms only quite roughly by estimation and comparison, the mathematical expression of a relationship a priori cannot be exact. The formula could be highly symbolic—but then the reader would be inclined, as a rule, to take it as absolute and as allowing no exception, and finally the author himself might mistake the numerical symbol which ought to serve as an expression of the valid laws, as a genuine mathematical formula.[26] We will go along with Sombart who, in a polite and ironical manner, said of Alfred Weber's book, *Theory of the Location of Industries,* especially of its mathematical appendix, that he personally could get along without the mathematical constructions; they were often only an unnecessary complication of the problem, but if they allowed the author to have fun, they should remain.[27] Bortkiewicz proves precisely, in the same case in fact, that most of the formulas and geometrical constructions of Weber are unnecessary.[28]

It is customary to consider the relationship between the distribution and size of central places, and the factors of traffic. Then we can see the strong parallel between the intensity of traffic and the sizes and frequency of central places. Because the one can be explained only by the other, it is strange that many prefer to explain the size of a central place by the traffic rather than the traffic by the size of the central place. We said earlier, however, that both can be explained by a third factor which is purely economic: the division between those goods which are produced and offered centrally, and those which are not produced and offered centrally. This results in the division of settlements into central and dispersed places and in the need of effective transportation in order to accomplish the exchange of goods. The mistake of Kohl is that, like all geographers, he started with the effects of traffic rather than with the economic causes of traffic.

Alfred Weber rightfully admits that the industrial development is the main influence on the size of towns; but by "size," he means simply the number of inhabitants. The main reason a larger town grows faster than a smaller one, according to Weber, is that it offers a better labor market. He says that the "metropolitan" market "which strengthens its power of attraction by virtue of its central position in the over-all social life and the primary size conditioned by this power," [29] attracts a labor force by virtue of this same power and grows even greater. With this statement, Weber explains the reason for the large concentrations of population in the last century. But it is our aim just to explain the existence of that "primary size," for the primary size is the starting-point* for the size of towns. It is this that attracts the flow of those seeking work. The development of industry and transportation are greater influences on the system of central places, as we have developed it, because they both need starting-points, which comprise the existing net of central places.

The fundamental element in our scheme relative to the size, number, and distribution of central places is the range of the central goods. There is an obvious objection: The range itself is not an independent factor, but rather is dependent upon quite a few other factors, among them the distribution and size of the central places. How can we say that the range has a key position in the explanation of the distribution and size of central places? Is it not circular reasoning with one unknown remaining? Not at all. In all economic theory the same sort of situation arises, e.g., the price of a good depends upon the demand and supply, the costs of production, the scarcity of the good, and the income and other conditions of the purchaser. But on the other hand, both the supply and the demand are themselves determined by the production costs, the (relative) scarcity, and finally, to a very great extent, by the price-willingness of the purchaser. Where is one to find a beginning and an end? The secret is that the mechanism will unfold itself in due time for it is a continually changing relationship. And that which is a consequence of a certain system of interdependent economic relationships, at the same time causes the next system of interdependent economic relationships. If such a process were demonstrated graphically, it would not be shown

---

* The starting-point, or initial size, is the reason larger towns usually become more important than smaller towns.

by a closed circle without beginning or end, but rather, taking the pass-
ing of time into account as a third dimension, it would be shown by the
more or less strongly expanding spiral which we have come to know as
the economic curve.

Thus, the theory which has been presented up to this point is imperfect in three respects. We can almost say that it is basically incorrect
and therefore requires correction. First, the simple fact of variability
and the further fact that every factor has varied must be considered, i.e.,
the time element must be incorporated in an abstract form. This brings
us to a dynamic consideration. Second, the actual concrete time of the
passage of history with its determinations and realities is to be considered
inaccessible and incalculable with respect to the theory. Third, in reality
that part of the earth's surface used to illustrate concrete space is the
result of special geographical conditions. Only after considering these
three points will we have a complete picture of the actual relations.

The system of central places has been developed, on the basis of
the range of the central goods, from the point of view that all parts of
the region are supplied with all conceivable central goods from the
minimum possible number of functioning central places. Therefore, we
shall call the principle on which our system has been exclusively developed the *supplying* or *market principle*.

But there are still other factors, besides the principles in respect to
the supplying of central goods, which affect the distribution, number,
and size of central places. These are chiefly principles which result from
traffic and human social life.

First, let us consider the principles of traffic.[30] Considering that our
scheme is being developed according to the market principle, it occurs to
us how difficult it is to establish satisfactorily the traffic system in such a
system of central places. There are fundamental problems involved in
drawing communication lines between places.[31] The more important
places—the A-, K-, and B-places—are not in the position the hexagonal
pattern calls for, but rather are offset in their directions.* If the desire
to create long-distance lines is prevalent, then the communication line
from one G-place to a neighboring G-place will be preferred, for that is
the most direct route possible. However, within the G-system, these lines
touch only one K- and three M-places, while the places of greater importance below the G-places, i.e., the B-places, do not lie on this long-
distance line. For them, there must be special secondary lines from G,
which, if they also are straight, connect two A-places and one B-place
to G. Between one long-distance line and one secondary line, there lie

---

* See Figure 3. Note how the traffic routes zigzag between the center G-place and
the B-places.

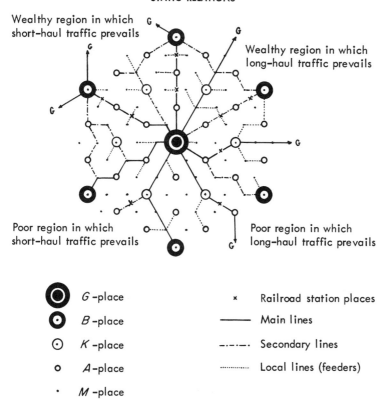

Wealthy region in which
short-haul traffic prevails

Wealthy region in which
long-haul traffic prevails

Poor region in which
short-haul traffic prevails

Poor region in which
long-haul traffic prevails

◉	G-place	×	Railroad station places
⦿	B-place	——	Main lines
⊙	K-place	–·–·–	Secondary lines
○	A-place	··········	Local lines (feeders)
·	M-place		

FIGURE 3

The Traffic Routes in a System of Central Places

one A- and three M-places which, in case they are not too far from one of the lines, will be connected by a feeder line or will remain unconnected. They are then represented by one of the station-points (in our example, 3.5 km. from an M-place).

It is possible, however, that the prevailing desire is to connect neighboring places, i.e., the market region, with G and to develop the line which touches as many of the important places in the region as possible into a main line. In this case, B-places will be connected with G first by a main line G–B, which runs in a zigzag direction touching two A-places and three M-places (while the less important K-places acquire only a secondary connection with G) and continues on to other junctions to connect the outer A-places with the system. The other M-places, not included in the traffic system, will be served by feeder lines.

But we are dealing with settlement-geography, not traffic-geography;

therefore, we must not dwell on these very interesting problems any longer. It should suffice to have shown that it is difficult in a system developed according to principles of marketing to come to a simple and satisfactory solution of the traffic problem. The following arrangement is the result: In a system of central places developed according to the marketing principle, the great long-distance lines necessarily bypass places of considerable importance, and the secondary lines built for short-distance traffic can reach the great places of long-distance traffic only in a roundabout way—often even in remarkably zigzag routes.[32]

There is also, however, an independent traffic principle. Kohl wrote his main work on this subject.[33] He began with many correct considerations, but failed to apply them in the correct order, which the well-developed theoretical construction of economics required, and thus did not receive his guidance from them. Traffic can only be economic, not genetic as was Kohl's belief.* The economic principle of traffic is to satisfy as many demands for transportation as possible with a minimum cost (in establishing traffic routes as well as in the operation of the transportation system itself). Also, the demands of the population, the cost of transportation, the cost of invested capital, etc., decisively influence the formation of a traffic system. But we should not understand by this that such economic rationality was always followed, e.g., in the location and construction of the medieval roads. In this special case, the traffic principle is not given *a priori* as the principle of the highest economic rationality; instead it acts as a selective principle, e.g., those routes which are connected with expensive transportation are discarded and the more advantageous ones are used. Hence, we find people shifting from inferior roads to better roads, i.e., the most favorable ones from an economic point of view will be used and the less favorable ones will perish. One must develop deductively a traffic system which is the most favorable according to economic principles in order to analyze the present traffic system by the use of such a rational scheme and insofar as it is possible to explain it—as we did in our investigation of the supplying net. Yet this is a test of the theory of traffic-geography.[34]

For the present, let us assume, in a less exact form, the following: The traffic principle states that the distribution of central places is most favorable when as many important places as possible lie on one traffic route between two important towns, the route being established as straightly and as cheaply as possible. The more unimportant places may be left aside. According to the traffic principle, the central places would thus be lined up on straight traffic routes which fan out from the central point. The central places on this line would be equidistant from one

---

* When he used the term, *genetic,* Kohl may have thought of the traffic principle as independent of any economic implications.

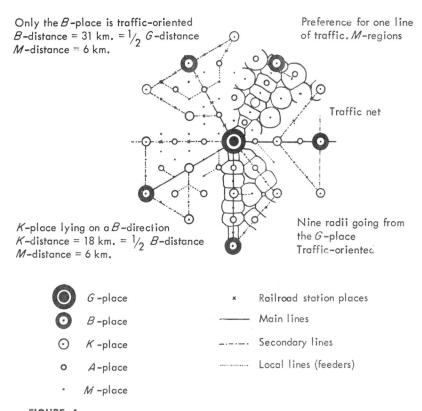

Only the *B*-place is traffic-oriented
B-distance = 31 km. = ½ *G*-distance
M-distance = 6 km.

Preference for one line
of traffic. *M*-regions

Traffic net

K-place lying on a *B*-direction
K-distance = 18 km. = ½ *B*-distance
M-distance = 6 km.

Nine radii going from
the *G*-place
Traffic-oriented

◉	*G*-place	×	Railroad station places
◉	*B*-place	——	Main lines
⊙	*K*-place	–·–·–	Secondary lines
○	*A*-place	··········	Local lines (feeders)
·	*M*-place		

FIGURE 4

A System of Central Places Developed According to the Traffic Principle

another—that is, Schrader's system of stopping place (*Etappenorte*).[35] *
It is questionable, therefore, whether four (or eight) radii are theoretically correct, as Kohl thinks.[36] Haufe says that six main radii are theoretically the best solution,[37] which is correct.

Figure 4 shows how the distribution of central places affected by the traffic principle would be. (Railroad traffic is assumed.) On the main lines from *G* to G_1, G_2, etc., there are in each system one *B*-, one *K*-, two *A*-, and four *M*-places, one behind the other, as stopping places, and at the same time according to the market principle, as central places. Other central places in a sector of the region, one *K*-, one *A*-, and two *M*-places, are connected with another traffic line by a secondary railroad; and four

---

* *Etappenorte:* Provisional halting places for soldiers or posts on the line of communications—places a day's march apart. From this definition we may think of Christaller's *Etappenorte* as central places along a traffic route which are approximately a day's journey apart. They are usually along fairly straight routes.

M-places are connected by a feeder line. The complementary regions of central places—only those of the M-regions appear in Figure 4—do not have the most rational hexagon form, but rather are very irregular in form. On the main line, they have little depth but greater extension to the side; away from the main line, they are more consistent and larger. One sees immediately that if the central places are distributed according to the traffic principle, a considerably higher number of central places of each type will be necessary in order to supply the region with central goods of a particular range. This contrasts with the marketing principle, which economizes on the number of central places required to supply the whole land. Both principles are theoretically correct, as both are, in a certain sense of the word, of the highest rationality. But there can be only one possibility with the highest economic rationality. Which possibility it is will depend upon the concrete circumstances. Either the traffic principle has such a weight that it outweighs the marketing principle, advantage for advantage, or the marketing principle is the stronger one, or finally, the most favorable system is obtained through a combination of both principles, i.e., through a compromise.

We will be able to observe, in Part III, which is on the regions of southern Germany,* how one principle prevails, how the other prevails, and how a compromise was reached. Nonetheless, at this point, theoretically we should discuss the question: When does one or the other principle probably prevail? First, it is important whether the demand for long-distance traffic or the demand for short-distance traffic is stronger, e.g., for the weekly market. In typical between- or through-traffic lands,† the former will more frequently be the case. In lands which lie far from the great economic thoroughfares or which are economically self-sufficient and closed within themselves, the latter will frequently be the case. Furthermore, only a densely settled, wealthy country with a population enjoying a high level of culture and which is mainly industrial, can support many central places; here, consequently, the traffic principle may gain the upper hand. Densely settled, poorer agricultural regions, on the other hand, consume fewer central goods and can support fewer central places. A higher rationality is more likely to be obtained with a minimum number of central places; therefore the marketing principle prevails. Finally, the topography of a country may also bring about a system as it would exist according to the traffic principle: In the valleys the towns are attracted by the preferred locations, whereas among the

---

* See Part III, "The Regional Part." (Actually, only "The L-System of Munich" was included in this translation.)

† Between- or through-traffic lands refer to those traffic areas in which the traffic lines bypass some important places so that the lines will be direct, i.e., follow the traffic principle.

high mountains the only parts of the land on which towns could be located cause them to lie in a long row, one behind the other. In densely settled, wealthy districts, this would be admissible from the standpoint of supply, but in thinly settled, poorer regions having the towns in long rows in the valleys seems to be disadvantageous because large parts of the mountain regions on both sides of the valleys now lie outside the supplying range of the central places. That means that the mountain-dwellers must either waive their demand for a great number of vital central goods or obtain them at higher costs. Thus, the central places are not going to have a favorable development if they are in rows in the valleys.

The fundamental difference between the traffic principle and the marketing principle is that the former is linear and the latter is spatial. There is, therefore, formalistically speaking, a basic incongruity between these principles.

Of quite another nature is the third principle, the sociopolitical one. It begins with the proposition of the separateness of human communities, by which they are kept together in a forceful way and protected against influences which are hostile to the community.[38] The ideal of such a spatial community has the nucleus as the capital (a central place of a higher rank), around it, a wreath of satellite places of lesser importance, and toward the edge of the region a thinning population density—and even uninhabited areas. Here, not only does the idea of the community, i.e., a centralistic order of individuals, play a role but so also does the idea of defense and protection. Therefore, we find this sociopolitical separation principle demonstrated not only in insecure countries, but also in countries in which the idea of the community is strongly emphasized. The old Germanic *mark* (border place) was, for example, such an organized community; its effects on location results are evident to this day, especially in the topographical location of the central places which, while they are central and regional, frequently guarantee protection at the same time. Another instance is in the large continuous forest districts (at the borders of such communities) which were deliberately not populated or partitioned in order to achieve protection.

Let us see how this separation principle contrasts with the marketing principle. From a modern point of view, this separation principle is like the administration principle: for purposes of administration, the whole, which is practically without limits, is organized into single administrative districts. Thus, where formerly synthetic community-units existed spatially, recently many have assumed analytical administrative order (e.g., the old counties or *Gaue*). The leading idea of this administrative order is the creation of virtually complete districts, districts of

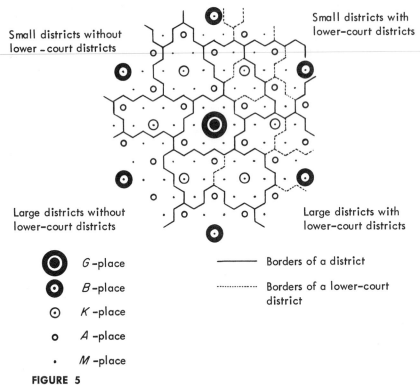

Small districts without
lower - court districts

Small districts with
lower-court districts

Large districts without
lower-court districts

Large districts with
lower-court districts

⊚ G -place

⊙ B -place

⊙ K -place

o A -place

• M -place

———— Borders of a district

.... Borders of a lower-court
district

FIGURE 5

The Distribution of Administration in a System of Central Places

practically equal area and population, in the center of which lies the
most important place. The borders lie in the thinly settled regions and
should follow closely the natural borders and barriers.[39] This idea is
partly realized in the system developed according to the marketing principle. But it is never realized in those cases in a system where a central
place of the next lower rank lies at the border point of provinces of
three central places. To which district will it be distributed? Because
the border place itself cannot be divided into three parts, the district
which is forced from the ideal circular form will be the one to receive it.
In any case, the complementary regions of this border place will be distributed to the three regions of the central places of a higher rank. Yet this
is also a disadvantage; Figure 5 shows the problem which is thus created.
The organic complementary regions are always cut by those borders, and
important places come to be situated at the peripheries of the administrative districts. The progression of ranks of types of central places can
be more easily determined by the importance of administration centered
there: two A-places, together with one higher ranking place and their

respective regions, form a lower administration district; two of the next higher rank, K-places, with a B-place, form the next higher administration district; two B-places, with one G-place, form a medium-sized administration district, etc. In fact, we find that each group of three units of a lower order very frequently make a unit of a higher order in the administration classification; this is clearest in France where one *Département* is usually formed by three *arrondissements* and one *arrondissement* is formed by three *cantons*. It is also found in Prussia where three *Regierungsbezirke* make a *Provinz* and three *Amtsgerichtsbezirke* make a *Kreis*.

The exact laws of the structure of the system of central places will be developed according to the separation principle by theoretical political-geography.[40] We wish only to give an idea of how the region would be constructed according to the separation principle (see Figure 6). It is

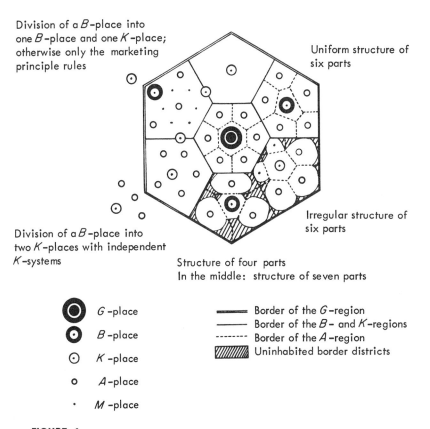

Division of a B-place into one B-place and one K-place; otherwise only the marketing principle rules

Uniform structure of six parts

Division of a B-place into two K-places with independent K-systems

Irregular structure of six parts

Structure of four parts
In the middle: structure of seven parts

◉ G-place	▬▬ Border of the G-region
◉ B-place	—— Border of the B- and K-regions
⊙ K-place	------ Border of the A-region
o A-place	▨ Uninhabited border districts
· M-place	

FIGURE 6

A System of Central Places According to the Separation Principle very clear that, according to the separation principle, the number of central places necessary to supply the region with central goods is increasing rapidly, and thereby quite a few other types are developed; not two *B*-places but six places of the next lower rank are to be counted for each *G*-place, but only three of them have full *B*-importance. No longer will 3 (3 × 3) lower units form a higher unit;* rather, six or seven are necessary. Also, we find this number very frequently in the distribution of administration (e.g., the number of *Kreise* in the Hessian provinces, Starkenburg and Oberhessen, the number of *Amtsbezirke* in the Baden *Landeskommissariatsbezirk,* Karlsruhe, the *Amtshauptmannschaften* in four Saxon *Kreishauptmannschaften*); frequently, however, twelve to fourteen (or eighteen to twenty-one) lower administration units form a medium-sized administration district, so out of thirty-one Prussian *Regierungsbezirken* (without Berlin or Hohenzollern) only twelve have twelve to fourteen *Kreise,* while in Bavaria there are, at most, approximately twenty *Bezirksämter* to a *Kreis.* There are then, according to the administration principle, two or three systems, each consisting of six or seven members.

Thus the separation principle is added to the traffic and the market principle. The three principles determine, each according to their own laws, the systems of central places. Two are economic and one is political. This community-and-governmental principle has neither the authority nor the rationality of the economic principles, but it has the authority of stately and sovereign might. It has already been mentioned when and under what assumptions any of these three principles can decisively influence the distribution of central places. In most cases, however, the principles must fight for the predominant position. The dynamic theory will have to develop the foundations by which the examples from reality in Part III, "The Regional Part," are to be found.

NOTES

1. Franz Oppenheimer ("Theorie der reinen und politischen Ökonomie," *System der Soziologie* (Jena: 1923), Vol. III, p. 109) regards the total "transportation costs" as "transportation-obstacles" and speaks of a law of transportation-obstacles.

2. M. Aurousseau ("The Arrangement of Rural Population," in *Geographical Review* (New York: 1920), 223ff.) gives three general types of settlements: (1) agglomerations (small towns, villages); (2) partial agglomerations (village communities, hamlets); and (3) disseminations.

3. Also, Schlüter concludes that "the mere fact of living together in villages creates an opportunity for an increase of the always existing small percentage of nonagricultural population." He thus affirms the distinctness of re-

---

* See p. 65.

gions with segregated single farms or of such villages in regard to the existence of central professions. (Otto Schlüter, "Beiträge zur Bevölkerungs- und Siedlungsgeographie Deutschlands," in *Petermanns Mitteilungen,* 58th year, 2 (Gotha: 1910), 65.)

4. Dörries invites attention to the "unequally greater frequency" of towns and places in the mountain region in contrast to the plains region of northwestern Germany; in southern Germany the situation is usually reversed. One can thus see how incorrect it is to explain this frequency only by the formation of the topography. (Hans Dörries, "Entstehung und Formenbildung der niedersächsischen Stadt, eine vergleichende Städtegeographie," in *Forschungen zur deutschen Landes- und Volkskunde,* 27 (Stuttgart: 1929), 18.)

5. Compare note 4 above with the elaborations of Johann Georg Kohl (*Der Verkehr und die Ansiedelungen der Menschen in ihrer Abhängigkeit von der Gestaltung der Erdoberfläche,* 2nd ed. (Leipzig: 1850)) and V. Furlan ("Die Standortsprobleme in der Volks- und Weltwirtschaftslehre," in *Weltwirtschaftliches Archiv,* 2 (Jena: 1913), 1ff).

6. The very titles of Kohl's works betray his fundamental attitude. See note 5 above.

7. Ratzel speaks, in fact, about the "town-procreating power of traffic." (*Anthropogeographie oder Grundzüge der Anwendung der Geographie auf die Geschichte,* 2nd ed. (Stuttgart: 1912), Vol. II, pp. 302-323.)

8. Erich Schrader, "Die Städte Hessens," in *Jahresbericht des Frankfurter Vereins für Geographie und Statistik* (Frankfurt: 1922).

9. Ferdinand von Richthofen, *Vorlesungen über allgemeine Siedlungs- und Verkehrsgeographie,* version and edition of Otto Schlüter (Berlin: 1908), pp. 259ff.

10. Robert Gradmann, "Die städtischen Siedlungen des Königreichs Württemberg," in *Forschungen zur deutschen Landes- und Volkskunde,* 21, Part I (Stuttgart: 1926).

11. Above all: Friedrich Metz, "Die ländlichen Siedlungen Badens. I Unterland," *Badische geographische Abhandlungen* (Karlsruhe: 1926), Part I.

12. See also Erwin Scheu (*Deutschlands wirtschaftsgeographische Harmonie* (Breslau: 1924), p. 3), who says that "conveyances . . . are only servants for overcoming space."

13. See Oskar Engländer, *Theorie des Güterverkehrs und der Frachtsätze* (Jena: 1924).

14. In fact, a workers' residential area of 2000 inhabitants has at most one movie, and a purely agricultural village of 2000 inhabitants has none. See "Statistik der Lichtspieltheater," in *Mitteilungen des hessischen landesstatistischen Amtes* (Darmstadt: 1928).

15. Oskar Engländer, *Theorie des Güterverkehrs . . . ,* and "Volkswirtschaftliche Theorie des Personenverkehrs," in *Archiv für Sozialwissenschaften und Sozialpolitik,* 50 (Tübingen: 1923).

16. See the sketch in Johann Heinrich von Thünen, *Der isolierte Staat in Beziehung auf Landwirtschaft und Nationalökonomie,* 2nd ed. (Jena: 1910).

17. See S. Daggett, "Theories of Location," *Principles of Inland Transportation,* 3rd ed. (New York: Harper & Row, Publishers, 1941), pp. 471-473.

18. If one considers the Thünen rings of the free economy, the forest economy, and the crop-rotation economy essentially as types of economies adjacent to the central town and simply as the complementary region of the town; see Johann Heinrich von Thünen, *op. cit.,* Table 2, p. 387.

19. "Auerbach's Law" (Size of place $= \dfrac{\text{Size of largest city}}{\text{Rank of place}}$) is not much more than playing with numbers. (Felix Auerbach, "Das Geset der Bevölkerungskonzentration," in *Petermanns Mitteilungen,* 59th year (Gotha: 1913), 74ff.) See also the rejoinders by Hans Maurer and Ludwig Weise in *ibid.,* 229ff.

20. Robert Gradmann, *Süddeutschland* (Stuttgart: 1931), Vol. I, pp. 159f.

21. See also Max Weber, "Die Stadt," in "Wirtschaft und Gesellschaft," *Grundriß der Sozialökonomie,* 2nd ed. (Tübingen: 1925), Vol. III, Part II, as well as his *Allgemeine Wirtschaftsgeschichte* (Munich and Leipzig: 1923).

22. This method for determining the single types and their characteristics is applied in the second part of the book; it is, however, a purely statistical method, and therefore, its application is not quite without shortcomings.

23. A. F. Weber states, also in another connection and based on a historical aspect, the following proposition which fits very well here: "The boundary stone was the predecessor of the market-cross." (Adna Ferrin Weber, *The Growth of Cities in the Nineteenth Century* (New York and London: 1899), p. 171.)

24. See Part II, "The Connecting Part," for the meanings of the letter designations of the types, pp. 154-158.

25. According to the classification of Sombart, this is a *"Fiktionsgesetz,"* that is, a scheme which concerns the "purpose-means-relationships" [the relationship between the aims to be reached and the methods and means to be applied in order to achieve these aims]. (Werner Sombart, *Die drei Nationalökonomien, Geschichte und System der Lehre von der Wirtschaft* (Munich and Leipzig: 1930), pp. 258ff.) These "fictitious laws" are demonstrated by "rational schemata" —such schemata have been developed here; simultaneously the classification concerns the "part-sum-relationship" [between the part and the whole] *(ibid.,* pp. 253ff).

26. Compare Thünen's formula for the just labor wage: $\sqrt{a \times p}$, in which a is the demand and p is the labor product of a worker's family of four. (Johann Heinrich von Thünen, in *op. cit.,* Part II, p. 549.)

27. Werner Sombart, "Einige Anmerkungen zur Lehre vom Standort der Industrien," in *Archiv für Sozialwissenschaften und Sozialpolitik,* 30 (Tübingen: 1910), 752.

28. Ludwig von Bortkiewicz, "Eine geometrische Fundierung der Lehre vom Standort der Industrien," in *Archiv für Sozialwissenschaften und Sozialpolitik,* 30 (Tübingen: 1910), 775.

29. Alfred Weber, "Die industrielle Standortlehre (allgemeine und kapitalistische Theorie des Standortes)," *Grundriß der Sozialökonomie* (Tübingen: 1914), p. 78.

30. Compare the following to Figure 3, p. 73.

31. Those questions are considered in Wilhelm Launhardt, *Theorie des Trassierens* (Hannover: 1887), Vol. I, but the author lacks theoretical foundations and also the clear insight into problems which can be formulated exactly only from the economic point of view.

32. Gradmann calls them "long-distance lines which consist of pieces." (Robert Gradmann, *Süddeutschland,* Vol. I. p. 185.)

33. Johan Georg Kohl, *op. cit.,* p. 12.

34. A worthwhile discussion of this subject is Helmut Haufe's "Die geographische Struktur des deutschen Eisenbahnverkehrs," in *Veröffentlichungen des geographischen Seminars der Universität Leipzig,* 2 (Langensalza: 1931). I

am sorry to say that the "theory" in this discussion falls short, although the fact that the author bases his discussion on it as well as on the theoretical basic thoughts given by him should be fully acknowledged.

35. Erich Schrader (*loc. cit.*) finds a fixed cross-country distance of about 21 km.

36. Kohl does not start with the distribution of the area only, but with the limitation of the area; thus, e.g., he gives the square region four main lines and gives the hexagon six main lines, etc., (*op. cit.*, pp. 104ff.).

37. Helmut Haufe, *op. cit.*, p. 15.

38. See especially Rudolf Kjellén, *Der Staat als Lebensform* (Leipzig: 1917), p. 70.

39. See Herman Gruber, *Kreise und Kreisgrenzen Preußens, vornehmlich die Ostpreußens, geographische betrachtet* (Königsberg: 1912). Especially, in referring to this work do we find the publications of government regulations.

See also Friedrich Nüssle, *Die administrative Einteilung des unteren und mittleren württembergischen Neckargebietes. Ein Beitrag zur wirtschafts- und politisch-geographischen Landeskunde von Württemberg* (Stuttgart: 1930). Nüssle suggests as significant signs of a "good" *Oberamt* [a certain administrative office of an area] prominent central location in the area, eminent center as *Oberamt*-town, and favorable development of the boundaries (pp. 229f.).

40. A theoretical political-geography is just as possible and may be approximately as "exact" as a theoretical economic-geography, although the rationality of action which is easily accessible in an exact understanding falls to the background, in contrast to the determination by reason of power in the action; with the help of the "understanding method" it is, however, also possible to obtain laws, rational schemes, and tendencies.

C
Dynamic Processes

1. Introduction: The Dynamic Point of View

By now we have shown, although not exhaustively, those relations which one may define as static. However, one such static position—e.g., a densely settled region here or a thinly settled region there—is only a consideration of the moment, a snapshot of the existing world in continued change; the stationary state is only fiction, whereas motion is reality. Every factor which adds to the importance of the central place— region, population, supply and demand of central goods, prices of the goods, transportation conditions, sizes of the central places and competition between central and dispersed production of a good—is subject to continuous change. The individual factor either creates the change out of itself according to its own nature—then the change is endogenous —or the change is forced by other elements—then the change is exogenous. The effects of continuous variation in these elements on each other are, as a rule, quite different from the effects when these elements are in a state of rest. The physicist knows that, for example, water in motion has a quite different influence from water at rest on the soil, on animals, etc., or that increasing pressure has different effects from constant pressure. In economic relationships, especially in the cultural sphere, the same is true; it is known that deflating or inflating currency produces different economic results than does a stable currency; and also that a rapidly deflating currency has different effects than a slowly deflating one. We shall speak, however, of the mutual relationships of the changing elements and indeed, better yet, of the processes— not the historical, concrete processes, but the individual concrete causes abstracted from general typical processes, in which time appears as an abstraction. These processes are nearer than the purely static relationships to reality. They are the real part of the theoretical discussion and should be incorporated into dynamic theory.

2. The Population

Let us begin with the population. Suppose that the population increases. Up to now it has amounted to 4000 inhabitants in a region of 80 sq. km. of whom 2000 live in the central place. This is Case 3, in which we assumed that there were 6125 consultations with an income of 18,375 marks for the doctor. Now let us assume that the population increases 20 per cent quite uniformly throughout the whole region as well as in the town. This will result in 7350 consultations. The importance of the central place consequently increases in the same proportion as the population. If the population increases a further 20 per cent, the number of consultations would be 8575. At this point, something fundamental changes. Assume that the doctor needs a minimum income of 8000 marks a year if he is to make a living. He is not, however, physically able to manage more than 8000 consultations a year. Either 575 desires for consultations must remain disregarded; or they must be satisfied at the neighboring central place; or, a second doctor must open a practice. But will the second doctor begin his practice at the central place or at some dispersed place in the region? Will the old center become strengthened or will a new center be formed? If the new doctor settles in the town, then he surely will get the 575 desires for consultations which have been disregarded. Whether he will be able to take still other patients from the first doctor depends mainly upon circumstances which should not be considered here. We shall assume an extreme case, in which the second doctor gets no other patients. The second doctor cannot live, however, on the 1725 marks from 575 consultations.

If, in the neighboring region, the population has grown to the same degree, and if this region also has one doctor, then it will be possible for the third doctor (the new one) to settle between both central places, or more exactly, midway between them. The computation would then be as follows:

	Area (sq. km.)	Population	Consultations per capita	Number of Consultations
In the town	5	2800	2	5600
Ring I	15	700	$1\frac{1}{2}$	1035
Ring II	39	1365	1	1365
Total		4865		8000

And for the third doctor (the new one):

	Area (sq. km.)	Population	Consultations per capita	Number of Consultations
Place located	5	175	2	350
Ring I	15	525	$1\frac{1}{2}$	$787\frac{1}{2}$
Ring II	22	770	1	770
Total		1470		$1907\frac{1}{2}$

These 1900 consultations for the third doctor give him an income of about 5700 marks, on which he cannot live. But if a third region of equal kind is added and if the new doctor settles at the intersection of these three regions, then he will receive about 2850 consultations and an annual income of 8550 marks. Thus, he will settle at that intersection; and an auxiliary central place will develop there.

Hence, with three doctors in the three regions, $3 \times 8575 = 25,725$ consultations a year will occur; with four doctors, there will be $3 \times 8000 = 24,000$ consultations for the old doctors and 2850 for the fourth doctor. Thus, there will be a total of 26,850 consultations in the region, i.e., more than there were with only three doctors. This occurs because persons who formerly, because of the longer distance to the doctor, could afford only one and one-half, or one-half consultations can now go to the new doctor located nearer to them for one and one-half or two consultations—a greater number of central places always brings a greater consumption of central goods.

If the population does not increase evenly over the whole region, and if in our example an increase of 40 per cent occurs in only the central place, then the result is similar. The region originally had 4000 inhabitants and the central place 2000 inhabitants. The 40 per cent increase of 1600 inhabitants occurs only at the central place; it now has 3600 inhabitants. The computation is as follows:

	Population	Consultations per capita	Number of Consultations
Nucleus	3600	2	7200
Ring I	500	$1\frac{1}{2}$	750
Ring II	1250	1	1250
Ring III	250	$\frac{1}{2}$	125
Total	5600		9325

The first doctor manages 8000 consultations; 1325 consultations remain disregarded. The second doctor, however, cannot live on such a small number of consultations. If he settles, as before, on the border between two regions, he will have 2562½ consultations and 7687.50 marks of income, which is not quite enough for him to live on.

	Area (sq. km.)	Population	Consultations per capita	Number of Consultations
In new nucleus	5	125	2	250
Ring I	15	375	1½	562½
Ring II	40	1000	1	1000
Ring III	60	1500	½	750
Total		3000		2562½

But if he is temporarily satisfied while expecting further increases in the population, he will establish his practice on the communication line of the two regions; i.e., the new place will be created according to the traffic principle. If the population increases slowly, then the new doctor must establish his practice at the intersection of three regions; i.e., the location of the new central place is determined by the marketing principle.

Fundamentally, we receive different results if the central place had 3000 inhabitants and the region had 2000 dispersed inhabitants to begin with. In that case, the central population provided 6000 consultations and the dispersed population 2125, i.e., 8125 consultations minus 2125 which could go to a neighboring doctor. If the population of the region increases 40 per cent and if the entire increase of 2000 inhabitants occurs at the central place, then there will be 10,000 consultations at this central place alone and an additional 2125 consultations from the dispersed population, for a total of 12,125 consultations. Of these, 8000 are claimed by the first doctor and 4125 by the new doctor. Thus, the second doctor establishes his practice at the central place also. No new central place is created, but the importance of the old central place, which formerly played a great role, increases. It is not important whether the increase in population occurs slowly or quickly.

Generally, the result of the foregoing reasoning is that if the population of a region grows evenly in town and country or if there are originally small towns which receive the whole increase of population, then it is certain in the first case (and probable in the second case) that a new auxiliary central place will develop at a point which lies as far away as possible from the old central places. The central importance of the old central places does not increase—or it increases very little— despite the increase in population. If, however, there is from the beginning a large town which receives the entire increase in population, then no new central place will be formed, and the importance of the single central place will grow correspondingly greater.

Now, suppose that the population does not immediately grow by an increase of 40 per cent but does so only in the course of fifty years. This does not fundamentally alter the future chances either of the large and growing place in the one case or the remote dispersed place in the other. That is, it does not limit their future choice of action. On the other hand, the possibility exists for the case of very quick increases, especially in the central places, that the location of the new central place will be determined in accordance with the traffic principle; with slow increases, the location is determined only according to the marketing principle.

The mechanism works quite similarly when the structure of the population changes, e.g., when the inhabitants transfer from agricultural to industrial activities, a change usually occurs, paralleled by a concentration of the population in the industrialized activities, with little change in the agricultural population (or when the income conditions of the population, especially of the center-living population, improve while those of the dispersed population may even decline). Both of these are frequent cases: when the scale of wants—the rank in which the consumer arranges his demands according to their urgency—changes, then the demands for central goods appear more urgent than those for dispersed goods. This means that an increase in the consumption of central goods results from the *lower** costs of the consumption of dispersed goods. We will call this *urbanizing,* i.e., the dispersed-living population becoming accustomed to urban demands, with the result that the same situations exist as we have seen in the case of an increase in the population. But it is to be observed that with an increase in incomes, relatively more central goods are bought than dispersed ones, and correspondingly with a decrease in incomes relatively less are bought.

But what of a retardation in the growth of population density? Let us assume that the population decreases equally in town and country, and that the consumption of central goods likewise decreases. To be sure, this may not be the case, since the tendency to decrease may be balanced by a countertendency of the consumption of central goods to increase because of the increase in the incomes of the smaller population or because of phenomena which will be discussed later. We assume, however, that the decrease in the consumption of central goods parallels the decrease in population. It is certain that a decrease in the importance of the central place (or central places) goes hand in hand in this region with these developments. The question which especially interests us is this: Does the decrease in importance occur at the auxiliary central places first—insofar as such places have developed—or does it occur at the central places, i.e., will the total number of central places be re-

---

* Italics mine—Ed.

duced, in which case the remaining ones will maintain their central importance at the old level, or will all places be reduced in importance? And as a further possibility, perhaps a migration of central demands occurs towards neighboring central places which lie in a region where no retarding development of the population has taken place.

We shall clarify this with the help of the doctor example. There are three regions at the intersection at which an auxiliary central place lies. At each of the central places 8000 consultations are managed and at the auxiliary central place 2850. If the population decreases by 20 per cent in both the town and in the country, then only 6400 consultations remain at each central place and 2280 at the auxiliary central place. But the doctor at the auxiliary central place cannot live on an income of 6840 marks (2280 $\times$ 3 marks). Hence, the auxiliary central place dies. The 2280 consultations of the auxiliary central place are now distributed among the three central places. Each receives, however, less than a third of the 2280 consultations, for fewer central goods are consumed because of the long distances from the region of the former auxiliary central place; perhaps each central place will gain only 380 consultations in addition to the 6400 consultations it already had, or a total of 6780 consultations. In other words, with a general decrease of population in a region the weaker auxiliary central places die away, but the importance of the other central places does not increase proportionately to the added population, but rather, less than proportionately; nonetheless, under certain circumstances this importance might even be intensified because of the increase in demand of central goods which have been released following the death of the auxiliary central place. If the population in the dispersed border regions decreases markedly, and the population of the central places decreases very little, then the process just described will occur to a still greater degree. This last case, of relatively small decreases in the population of the central places, will be called the regular case, as these central places are usually able to maintain their importance through the acceptance of other demands which have become available.

In the case of central goods augmentable as desired with variable prices—our earlier shoeshop example—the price (of the shoes) will fall with a decreased demand which resulted from a decrease in population, because the seller hopes to prevent a reduction in consumption by means of reducing his price. As a result of these cheaper prices, purchasers from a neighboring region will now appear and purchase. The importance of the central place in the declining region would perhaps increase. But this can only be temporary—a kind of clearance sale. Rather, the tendency is for the demand for central goods to migrate to the central places in the neighboring regions with increasing populations, because these places increase production and reduce prices accordingly. The first re-action to a decrease in population is a reduction of prices; and the first reaction to an increase in the population is an increase of prices. But the permanent reaction to a decrease in population is a rise in the costs of production; and the permanent reaction to an increase in population is a reduction in the costs of production—as a result of these differing price trends, the marketing region of the growing central place is extended at the expense of the marketing region of the declining central place. Hence, the rate of population change is highly important, as we shall see when we discuss it later.

3. The Central Goods

The processes just mentioned result in a change in the demand for central goods. It is not necessary to discuss the effects of these processes any further. On the other hand, a change of demand might be caused by a change in the price of the good. But there will be more about this later.

New for us is the problem of the influence of a change in the supply of central goods on the development of central places. Let us assume a case in which, by means of an increase of those doing academic study —a sociological and economic phenomenon—the number of doctors who offer their services has increased more than the demand for their services (which are to be considered as central goods). Incidentally, the largest number of college graduates go into central professions. An increase in college graduates thus generally increases the offering of such central goods, as the services of lawyers, higher officials, teachers, ministers, and other professionals. An increase in the offering of central goods is doubtless caused by an increase in demand. This increase may result from the fact that the central good also becomes offered at places or in regions in which a direct offering of these central goods was previously absent, and the demand for those goods consequently less. Or it may have been caused by a generally higher regard for central goods, which is manifested not only by the attraction towards the central occupations but also by the stronger demand for central goods. But above all, the demand is increased by the fact that the central goods become cheaper as a result of an increase in the offering of them (in consequence of the sellers cutting the price—sharpened competition—or in consequence of a general reduction of the prices in order to gain the patronage of buyers who could not buy at the higher prices) or of the public being approached through advertising.

The larger supply of central goods is in any case the consequence of increased consumption. Therefore, different possibilities can be distinguished:

Case 1. Despite the greater quantity of sales of central goods, the receipts remain the same, because the goods are per unit sold for less; with production costs remaining constant the profit of the seller of central goods declines.

Case 2. With receipts the same, and the production costs declining accordingly, the profit remains the same as earlier.

Case 3. With increased receipts (the cost of consumption of dispersed goods), the profit will increase, as a rule.

In Case (1) the importance of the central place declines with a higher supply; in Case (2) its importance remains the same; and in Case (3) the importance may increase. If more persons take part in the increased supply than in the former lower supply—as in the case of the increase in the supply as a consequence of the expansion in college training—the receipts may increase; but every one of those who offer the central good will receive a smaller profit. Thus, the number of middle and higher incomes at the central places declines, and the number of smaller incomes increases, as a result of which the importance of the central place is reduced. This decline in importance occurs because only the middle incomes (because of their number) have a greater influence on the consumption of central goods.

Whether an increased supply causes an apparent weakening or strengthening of the importance of a central place cannot generally be determined. But this, too, depends upon the types of goods offered. If the demand for a certain type of good (a movie, for example) is very elastic, then an increased supply will mean a large increase in consumption, perhaps so large that the demand for similar dispersed goods (e.g., books) will be waived, resulting in a strengthening of the central places. If the demand for a certain type of good is inelastic (medical care, for example), an increased supply will not bring about a proportionate increase in consumption. The central place, therefore, will become weakened, at least insofar as its importance is determined by the supply of goods the demand for which is inelastic.

An increased supply as well as an increased demand for central goods may lead to favorable development of the central places. The controlling power of supply and demand is different, however, with regard to the type of development of the central places. If increased demand leads in most cases to a strengthening of existing central places, then an increased supply usually will lead to an increase in the number of central places through building of new central places or revival of central places which were "lost." An increased supply of the central goods offered sells best if the increase does not occur at all existing central places. Finally, there are cases in which, in contrast to the effect of the increased demand, the importance of the central place declines with an increased supply.

A decrease in the demand for central goods works in the same manner as decreases in the population, incomes, etc.; that is no new problem for us.

The effects of a reduction in the supply of central goods are much more manifold. For goods for which the demand is urgent and inelastic, the demand will exceed the supply. For goods with a fixed supply, the previously mentioned consequences appear: Consumption migrates to neighboring places and, even though the prices at the original selling place are stable, high, or variable, the demand declines until it is fully covered by the increased supply; the profit on these central goods increases, sometimes so much that it is altogether higher than before and thus favors the central place. It might also be that with a reduction in the supply of central goods, a transfer from central to dispersed production will occur, as we observed so often during the War;* and the importance of the central place will thus be reduced.

The processes with regard to goods with nonurgent, elastic demands are somewhat different. The reduction in the supply of goods with fixed supplies and firm prices results simply in a reduction in consumption. With goods of fixed supplies and variable prices, it results in a price rise, less than proportionate, however, until the supply is again sufficient to cover the demand. As a result of this fact, many would-be purchasers of the scarce nonurgent good buy a substitute central or dispersed good instead; and the importance of the central place probably declines.

We have already discussed the importance of prices; there are only a few things to be added here. We said in the chapter on static relations that the central place with lower prices has a larger range for its central goods, i.e., it has a larger complementary region, than the central place with higher prices; the former place is better developed than the latter one. The question in dynamics is: What influences do rising or falling prices of central goods have (generally) upon the development of central places? First, we must investigate the factor of price-instability. We are not interested in the causes (which may vary greatly) but in the duration of a price-fluctuation, which is significant to our discussion.

There are first the fluctuations of short duration, the seasonal fluctuations. They have almost no significance on the development of central places, except insofar as the central place must adjust itself to the price-fluctuations and, consequently, to the consumption of central goods gen-

---

* World War I.

erally. Its central institutions must be relatively flexible in order to satisfy demand when it increases and must also be able to suffer slumps in business activity. Since this is valid for all central places, it is of little significance here.

An exceptional case involves those central places which are usually more concerned with seasonal price fluctuations than the neighboring places. This case includes all those places in the vicinity of which a seasonal production (a "campaign")* occurs, for example, in agricultural production (sugar beets, for instance) and in areal-collective-economies† (fishing, logging, etc.); and central places in the main tourist regions (the Alps, the Black Forest, the seashore). The increase in demand for central goods during the season, because of an increase in the population or an increase in their earnings, raises the prices. Such central places will have, as a consequence of the increased prices and still further as a consequence of the factors which cause the increase in prices, a stronger development than places not subject to the seasons. Hence, because of what we have said before about the development of the auxiliary central places of such regions being regularly small, and because the increase in the consumption of central goods happens mostly at the dispersed places of the region, we shall discover additional auxiliary central places which are often only fleeting, i.e., only for the duration of the season. Also, those central places which lie at the periphery or outside of the region dependent upon the seasons are responsible for part of the favorable development, because, during the season, they are able to sell an additional quantity of central goods in consequence of the migration of consumption to places with lower prices. This seasonally-conditioned upswing of the business cycle appears spatially to affect two regions: an inner one which is affected immediately and an outer one which is affected indirectly. There are also seasonally-conditioned business cycle troughs which have corresponding results (e.g., local declines in prices, migration of consumption from the neighboring regions which do not undergo the fluctuation in the business cycle), by which a certain balance becomes established.

The second type of price-fluctuation with respect to duration is the cyclical variation in the proper sense.‡ We have written a special section on the problems of the business cycle.§

A third type of price fluctuation—secular changes in prices—has historically had a significant influence on central places. The general increase in prices of agricultural products and raw materials in the re-

---

* A temporary sales promotion.

† That is, economies in which goods are collected over large areas and brought to one or to a few points for sale.

‡ The business cycle proper usually takes several years for completion.

§ See Section 9, p. 126.

cent epoch of industrial development, chiefly during the nineteenth century, with simultaneous increases in the prices of labor, belongs to this type; but at the same time a considerable reduction in the prices of industrial products occurred. Since the end of the nineteenth century, there has been a general price decline, at least with regard to agricultural products and raw materials. In the first sketchy period of industrial development, along with the increase in agricultural prices, there was a clear upward development of central places, and central places of more local importance, in agricultural regions, were revived. Far stronger have been the influences of price declines in industrial products, the increase in the number of industrial workers, and the rise in their wages; these phenomena are chiefly responsible for the rising importance of central places of a higher order. It is too difficult to pass judgment on the present period because of its proportionately short duration. It is still not practical at this point to state how much the price development is related to the secular causes and how much to the cyclical causes. Besides, the price development trend might have still less influence on the development of central places because of the short duration of its effects. In any case, the decline in prices of agricultural products at the turn of the century[1] led to a decline in the importance of the central places of a lower order because the nonagricultural population then spent a smaller part of its income for agricultural products, i.e., for dispersed goods, and spent a larger part of its earnings for central goods.

What is the effect if the number of types of central goods which are offered or produced at a central place increases or decreases? Let us assume that a central place had up to now two central goods, A and B. The inhabitants of the region spend 20,000 marks for A and 20,000 marks for B, a total of 40,000 marks. Of the 40,000 marks, 5000 are for travel expenses (loss of working time, travel costs, valuation of other burdens, etc.). The rest (35,000 marks) is spent for the central goods themselves, which determine the receipts of the central place, that is, 17,500 marks for each of the goods. If for any reason the central place can no longer offer the good B (e.g., because of the elimination of the post office or the bankruptcy of a dairy), then the population can spend $20,000 - 5000$ (travel costs) $= 15,000$ marks for central good A, and only $20,000 - 10,000$ (travel costs) $= 10,000$ marks for good B because it now has to be bought at a more remote central place to which the travel costs are 10,000. Consequently, the central place loses not only the 17,500 marks spent for good B but also 2500 marks spent for good A, while the more remote central place gains not 17,500 marks, but only 10,000, for good B. The loss to the nearer central place will be even greater if the more remote central place also offers good A, so that those who wish to buy good *B* can now buy both goods in one trip to the more remote central place.

According to similar considerations, a central place which offers a *new* type of central good will show a greater increase in sales of central goods than normally because the increase falls to the new central good alone, first, through the saving on travel costs for the dispersed population and, second, through the migration from the neighboring regions of the demand for the old types of central goods.

From the processes mentioned here, we may conclude: First, with a general increase in the number of types of central goods, observed virtually over centuries and especially in the last 100 years, towns gained importance while the country outside remained stagnant or declined. And second, a decline in the offerings of central goods has more disadvantages for the central place concerned than is normally assumed to be the case. Thus, it is also understandable why small towns, especially, resist so violently the removal or elimination of administrative offices.

4. Production Costs and Technical Progress

We must now consider the influences and procedures of production costs and technical progress. These influences are well-known with regard to the location of industries; but what we are most concerned with is the specific influence of these interrelationships on the size and distribution of central places.

The price of central goods is, as we have seen, to a great extent the deciding factor in the size and area of an individual central place. Prices have different origins, depending upon whether the supplies of the goods in question are elastic or inelastic. In the former case, costs determine the price, while in the latter case, costs are determining only if there is a set minimum price. It is, therefore, vital to consider closely the influence of production costs on the price of central goods and significance of central places.

Customarily, production costs are subdivided into capital costs (interest), labor costs (wages), revenue costs (profits), and land costs (rent). We shall use this division here.

First, the capital expenditures. Capital includes not only borrowed funds and other cash funds, but also buildings, machines, storage areas, and inventories. The cost of these includes the payment of interest and insurance and the amortization of debt; within a national economy, they are fairly uniform, differing only slightly between local and regional areas. Only in interest is there any strong variation, due to the coverage of risk. On the local level, this element of uncertainty causes a higher cost, as can happen, for example, in border areas (especially if they are fought over, or otherwise endangered (e.g., East Prussia). A high interest rate for capital means higher production costs and, therefore, higher prices for variable cost goods,* or lesser profits for goods of fixed supply.† Therefore, central places in such areas must sell their goods at higher prices, which, as a rule, leads to a migration of consumption to neighboring central places (with a higher centrality) where prices are lower. Near unstabilized borders, the central places will have, therefore, small complementary areas and will show limited development; central places near stabilized borders, on the other hand, will have, as a rule, greater development, since the border traffic stimulates action. To an even greater extent, these same factors (stable or unstable borders) influence the price of insurance and the amount of depreciation. (The latter has received too little attention.) A change in the interest rate usually affects the whole economy uniformly, and therefore has little influence on the relative development of central places. To be sure, however, a change in the risk premium contained in the interest rate changes differently, regionally and locally, and therefore does influence the relative development of central places.

Capital costs have great importance in the development of central places, inasmuch as they chiefly determine the lower range limit of central goods, particularly of those which have a high proportion of capital costs to total costs. A central good with relatively high capital costs is necessarily a central good of a higher order with a wide range and a larger consumer area. High capital investment, therefore, forces a higher centralization of production (that is, of supply). Thus, dynamic reactions are naturally much more noticeably felt; there is a greater change in the cost of capital for the central good of a higher order with a high proportion of capital costs, as compared with central goods of a lower order which use little capital. The result is that central places of a higher order are subjected to greater variation in importance than are central places of a lower order with more stable importance.

The way in which the production cost factor of labor influences the location of industry is excellently described by Alfred Weber.[2] This is important to us for two reasons: first, because labor markets develop, and second, because the level of wages is determined for the compensation of labor. Out of the conditions that develop, the labor force develops into one of the most important consumer groups (already discussed in

---

* Goods whose production is subject to economies of large-scale production.

† Like land, the quantity of the factor is fixed. Therefore, its rent (profits) is determined by the value of the final product.

the chapter on population).* We are not concerned here with the question of the industrial site, but rather with the question of the development of the central places.

What is to be understood by the term, *labor market?* The term applies to that place where the demand or supply of labor is large enough to create an exchange of supplies and demands of labor—in the first case (demand), places with many work possibilities, especially industrial places, and in the latter case supply, locations with greater population. From this, it can be seen that neither the supply nor the demand has anything to do with the central places, even though the industrial places and the heavily populated places are central places. Only the exchange is a central function; and the place of this exchange is a *labor market.*

Whether this *market* is at the place of demand, the place of supply, or a third place depends on several factors. It will evolve at the place of demand—an industrial place—when unemployment is general, or exists regionally; that is, if the supply exceeds the demand. On the other hand, if there is a labor shortage, the labor market will evolve at the source of supply. With the existence of organized labor agencies, this can occur at other central places. Therefore, the central function of the industrial site is increased if unemployment exists; the central function of the heavily populated place is increased if there is a labor shortage; and the central function of the more generally located central places is increased if organized labor agencies are located there.

Wages will be higher at places of labor shortages than at places of labor surpluses, especially if these conditions are chronic rather than seasonal or cyclical. Wages may be lower in one place than in another if demand is less or if standards of living are lower. The cause of this does not interest us here; it is sufficient to know that somewhere generally lower wages are present and somewhere else generally higher wages are present. Usually, wages are lower in smaller places and higher in larger places; but they are lower in overpopulated places with a small labor market. In places of lower wages industries have lower production costs and prefer such locations for sites to the extent that, according to Weber's terminology,[3] labor-oriented industries are concerned. For specialized central trade, lower wages mean lower production costs and lower prices for the central goods, whereby such locations can expand their complementary regions at the expense of regions with higher wages. This is especially noticeable in resort regions.

Central places lying outside of the resort area show a more favorable development, since they have lower wages than the resort area; therefore, their products have wider ranges, and they have larger comple-

---

* See Part I, Chapter C.2.

mentary regions. This is particularly evident in the case of flourishing central places which are near spas. As a matter of fact, lower wages in the smaller or less preferred places tend to counteract the factors which cause the larger central places to be preferred.

Changes in wages and capital costs have similar results; but along with changes in wages, local consumption also changes. (This has already been discussed in the chapter on population.*

In the consideration of a geographical area, the most important production cost is the factor connected with land. This factor, in private enterprise, is nothing more than capital—for example, machines, money, and credit. However, because it cannot be multiplied or transported, it demands a special position. General rent results from nonreproducibility, and special rent results from nontransportability. Both kinds of basic revenue find their expression in the price of the land: the more favorable land, which brings in the higher revenue, has a higher price. Where the price of the land is higher, the costs of production are higher, because both the land on which the production takes place and the land on which dwellings are built are costlier. Therefore, higher rent demands must be made, and wages must also be higher.

In general, rents for land in the central places of a higher order are higher than in the central places of a lower order, due to the higher prices for lots resulting from the additional need for real estate in the production of central goods of a higher order. From the beginning, the production and supply of central goods of a higher order has to reckon with higher rents and, therefore, with higher production costs, which influence in a different manner the location of the production of goods which require a high proportion of capital (previously considered). Like higher wage cost, the higher rental counteracts the excessive centralization of the central goods of a higher order in the larger cities. At the same time, it leads to a higher capital investment through the correspondingly greater exploitation of the land, by which the central installation is made as large as possible, increasing the supply of local goods in order to divide the overhead of expensive real estate costs among a greater output of produced goods. Which tendency will be the determining factor cannot, generally, be established; ordinarily, one can say, however, that rents serve as a brake on strong centralization, and are therefore decentralizing.

A special case may be of interest. The central place A, with a small area of eighty square miles, may, because of a special topographical condition which prevents its expansion, have relatively higher rentals than the neighboring central place B, approximately 10 kms. away. If we have a central good whose range is no more than 15 kms., it would

* See Part I, Chapter C.2.

have to be offered at the central places of both regions. Thus, the choice exists of whether to produce and offer the good at location A with a higher rental or at location B with a lower one. Provided no other reasons against it exist, location B will be chosen, since the production costs there are less. The location with the lower rentals, therefore, will develop more favorably than the location with higher rentals, and can overtake the latter. In this manner, the centrality of the smaller central place increases along with its land rents; and, in the end, both central places may have the same land rents. In spite of this, location B will be preferred over A as the place of increasing development. A central place, therefore, may be outdistanced in its development as a central place, if the rental cost is not the result of the high centralization, but rather of particular natural or other circumstances. Yes, it can even be said that a new central place may develop near the central place with higher land costs, especially where the line of traffic enhances its development. (For instance, because of a closely located railway junction, the city of Oos developed near Baden-Baden.)

Not only are the three major factors of production costs—interest, wages, and rent—usually mentioned, but also other cost factors such as taxes (state and local) and the advantages of organization are important in the development of central places. The latter are often influential. For example, a place close to the border can take over central functions if its levies and taxes are lower than in a neighboring, original central place. Examples include Frankfurt and Offenbach, Mannheim and Ludwigshafen, and Basel and Loerrach. In such cases, the centrality usually attached to a central place is divided among two or more neighboring places. As an isolated case, such a split may bring advantages; but in the larger view, it is mostly uneconomical. The advantages of cooperation are especially felt in larger cities through combined wholesale purchases by grocers, milk cooperatives, and others.[4]

Something, with many meanings and not precisely definable, is involved in all considerations of dynamic economic association. If this something is not considered, all speculation must end. This something has been assigned the general and vague expression of *technical progress*. In detail, it includes every little technical and organizational improvement. Seen as a whole, it is the one process which can be followed throughout human history as the increasing perfection of goods by which life has been made more pleasant and nature has been better exploited and controlled. Insofar as technical progress brings a continuing expansion of human skills, it can be described graphically as a continually rising curve. Only very seldom, and usually only for a brief span, does this curve sink, indicating a decrease in technical ability, as occurred, for example, in medieval Europe, when the highly developed Roman skills were almost completely lost following the mass migrations. The rise of the curve is sometimes fairly even, and, at other times, steep. The influence of technical progress on the course of economic activity is one of the most important topics of dynamic considerations, which, especially and impressively, shows how unsatisfactory is a simple statistical consideration of the relationships between technical change and economic development.

Technical progress is represented mainly as an increasing division and specialization of labor; and as the substitution of the more efficient mechanical "labor" of machines for insufficient human and animal labor. Therefore, in connection with the increasing shift from labor to capital (in the sense of an increase of capital's share and a decrease in labor's share in production), resulting in a tremendous increase in production and a rapid decrease in the prices of goods, there is an increase in practical knowledge and ability, and an increase in the rational control over the origin and more refined shaping of the economy. Generally and briefly (but by no means necessarily by force) an impoverishment of the intellectual and cultural life goes (although not necessarily by force) hand in hand with the growth of technical and rational development of the economy.

Parallel to this technical progress, and born from the same mental attitude and intellectual endeavor, there is an increase in demands on life, an increase of the desire to possess goods, a multiplication and differentiation of needs, and a rise in living and intellectual standards.

From the supply side of production, this development indicates a transition from the more individual type of handicraft production at dispersed places to the more centralized and mechanical type of central goods production. That is, in the sense of supply itself, there is a preference for central (more convenient for business) over dispersed (more convenient for consumers) supply. From the demand side, this development indicates a change in needs and tastes, in the sense of a preference for central over dispersed goods. Supply and demand both prefer, therefore, central locations, and a general urbanization takes place. This is illustrated statistically by the great increase in urban population and a much lesser increase (or possibly a decrease) in rural population. However, there are certain observable trends (brought on by the automobile, radio, telephone, and others) which suggest that technical progress may possibly have completely different effects during the next decade or century.

As far as the central places are concerned, how significant is this development? Will it benefit all central places equally? Will it favor the larger agglomerations, the central places of a higher order? Or will it let new central places spring up next to the old ones, so as to satisfy the continually increasing demand for central goods? As far as technical progress brings an increase in supply, our earlier observation will hold here: The development will in general benefit all central places equally, but will also call new ones into being to fill the increasing supply. Although the increase in the demand of central goods favors existing larger central places in the existing, lesser developed areas, new central places may develop.

We must also state the following reflection: Technical progress tends to increase the range of central goods by decreasing transportation costs and production costs through increased specialization of types of goods and through mass production. The result is continued development. The increase in the goods of a higher order offered at central places of a higher order is especially evident in the introduction of new commodities. The transition of central goods of a lower order to ones of a higher order can be illustrated by the warehouse with central goods of a higher order which are widely bought in the countryside while the same goods as central goods of a lower order, and sold in the ordinary stores, are gradually supplanted. It can also be illustrated by the increasing specialization of medicine whereby the specialist offers services of a higher order which were formerly offered by the general practitioner as services of a lower order. These facts signify a distinct preference for the central places of a higher order over those of a lower order, which is a well-known phenomenon apparent in the great increase of the population of major cities and relative stagnation or decrease of population in small cities.

5. The Region

The complementary region of a central place is determined ideally and fundamentally by the range of the central goods at that place. This ideal complementary region is, however, substantially pared in concrete cases: first, by the proximity of neighboring central places, which in the most favorable circumstances—with their distances from one another no greater than necessary to enable them to supply the entire land with central goods—a segment is cut away from the ideally circular complementary region, so that in a system of central places the complementary regions are shaped hexagonally; in individual cases this segment may frequently be larger. On the other hand, this ideally constructed complementary region becomes corrected basically by the topography and the transportation facilities (*Wegsamkeit*); this correction, however, is already incorporated in the meaning of *range,* because the range is not a mathematical but an economic distance.

It is obvious that the size of the complementary region changes when the ranges of the respective central goods change. This, however, belongs to the sections concerned with changes in the range;* the change in the region is only a consequence of it. The size of the complementary region is, in fact, changed only when the number of central places increases or when a change in the size-types of the central places occurs. We want to investigate individual changes in the sizes of complementary regions, and the consequences of those changes. We are thinking, for instance, of border regulations, cessions of regions to neighboring states, etc.

It is well-known that towns the sales of which are reduced by changes in the borders must suffer extreme economic distress. The whole apparatus of such a central place, which serves to produce central goods and to keep them in stock (e.g., members of firms and of the labor forces who produce and offer central goods, estates and homes—fixed capital, machines, establishments, and warehouses) is still existent. However, demand is strongly reduced; capital values and incomes at the central place decline; prices of central goods decline; and the central place suffers. In certain cases the central importance of border places is altogether destroyed.

On the other side of the border, what of the existing central place which must supply an additional part of the region with central goods? The inhabitants of this separated part now must spend a greater amount on travel and are thus able to buy fewer central goods. The weakening of the central place on one side of the border is not balanced by the strengthening of the central place on the other side. In any case, a reduction in the consumption of central goods occurs. Very probably an auxiliary central place will develop in the separated part, as a result of which the consumption of central goods will rise again; however, it will have unfavorable conditions because the region can hardly support it.

If the influence of a change in the transportation facilities of a region is scrutinized in respect to the development of the central places, all those cases which have new transportation facilities or an improvement effected by technically more perfect transportation institutions should be disregarded. We shall deal with these cases in connection with the importance of traffic, as tariff questions and other considerations play a role. We shall assume uniform transportation in all parts, namely walking. Previously the region was very difficult to traverse; today, through the drainage of swamps and the building of bridges and roads, it has become traversable. The consumption of central goods, following our former example, was 3875 consultations annually in such an almost impassable region. After it was made more easily traversable, consumption increased to 5250 consultations. Which does this increase benefit, the old central place or the new auxiliary central place?

In the region of poor transportation (a pathless region) there is a

* See Part I, Chapter B.7, and Part I, Chapter C.7.

certain tendency to form auxiliary central places, each of which is quite isolated. Therefore, in our example, each dispersed inhabitant could afford an average of only 0.625 consultations annually (1875 consultations divided by 3000 inhabitants), in contrast to the central inhabitant who could afford 2 consultations. This difference is so great that it makes possible the offering of the central good at the dispersed place. As the consumption of central goods will suddenly rise more than threefold, the consumption may be enough to permit the existence of an auxiliary central place which produces or offers this good. If, however, this region is made easily passable, then each dispersed person can afford 1.1 consultations annually (3250 divided by 3000 inhabitants). The formation of an auxiliary central place no longer meets with the same success because the consumption there can increase only from 1.1 to 2 consultations. That means, generally, that in a traversable region there is a considerably lesser tendency for auxiliary central places to develop than in an impassable region—assuming that the same wealth exists in both. After the region has been made passable, the central place of this region will become preferred beyond a doubt as it has, *a priori,* its own consumption of 2000 consultations. If it can offer central goods at lower cost for any other reason (insofar as the goods are based on production costs and have a variable market price), other places will not be able to compete with it. This will result in death for the auxiliary central places formerly developed, because the central place with its cheaper offerings and its better transportation facilities overshadows the more expensive offering of the auxiliary central place.

The natural endowments of a region can undergo manifold changes; the fertility of the soil can be exhausted by poor agronomy and the minerals can be exhausted by poor economizing. This leads to impoverishment or to emigration of the population with the same consequences as previously mentioned in the section on population* for the development of central places. A change in the valuation of the natural endowments of a region has the same effects. As a matter of fact, the valuation of the soil and minerals and not the natural endowment of the region is decisive in regard to whether these natural resources can be used with economic advantage. If one does not know how coal can be utilized, it is worthless and attracts no one. The valuation of the natural endowment can be increased by technical progress which discovers new utilizations; that is, land which previously has been worthless can suddenly become valuable if, for instance, ores are mined and used to make iron. Or tastes may change, for instance, to mountainous landscape; seeing its beauty, we travel to it. On the other hand the valuation can fall, as when we prefer coal to wood as a fuel, and iron or concrete to lumber as a build-

---

* See Chapter C.2.

ing material. These facts bring about increase and enrichment for some, and reduction and impoverishment for others, with known consequences. These consequences need not necessarily occur in every case, for impoverishment can result in the development of a more favorable labor market with lower wage demands, and thus in the attraction of other industries. A higher valuation of the natural endowments of a region can result in such an (most speculative) increase of the rent that enrichment of the entire population becomes impossible. Or, the increase in population may be so pronounced because of immigration that the enrichment does not occur, and a wage-pressure is even created. In the case of lower valuation, the emigration may become so pronounced that the few remaining inhabitants continue to be wealthy in spite of the impoverishment or devaluation of the soil.

6. The Traffic

We shall now consider the significance of transportation for the development of the central places under dynamic conditions. First, in general, lower transportation costs mean that, out of that part of income allotted to the acquisition of certain types of goods, a greater part can be spent for the goods themselves and a proportionately smaller part for transportation. The increasing security and comfort of the means of transportation have the result that the obstacles (such as the distances to be covered and the discomforts resulting therefrom) preventing more frequent acquisition of these goods are diminished. This twofold tendency is still further strengthened by technical progress, in that more central goods are acquired as a result of the reduction in the production costs of goods. But this results, with respect to central goods, in not only a higher consumption of central goods already produced, or in a greater number of kinds of goods offered, but also in greater—and more advantageous—centralization of production or offering of goods previously produced dispersedly. Therefore, not only the amount of the central good of the same kind is increased but also the number of types is increased, which means an increased preference for the town and the growth of the central places. This results, at the same time, in a shift of the distribution of the population, with a greater density at the central places, and stagnation or decline at the dispersed places (as a consequence of the transfer of the production from dispersed to central places as agricultural labor is freed), which causes an additional increase in the development of the central places.

This is all which we shall say generally on the influence of progress in transportation. Now we turn to more specific questions. Let us assume that, in an area of 80 sq. km., there is a central place in a position which was chosen in accordance with the former road traffic and the area's former military insecurity—positions, e.g., in higher situations, the *Spörn* or mountain positions, or on high plains in the vicinities of large river valleys on highways which avoid the meandering river valleys. Let us further assume that a railroad is built through the plain or the river valley, so that the station for the aforesaid central place was perhaps three-quarters of an hour from it. What influence has this on the central place?

The station itself is already a central institution. Next to it, a restaurant may be opened and perhaps a post office and most likely a storehouse of an agricultural cooperative will be added. Thus, we already have three or four kinds of central goods which are offered at the station place rather than at the central place. The station place already must be considered an auxiliary central place. Perhaps a veterinarian, who does not have to live at the central place because he hardly has any customers among the urban population, may be added, together with a construction materials store, a coal yard, and a transfer company. Perhaps living quarters and stores for railroad employees may be added. The station place may develop, in this manner, into a central place. But what happens to the existing central place? It will retain its existing central institutions—stores, physicians, tax collector's office, police station, etc.—because their customers live, to a larger extent, in the central place itself; it will also retain other institutions, which are not so strongly dependent on the railway, especially the goods traffic. But an increase in these central institutions will occur only when the customers of these new institutions are predominantly urban; otherwise the station place will normally be preferred.

But yet another factor will most likely be decisive: All dispersed places in the vicinity of the station are, as a result of the railroad connection, generally more easily able to buy in a central place of a higher order not too distantly located from the railroad. This central place is perhaps farther away in kilometers, but, by means of the inexpensive and comfortable railroad, it has become economically nearer, especially if one takes into account the fact that the prices of central goods are likely to be lower at this central place of a higher order; and, most definitely, the number of types of goods offered is greater, so that, with travel costs of one trip, several kinds of goods can be acquired at the same time. Therefore, a railroad connection which does not directly touch a central place of a lower order weakens it in two ways: through the development of an auxiliary central place at the station and through emigration of consumption of central goods to a nearby central place of a higher order. For the station place, it means development into an auxiliary central place or into a central place with a complementary region in common with the former central place. For nearby larger towns, it means, finally, important strengthening. Here again, as we have already established in another connection, there is a preference for the larger towns at the expense of the smaller, with regard to strictly economic considerations.

Another interesting case involves the rise in automobile traffic. Its significance lies in the fact that it is not restricted to the permanent rail network existing in the low-density areas and to the stations existing only at certain intervals, at which goods are transferred to other means of transportation. It is, therefore, more mobile, more general, and frequently cheaper. It is rightly said that automobile traffic results in decentralization. Herein lies the most important difference from the effects of the railroad, which, by necessity, preferred the centers and enabled them to gain importance.

How is the tendency of automobile traffic to produce decentralization to be understood, and what results does it have? Mainly, two series of events must be distinguished: the use of the automobile to serve the customer and its use as transportation to places where central institutions exist. Each of these series has different effects. Used as a delivery car, the automobile brings an advantage to the more favorable market, that is, as a rule, to the greater central place, and a disadvantage to the smaller market; for the speed and simplicity of delivery by car increases the economic radii of the goods offered in the larger central places. In smaller central places with lower consumption, the use of a delivery car will hardly pay. The store from which delivery is made need not necessarily be at the place of greater consumption; it can also be at a dispersed place of production where more favorable production conditions outweigh the increased costs of transportation (delivery directly from the factory and not from an urban delivery store). Therefore, to an increasing extent, centain types of goods which were previously offered centrally are offered dispersedly by means of the delivery cars. But that causes a general decline of the central places, especially those of the lower and the lowest order, because they have become unnecessary (because, for example, of the delivery of bread far into the country from a large bakery which need not be situated centrally).

The other series of events involves the services of the car, which brings the worker and the public comfortably to the central work, administration, and recreation places of the large towns. The advantage of residence at the central place over residence at a dispersed place is diminished. This can gradually lead to a certain disintegration of the town, or at least to a decentralization. Most of the central goods of the lower order, which serve daily demand, will be acquired at the residence-place and not at the working-place—insofar as they are not transported by delivery cars. On the other hand, the central goods of a higher order will be demanded from a wider circle of persons, for which reason the places of their supply will increase in importance. This tendency works mainly to produce favorable development of the central places of a higher order, with respect to goods of a higher order, but it works unfavorably with respect to those of the lower order.

7. The Range of Central Goods

We have already seen in the static theory that the range of a central good from a central place is variable. Every change in a factor determining it brings about a change in the range. Four main factors are involved: the size and importance of the central place, the price-willingness of the purchaser, the subjective economic distance, and the type, quantity, and price of a good. A change in the ideal range (from an isolated hypothetical central place) is at least constant, while the real range (formed by the competition of several central places) does not undergo constant or immediate change.

By now, we should have gained a satisfactory idea of the variability in the importance of a central place—and perhaps even an exaggerated picture of it. The obstacles to a quick or decided change in the importance are often very great, sometimes so great that the change does not fully occur, especially when the conditioning processes (depression or boom) at the central place are only temporary, and local. A temporary depression does not bring about an emigration of central professions; instead they remain at the place, restrict themselves, and await the return of prosperity. And similarly, in times of prosperity, a great flow of new professions does not occur immediately. The other processes, however, occur more slowly, so that they cannot be observed; only a historical review makes their effects clear. The obstacles to any one of the fundamental factors mentioned are sometimes of a more negative and sometimes of a more positive nature; i.e., the restraints occur in some cases where a higher rationality results, and in other cases where a more temporary fluctuation brings about a sudden and/or catastrophic result. Some restraints of the first (negative) type are: ignorance of the most rational organization and production methods, customary techniques and tastes, and other negative restraints such as advertising, organization of trusts, monopoly agreements, etc. These are all means by which the capitalistic economic system gives rational direction to the economy through the price mechanism; or, when the price mechanism fails, it creates substitute mechanisms. Restraints of a more positive nature are: the customs which support certain business and economic combinations, personal adjustments, the inventive and organizational spirit of the entrepreneurs, the adjustment of the population to changes in the economy, and also, in part, other phenomena previously mentioned (such as the rational traffic system, the administration, and normal economic change).

A change in the importance of a central place causes an immediate change in the range of the central goods, except that, as we have seen, several types of central goods may be obtained in one trip, that is, with round-trip expenses. In that latter case, the change in the importance of a central place takes the form of a change in the price-willingness of the purchaser, a change in the distance (in the subjective economic distance), or a change in the prices of central goods. An increase or a decrease in the number of types of goods which are offered at a central place also causes an increase or a decrease in the importance of the central place. It increases or decreases correspondingly with the range of all types of goods offered in the central place, which is why the importance of the place increases or decreases proportionately more than the consumption of more or fewer types of goods.

The second factor which affects the range of central goods is the price-willingness of the purchaser. The price-willingness, that is, the favorable attitude of the consumer towards buying certain central goods, undergoes steady changes. It is always determined first by the quantity of money which is to be spent altogether for the acquisition of the central good itself, and second by that part of income which must be spent for travel; and the valuation of the central goods themselves and the valuation of the journey are individually, and perhaps locally, different because the two valuations stem from unequal motivations. The valuation of the journey, especially, is frequently not clearly expressed in monetary terms; e.g., inconvenience and fatigue play considerable roles here. The influence of the price-willingness of a purchaser will be discussed in individual cases below, in the investigation of the effects of the economic distance. Generally, it may be said that an increase in price-willingness enlarges the range and that a decrease reduces it.

The third factor which influences the range of a central good is the subjective economic distance. Among the changes of this factor the following are to be distinguished: (1) changes in the objective facts—namely, freight and passenger fares (general or local changes—the latter especially as a result of the establishment of new traffic institutions), the security in transportation and the corresponding insurance rates (general security of the country or special technical security of the transportation facilities), the methods and means of cargo handling (speeding up of cargo handling leads to a reduction in storage costs), the speed (saving of time) and all other technical contrivances (introduction of refrigerator cars); and (2) changes in the subjective factors—namely, changes in

tastes (types of central goods having been recently introduced are preferred to other types of goods—newer types are "nearer" to the consumer), changes in income conditions (general change in the sizes or in
the distribution of incomes—in the sense of equalization or of a stronger
differentiation), changes in professional activity (decrease in the agricultural population and an increase in the commercial and industrial
population, or an increase in the number of *rentiers* relative to the entire
population), changes in ideologies (materialism to idealism), or changes
in the variation of time (with the increasing Europeanization of Russia
and the Orient, time becomes more and more worthwhile there).

The objective factors are clearly recognizable, for example, as transportation costs, i.e., as transportation advantages expressed in monetary
terms—a reduction in them increases, while an increase reduces, the
range of a central good. The subjective factors are not quite so recognizable, but they similarly cause an enlargement or restriction in the range
of a central good. If the range is increased, then the respective central
good which was previously offered perhaps at all central places of a lower
rank in order to supply the whole region will now be offered at the more
important central places, where the offering may be in greater quantities,
for a larger region now lies within its range. A reduction in prices is
usually connected with a greater centralization of production of offering,
which is advantageous for the central places of a higher order rather
than those of a lower order with respect to this good. Thus the smaller
markets die. A reduction in the range, on the other hand, perhaps means
that the whole country will no longer be supplied with the central good
from the old places of offering. That means that additional places of
offering must be established in the lower ranks, i.e., a strengthening of
the central places of a lower order or the creation of new central or
auxiliary places.

What we have just said refers to change in the ideal range. Such
change simultaneously influences the real range only under certain conditions, e.g., when old central places are eliminated from the offering of
certain central goods or new places are added. But it is also possible,
through the competition of two existing central places for the position
of supplying the land, for the real range to change without a change in
the number of central places. Therefore, the objective causes of changes
in the economic distance play a lesser role, because the two competing
central places are, as a rule, equally concerned with these causes. Exceptions are the opening of new transportation routes and establishments, the local betterment of the conditions of handling and storing
goods, and changes of the political borders which may mean detours or
short cuts. On the other hand, frequently the subjective causes have
local effects, i.e., they favor or disfavor certain central places, e.g., changes

in income conditions (a favorable development of a region with textile industry) or changes in the structure of the population (industrialization of a region which previously was agricultural). The valuation of the distance differs locally because of these factors. Where the costs and the burdens of the distances are valuated less, above all in the vicinity of large towns, the central goods attain a larger range which causes more favorable development of the central places of a higher order. This development tends to be concentrated in those less important central places (lying in the vicinity of central places of a higher order) which lose their central position more and more, until finally they are wholly pushed away or absorbed by the more important place.

The fourth factor determining the range of a central good is the price of this good at the place of production or at the place of central offering. Two cases should be distinguished: the first occurs when price changes equally throughout the whole land, e.g., in consequence of national production which reduces the production costs of a certain product previously produced by artisans, because of a tax measure by which production costs are increased, or in consequence of a reduction in demand because of mass unemployment. The range of goods affected by the change in price will change correspondingly; the range of goods with elastic demands (nonessential goods) changes more than the range of goods with inelastic demands (essential goods). Under certain conditions the range is so much changed that there is a transfer from central to dispersed production, or, vice-versa, from dispersed to central production. Or, central goods of a higher order might be changed into central goods of a lower order, or vice-versa. At any rate, the ranges of other types of goods which are affected by the change in price will suffer repercussions, as the number of types of goods offered changes. The second case occurs when the price does not change throughout the whole land, but rather changes only locally or regionally. This will result almost always in a change in the range and thus be to the advantage of the central place with lower prices and to the disadvantage of those places with higher prices.

Also, the quantity of goods offered at a central place may change, and thus effect a change in the range of this central good. With goods of a fixed supply, a change in the quantity has a decisive influence on the range of these scarce goods. With scarce goods which have variable prices, a change in the quantity results immediately in a change in the price—but this is nothing new to us. With scarce goods which have stable prices, an increase in the supply is followed by an increase in the range, and a decrease in the supply is followed by a decrease in the range, due to migration of purchasers to or from the border districts of the regions.

As the upper limit of the range—which we had in mind up to now when we spoke simply of the range—is subjected to a steady change, the lower limit of the range also changes. This limit is determined, however, by the least consumption of a central good necessary in order to make the production or offering of a central good pay in a central place. Consumption depends on the distribution of the population and their demand, the prices of the central goods, etc. If one of these factors changes, then the entire consumption changes and the lower limit of the range changes correspondingly. If, however, the lower limit of the range is lowered at the central place, then the central good in question might be offered in other central places in the vicinity also; either new central places will be created or the importance of existing central places will increase. If the lower limit of the range is increased, then weak central places in the vicinity will disappear or their importance will be weakened. In the case in which several central places compete with one another, the one which has the lowest limit of the range will be successful—primarily, in respect to a certain type of central good. But, furthermore, the lower limit of other types of goods is generally lowered; the importance of this central place increases, and the growth of the place reduces its lower limit of the range.

8. The Dynamic Aspects of a System of Central Places

The scheme of central places developed in our discussion of static relations is unusually strict and appears to be stiff. The location and number of the central places is firmly determined; moreover, only certain typical sizes of central places are possible. The distances between the central places are set once a fixed or basic measure of distance of the system is determined. Can this scheme undergo any changes at all? If the economic facts permanently change, how does this scheme take such changes into account?

The system of central places is developed only on the assumption that there are many types of central goods, from the lowest to the highest order, each having a special range. The specific ranges differ with regard to time and location, and, as we found in the discussion on ranges of central goods, are themselves subject to steady changes soon after a change in any one of the factors determining the range. Every birth and every death, every change of profession by an individual, every change in fashion, every change in individual wants for certain goods, every invention, every price fluctuation, every new tax, etc., influences the size of the range of the central goods, even if only to a small degree. Every change in the range of any central good at any place causes simultaneous deviations within the system of central places. The rational scheme of the system is not itself changed; only the decisive factors are changed.

Changes can occur in the distances between central places, in the typical sizes of the central places, or in the locations and number of central places.

In the following discussion, we shall deviate methodically from the course we have taken up to now. Up to this point, we have formulated our theory on the bases of the simple, more or less isolated facts, population, number of types of central goods, etc. In the static theory we explained the mutual relationships; and in the dynamic theory, we explained the effects of changes in the simple facts, on central places. While up to now we have proceeded hypothetically, we shall now consider complex phenomena as found in concrete reality, and seek to discover all the factors and processes which serve to explain those phenomena. Preferably, the analytical method should also be applied, whereby a constant "theory" governs, i.e., such an ideal (in reality, frequently a complex appearance) is first imagined as hypothetical—then the factors involved are elaborated upon.

We assume that the system of central places is normal or ideal. When, and because of what, will the location of the central places be different from the scheme? What circumstances effect deviations from, or prevent the establishment of, the location corresponding to the scheme? Purely geographical factors, such as topography, cultivation of the soil, flora, and the climate, which cause deviations from the scheme, are disregarded in our consideration, as are purely historical, political, ethnic, and personal factors. Only those changes which are explainable with the help of economic theory will be considered, that is, those which are purely or predominantly conditioned by economics. In Part III, "The Regional Part," on the other hand, one or another of the non-economic factors will be mentioned when we demonstrate why the theoretical scheme does not fit a certain concrete case.

Small deviations in the location of a central place from the location in which it should be located according to the scheme can be caused by unequal distribution of the population. Such unequal distribution could make eccentric locations of the central place the more favorable ones as, for example, occurs if the lower parts of mountain valleys are densely populated and the upper parts only thinly populated or altogether unpopulated. We should look less for the geometric center and more for the population center, or, to be more exact, the center of the wealth of the population which from an economic point of view is the more central. Furthermore, we must consider that the distances on which the scheme is based are, practically speaking, not distances in kilometers, but economic distances; and that they are not simple time-cost distances, but rather subjectively valued time-cost distances. This fact causes considerable deviations, which are not easily determined, of the economic scheme from a purely geometrical scheme. These deviations, which we find on ancient or medieval maps, are based on a net of distances determined by walking or sailing. Under certain circumstances the day's journey through a tiring (monotonous, snowy, sandy) landscape might subjectively appear longer than a journey of the same distance in kilometers through a colorful landscape. We have based the scheme, however, on objective economic measures, linear measures as well as areal measures (the latter ones are partly determined by the number of inhabitants); in order to make matters simpler, we have used mathematical measures (12, 21, 36, etc., km. rings and 400, 1200, 1600, etc., sq. km. regions). The resulting deviations will be considered case by case.

The locational deviations of the central places, which are determined by the effects of the three principles determining the distribution of the central places, are very significant. It is known that the locations of places determined according to the market principle are fundamentally different from those determined according to the traffic principle. Let us imagine a country which has lived rather exclusively to itself and which consists of a net of central places developed purely according to the marketing principle, i.e., according to the scheme of Figure 1.* Let us assume that this country now enters into interregional commerce and trade, and thereby into long-distance transportation. The large towns of the country thus become connected with one another and with the large towns outside the country by long-distance railroads. These railroads, as shown in the static theory, necessarily bypass middle towns: these towns, which up to now were at the second rank of importance, are now in a disadvantageous position with regard to transportation, and other towns of lesser importance are now placed in a more advantageous position because they lie on the long-distance line. What is the result? We shall consider this example in separate stages.

In the first stage, the larger long-distance lines (connecting the G-places of the system) are built up. It is unimportant whether this was the first historical step, because it is only a hypothetical example. The K-places become important stopping places along the railroad. Some goods formerly offered in the middle towns, the B-places, are now sold with greater advantage at the smaller K-places, which means an increase in the importance of the K-places and a stagnation or decline of the B-places.

In the second stage, the railroad net becomes denser; the B-places are connected with the G-places by secondary feeder lines, and are thus placed in better positions, though not quite as good as the positions of the K-places. If the period of time between the first and second stage is so great that the K-places, by virtue of their unique locational position

---

* See p. 61.

in respect to the traffic system, succeed in acquiring the main position of supplying the country with central goods—above all, those which arrive by railroad and are then distributed to the country from the central place, then the fate of the B-places will be sealed. They will continue to produce those central goods which were produced at the places themselves and for the production of which they do not need to import raw materials from the outside. If the period of time between the first and the second stages is very great, then the K-places, the population and wealth of which will also have grown, will draw a part of the production of goods formerly conducted in B because production at these new population centers will offer greater advantages. If, on the other hand, the period of time between the first and second stages is small, i.e., if the formation of the traffic net occurs suddenly, then there will be insufficient time for the offering of central goods to change from the B-places to the K-places. The B-places will thus maintain or strengthen their importance (according to the proposition that the larger place wins as a rule), while the K-places will develop further, but never to the same degree as the B-places.

We may hence conclude that if train service develops slowly, and if long-distance lines are preferred, then the system of central places may be able to reform itself according to the propositions of the traffic principle. If the development is swift, however, or if local lines are preferred, then the scheme of markets will remain intact.

We are likewise able to show the reverse, which occurs very seldom, but still is not without importance: If the traffic lines system of central places, which has developed according to the traffic principle, loses importance (through reduction of trade or replacement of the railroad by automobile transportation), a certain impoverishment will occur with the result that fewer central goods can be sold, and a number of central places, which were previously in the business of supplying, are eliminated. Does this retardation apply more to the places which lie correctly according to the traffic principle but wrongly according to the marketing principle, or does it apply to all places equally? We have already seen, in the static theory, that a considerably larger number of central places is needed to provide the country with central goods uniformly, if the places are developed according to the traffic principle than if the places are developed according to the marketing principle. It also happens that all those central places in the system developed according to the traffic principle, the locations of which are most contrary to the marketing principle (and, to a lesser degree, those central places lying correctly according to the marketing principle), must suffer. If such a period of retardation lasts very long, the system of central places might finally arrange itself differently according to the marketing principle. That is, those central places lying off the traffic lines, but which have a better local market location, may assert themselves, while the places lying on the traffic lines decline. If these periods of retardation are only of short duration, the status quo ante will be maintained or restored.

The net of central places established by the Romans in Germany was largely oriented according to the traffic principle. After the traffic had ceased in the course of the barbarian invasions, the Roman towns more or less disappeared, and the country became impoverished. At that point, those central places which had arisen as consolidations of political and economic functions could have developed according to the marketing principle. Where the break was especially sharp and permanent, this transition may have been complete. Where the break was less complete, the Roman net established according to the traffic principle could have been preserved—even though the Roman towns were largely destroyed, at least memories and the names of the locations remained and later on determined the locations of future towns.

Besides the marketing and traffic principles there is still a third competitor, the separation principle. It is obvious that this principle has been much more important in federalistic Germany than in the more centralistic France or Russia. The small areas of the mid-mountain regions of Germany also favors the separation principle. The processes by which the systems change according to this principle are the following:* If, in a system of central places based on the marketing principle, a territory is formed around a G-place, the boundaries of which approximate the 36 km. ring, then two B-places which lie on this ring will be embodied in this territory. At the other four corners of the system, where the B-places remain outside of the territory, the nearest A-places will develop as substitute places for these B-places, because this region of the territory is no longer supplied with central goods from places lying outside, because of custom barriers, prohibitions, etc. Sometimes, new competitive enterprises may even develop. The old B-place naturally loses its importance, declining perhaps to K-importance; the substitute place climbs perhaps to K-importance; and instead of the one B-place which formerly existed, we will have two K-places, with the B-position distributed to two or three K-places where three territories converge. If the new K-place does not develop so strongly, and if the old B-place maintains its B-importance, then we can say that the new K-place takes the place of the B-place in the other territory. Such cases are very frequent, as will be shown in Part III, The Regional Part.

The reverse case is also frequent: as a matter of course, according to the separation principle, there will be no common border place of the three systems, but there will be a representative of a common border

---

* Refer to Figure 1, p. 61, for the discussion that follows.

place in each system. If the advantages which the separation principle offers are negated through, for example, the merging of several territories into a larger state, then there is a possibility that the place which is located most correctly according to the marketing principle will take advantage of the situation and gain the importance appropriate to its position in the system, while the other two places will stagnate and perhaps decline.

In the competition of the three principles, one of the principles will not necessarily clearly triumph. The competition between the traffic and marketing principles may result in a sharing of the function as a central place; in this way, the position occupied by the B-place in the system is distributed between a K-place lying on a traffic line and another K-place lying correctly in a market location. K_1 will offer some of the goods with B-range and K_2 will offer the others; thus, there will be two K-places offering B-goods. Such a situation is also frequently found. But the location of the central place itself may also be a compromise location, about halfway between the theoretical market location and the theoretical traffic location; the system of traffic lines helps to determine this compromise. Thus, we may find every possible transition of the location so that the analysis of concrete reality sometimes does not have a clear result. These matters will be considered in Part III, the part on southern Germany.*

When might the number of central places be different from that which we would expect according to the scheme? † First of all, the number might be different when the traffic or the separation principle is more dominant than the marketing principle; naturally, this would generally bring about a smaller development of central places in the poorer regions, especially of the central places of a lower order (because some parts of the region remain outside the range of central goods). On the other hand, an increased number of central places might develop in the wealthier regions.

In the latter case, a larger number of central places could also develop in a system governed by the marketing principle. This will occur when good income conditions exist (i.e., when middle incomes are especially prevalent), when the independent professions are very numerous, when industrial production is prevalent, when the production costs (and also the prices) of central goods are low (the profit must still be high), or when the transportation conditions are favorable and transportation tariffs are low. We can combine these concepts into one: More central places will exist when the lower limit of the range of central goods is low, that

---

* See "The L-System of Munich," pp. 170-188.

† Christaller means the scheme of central places developed according to a system of markets.

is, when the consumption of central goods at the central places is sufficient to provide a profit for the production and offering at these central places. And we shall find more central places in such regions, especially in those where, simultaneously, the traffic or the separation principle takes a greater part in the buiding up of the system of central places. The question of whether the added central places are distributed equally to all size-types or mainly to those of a lower (or a higher) order will be discussed later on.

If the presuppositions change in such a way that the lower limit of the range of the central goods is restricted, the number of central places may increase to the extent that the system of central places adjusts itself to the traffic or the separation principle—depending on which stands first in the consideration of interests. With an increase in wealth, artisan activity, education, etc., in the Middle Ages, the separation principle was a strong stimulus because, in those times, the formation and greater seclusion of territories began. The central places necessary in addition to the ones already existing in the system of central places might have been distributed according to the separation principle. A different development occurred during the Industrial Revolution in the last century when the separation principle lost much of its force because of the composition of politically-conditioned regions. Instead, the traffic principle was pushed to the foreground by the development of railroads. In this period, the traffic principle gained because newly added central places were configurated according to the traffic principle.

But there are also times of reverse development. Reverse development causes a widening of the lower limit of the range of central goods —perhaps in consequence of an increase in the intensive use of production capital, and perhaps because of the impoverishment of the population. A larger region is then necessary in order to make production with all of the necessary equipment (factory facilities) or offering pay. Some central places will not be able to keep up with this development; they are not able to extend their ranges because the regions of neighboring central places have already formed. These central places will fade away, and the number of central places will be decreased. Also, in this case, those which lie correctly in accordance with the principle prevailing in the region at the time of the reverse development will maintain themselves while the others will die. Thus, this process of selection may transform the existing system into a different system based on another principle.

Consequently, we can say that an increase as well as a decrease in the number of central places is usually accompanied by a certain transformation of the system, for the most favorable places will be sought or will maintain themselves for the longest time, and the most unfavorable ones will be neglected and will become dispersed places. Because increases in wealth, industrialization, etc., are frequently limited regionally, we can determine the regional frequency of central places. No matter in which historical period the increases or decreases in the number of central places occur, their distribution will conform to the traffic principle, the separation principle, or the marketing principle.

When are the distances between central places, which form the base of the system of central places, changed? They are always changed when new places acquire central importance or when old ones lose their importance. These new central places are created mostly at those locations which are most distant from the old central places, for instance, if the central places were up to now 12 km. apart, then the three new neighboring central places will be at the points of an equilateral triangle the sides of which are each 12 km. long. The point equidistant from these three places is $12/\sqrt{3}$, that is, 6.94 or about 7 km. from these three places. On the other hand, if the distances between the central places were 7 km., and if some of those places were to cease being central places, then the other central places would remain 12 km. apart from each other. But all of this is based on the assumption that the marketing principle alone was the determining principle. Correspondingly, the case is the same if the traffic principle or the separation principle is governing.

Obviously, there must be some basic time-distance measure, and it must be one which is determined by the time it takes for a person to go a certain distance.[5] Let us imagine a colonial land which is to be thoroughly settled. Certain prominent points on the landscape—bays, conspicuous points along rivers, forests with fertile soil, etc.—are starting points at which settlements may originate. Those places within a day's travel of these starting points will belong to this region. Such places can be no more than 35 to 40 km. apart. Other places which a person can reach and return from in one day will have a special rank. They will lie about 20 km. from the starting points.[6] Auxiliary central places, from which the dispersed points of the country can be supplied, will be created on these two rings. If the land becomes more and more populated and the demand for central goods increases, then these auxiliary central places will develop into full central places, and new auxiliary central places will be created in locations according to our scheme. These new auxiliary central places will be 12 km. from existing central places. If now two original starting points of settlement lie 90 km. apart, the new central places which are to be established will face a dilemma. According to the marketing principle their most favorable distance from the starting points would be $90/\sqrt{3} = 52$ km. (along the shortest communication line). According to the traffic principle, however, it would be 45 km.

(midway along the shortest communication line). This basic measure (a day's travel) as a practical measure is, however, 35 to 40 km. Thus, an auxiliary central place might be created at this distance from each of the two starting points. One would belong to the first system and the other to the second system, and further development would be normal. It could be the case that in the course of its development, the starting point which is 90 km. from the other starting point will be taken into the *L*-system of the first. However, this could result in its downfall as a central place, because it would falsely lie in the system of the first place and therefore would be displaced by the younger, more correctly situated place, e.g., the *P*-place, which would be 108 km. from the first place. Thus, in colonial lands, the oldest settlements frequently remained small because they lay incorrectly in the system as finally consolidated, according to the selection process previously described.

If the time measure—such as the day's journey—is decisive in determining the distances between central places, then it will determine whether it is easy or difficult to travel through the land. In the first case (plains, prairies), the mathematical distances are greater than in the latter case (forests, mountains).[7] It is of great significance how the population effectively values a day's journey; lazy people might value it at 25 km., and energetic people might value it at 45 km. But still a third factor is significant: the auxiliary means by which distance is overcome. If the means of transportation are speedy to start with—e.g., the horse on a plains landscape, then the distances between central places in the net of central places can be rather high. The same is true to a still higher degree for transportation by automobile. Hence, it is not insignificant in which time-stage the system of central places initially developed. In one system, the primary distance between central places might be great and in another it might be less. Therefore, we are able to establish the basic measure of the system of central places based on the historical time in which it finally began to develop itself; for example, we can conclude whether a riding people or a walking people determined the first starting points of the central places.

Let us assume that a system was originally formed according to a standard day's walk of 20 km. Then perhaps a fundamental change in the most significant mode of transportation occurred, e.g., the automobile (perhaps in Africa). Either the old basic measure of 20 km. was rooted so deeply in the minds of the population—that is, if this old system had existed for a long time—that the 20 km. measure will continue to be valid in the future, except that an automobile trip of half an hour will be scheduled instead of a walk of four hours. Or, if the system was still young and not solidified and the 20 km. measure was not rooted so firmly in the minds of the population, the system will be converted to the new time-measure created by the automobile, and an hour's travel of 40 km. by automobile will be the new basic measure. A new mode of transportation can create a change in newly settled regions but not in regions of old settlements—e.g., compare America, especially the American West, and the northwest of Argentina, with Europe.

The traffic principle and the separation principle also play their roles; but their influences are so complicated that we prefer to consider clearcut examples in order to find out which powers were at work and which processes led to certain results.

As to the size-types of the central places, the sizes (i.e., the importance) of the places are determined mainly by the number of types of central goods which is offered. We shall refer more than once to the significance of these details. Those types of central goods which have smaller upper limits of the range may predominate (for the most part they are significantly heavy and relatively cheap goods which are produced everywhere, such as beer and fresh meat). If the lower limit is also low, the central places of a lower order may be well and regularly developed; but at the same time, the places of a higher order may be relatively less developed. Such is the case in wealthy agricultural countries which are connected only very slightly to modern civilization. But if the lower limit is high, i.e., the population consumes only a few central goods because of impoverishment, lack of effective demand, etc., and if at the same time the upper limit of the range is low (little development and an expensive traffic net), then all central places both of a lower and a higher order will be less developed—such is the case in the poor agricultural countries.

If those types of goods with a higher upper limit of the range are prevalent, because of larger numbers of goods of lighter weights and a cheaper traffic system, then we shall be able to distinguish the following: If the lower limit is also high and if there is a high demand for the capital necessary for offering goods at all places (another possibility of clarification: The matter of limited wealth cannot come into question because the consumption of high valued luxury central goods is predominant), then the central places of a higher order will be developed strongly and those of a lower order consequently will be developed very weakly. And finally, if the lower limit is low—as in a wealthy and densely settled region, not only the larger but also the smaller central places will be very well developed. We could say that the whole system of central places would be raised one stage: the M-places will have A-importance, the A-places will have K-importance, and so forth. Thus, we could say that the whole system of central places would be raised to a higher level.

Let us compare these conditions schematically:

1. Types of goods with small lower limits and small upper limits: small places will be favorably developed and large places will be unfavorably developed.
2. Types of goods with small lower limits and high upper limits: all places will be well developed.
3. Types of goods with high lower limits and small upper limits: all places will be poorly developed.
4. Types of goods with high lower limits and high upper limits: large places will be favorably developed and small places will be unfavorably developed.

If a change results in the predominance of another category of types of goods—e.g., instead of small value and heavy weight of a central good, a high value and low weight is of primary consideration, such as a transfer from Category 1 to Category 4—then the fortunes of the individual types of central places change accordingly. In the above example, the importance of the smaller places diminishes and the importance of the larger central places increases. Also, when the same category of types of goods predominates but the ranges change, then, perhaps following a transition to mechanized mass production, the lower limits of the ranges will be extended; or, following a simultaneous reduction in the prices of the products, the upper limits of the ranges will be extended. The result is again an increase in the importance of central places of a higher order and a decrease in the importance of central places of a lower order.

These processes are also put in operation by the traffic or the separation principle. When the central places of a higher order formerly in a relatively unfavorable position enter into a more favorable position, those places which have the advantage of a correct location according to the traffic principle will profit by these opportunities. Those places will gain by acquiring the importance of a higher order, while the old central places of a higher order will gain nothing. As a result of this development, the system of central places might be converted to the traffic principle. Thus, several processes must occur simultaneously and concurrently: an increase of the upper and lower limits of the range of central goods (by mechanizing and lowering the cost of production) or a change in the nature of the transportation (from mail coach to railroad), together with a simultaneous increase in incomes. Then those central places which lie in a favorable traffic position will become, in a system which was formerly governed by the marketing principle, central places of a higher order. The old central places of a higher order will lose their character as places of a higher order, and the system will adjust itself to the demands of the traffic principle.

It would be interesting to discuss the historical development of the concrete content of the systems of central places (e.g., in southern Germany). To do so, however, would exceed the limits of this investigation. We shall mention only a few of the more fundamental points.

The establishment of any point (to be exact: of two points) on the earth's surface as a central capital or other important place determines simultaneously an entire system of central places, which is developed from below, from the smallest units up to the top of the pyramid of sizes; moreover, the fixed points of such a system are determined by such capitals. Thus, the locations of old Roman towns in southern Germany act as central places, even if the original settlements themselves are in ruins or have disappeared. Those Roman towns act functionally like fixed points. Some of them were exceeded in importance by other towns in the Middle Ages (e.g., Mainz by Frankfurt), and others were exceeded in importance in the modern age (e.g., Worms and Heidelberg by Mannheim). The locations of these new towns were, however, determined by the fixed points of the Roman towns, since these new towns developed not at arbitrary places but at important places determined by the locations of the Roman or other old towns. Thus, the rule is that the older system previously determined always determines the more recent system developed under other economic laws and conditions with other types of central goods and other ranges of these central goods.[8]

We observe a very great frequency of places called towns and market spots; and we may consider the central places of ancient times, of the Middle Ages, and of modern times, the results of the economic conditions, values, and production of each period. In certain regions such as the Neckarland in Württemberg, Unterfranken, the edges of the upper Rhine plain, and Hesse, the frequency is great. In other districts, however, such as the Hunsrück, Haardt, and Bavaria, we find a low frequency. As a rule, we find a greater density of towns in regions of old settlements than in the more recently settled mountain districts.[9] These differences resulted from varying demands at the time of the towns' development: because central goods had lower ranges, central places in the developed regions had to lie near one another; while in the less developed poorer regions which had only recently been settled, less demand existed for central goods and thus for central places.

The strong differences in the development of regions close to one another containing old or new settlements (as we find them in the distribution of settlements called towns) have disappeared almost wholly under the influence of intensive settlement, better transportation, technological progress, and the disappearance of frequent wars. A broad equalization has taken place, indeed, in the sense that numerous towns and markets in the regions of high town-density have lost their functions as central places, while in the regions of low town-density, numerous villages have gained central functions. This fact is considered all too little in orthodox geography, which restricts itself almost wholly to the historical form of central places because it lacks easy accessibility to and exact recognition of the present central places. Therefore, a wide area of understanding is closed to the geographer of settlements; he can consider the form of appearance of a town but not the functional connection between a region and its central place. The central place is, however, crucial in regard to economic geography.

Within the economy of a people united in one state, i.e., within a concrete national economy or within one territory, the conditions under which the individual factors determine the range of a good are fairly similar and manifoldly uniform: for example, in regard to the structure of the population (similar income conditions, standards of living, customs, and schedules of wants), the cost of the distance (equal tariffs, uniform systems of traffic), and prices, insofar as they are determined by the costs of production (which are influenced by the same system of taxes, revenues, duties, similar wages, etc.). Therefore, certain changes concerning the systems and size-types of central places, which are created by eventual changes of the ranges of the central goods, are rather similar. But the moment one crosses the border of such a national economy (state) and enters another national economy, one observes an important difference. The change is not too striking if the same people live on both sides of the border, because the composition of the population is relatively equal, and thus, so is their effective demand. But, where the political border is simultaneously a national border, not only the structure of the population but also the schedule of demands and other variables change. To a somewhat greater extent, beyond the borders we recognize other conditions under which the range of central goods is set by the determining factors. Accordingly, the values and the measures of sizes, etc., which are the determining bases of central places, will be different on each side of a border. That is, the distances between the central places and the size-types of central places and their progression will have different basic measures.

Such differing developments are less interesting, however, with regard to the investigation of the system of central places in southern Germany. Still, it should be considered that southern Germany is composed of individual states which existed for a certain time under quite differing economic conditions, e.g., during the era of mercantilism, during the decline in the unity of the Reich, and during the high points of the absolutely administered territorial states (mostly differences in customs, taxes, and subsidization of certain professions), and that each territory endeavored at the time to develop its own fixed point—a capital—in the system of central places. These factors have indeed greatly influenced the complete concrete picture of the system of central places in southwestern and central Germany—only compare the Rhine-Main region with, say, upper Bavaria. Since the elimination of most of the independent regions in 1805 and, still more, since the creation of the Reich in 1871,* the conditions have become unique. Thus we can now see how the old system of central places develops more and more in the direction of the purely rational form.

But every new alteration of the borders (e.g., the loss of Alsace-Lorraine, the losses of regions in northern and eastern Germany, and very obviously, the distribution of the Austro-Hungarian Empire,† especially in regard to Hungary) results in a nearly complete conversion of the system of central places, which involves immense material loss. New central places of a lower, a higher, and even of the highest order develop in large numbers. The old ranks of central places become rearranged and many central places lose their functions altogether. A considerable part of the present crises from which central and southeastern Europe, especially Austria and Hungary, suffer is the result of the forcible and sudden destruction of the old system of central places through the establishment of new borders, which brought a devaluation of old central establishments and institutions, frequently in a grotesque manner; and the compulsion behind the creation of new institutions and establishments—not only state institutions, but also those of a private, cultural, commercial, and/or industrial character. Also included are the general conversion of prices, tariffs, demands, etc., which is perhaps still more significant than the transformation of the more obvious central establishment.

We still have to answer the question—at least in the basic propositions—of how much planned measures of State economic policy, in the direction of a rationalization of reality and a promotion of the national economy, can influence the system of central places. When one recognizes that there is, in fact, sense to the development of central places, and that such development is not haphazard, but is ruled by forces of economic laws and propositions, then the possibility exists for actively promoting and influencing this development by planning.

Our scheme of the distribution of central places and their size-types

---

* That is, the unification.

† Vienna's importance as a center of a state remained high, but following the split, its total function as a center was shared with Budapest, whose total importance as a state center increased.

is a rational one, i.e., one which is directed towards the highest rationality in economics, the most favorable utilization of central institutions, and the least loss of value; in short, it is one in which the tendency of the entire economy is directed towards its realization, insofar as the principle of highest rationality prevails. Every single producer or seller of a central good selects the most favorable production or market conditions in order to promote the best interests of his own business; accordingly, he chooses the best site of production or offering of goods. The consumer also seeks those conditions which are most favorable for him. Ignorance, laziness, influences of power (monopolies, etc.), political influences, etc., considerably hinder the attainment of the most favorable conditions for the one who offers as well as for the one who demands.

The modern social state considers it a task of the state to eliminate these hindrances and to promote the economy of the producers as well as the economy of the consumers through economic-political measures.[10] The goal of such economic-political measures is to influence the present size and distribution of central places so that they approach as much as possible the scheme of highest rationality that we have developed theoretically; for, by this, the highest degree of effectiveness of the single economic activities as well as of the national economy could be guaranteed. In these respects, the advantages offered by a market-orientation of the location should be compared with the advantages of a traffic-orientation, and those of a separation-orientation; that principle should be preferred which guarantees the greatest general advantages—and simultaneously, according to Helander, the special advantages for the state as such.

In seeking to attain this goal, the following economic-political measures should be considered:

1. The setup of the administration should be formed so that the seats of the higher, middle, and lower official agencies and boards are at places which correspond with our scheme, and that the administration districts are bound so that they fit into the scheme of distribution; fragmentation of strength and power is avoided in this way, and those central places which require a higher importance according to the scheme are promoted.

2. The revenue and tariff system should be organized so that those places corresponding with the ideal centers of the scheme are not hampered in their development as central places of a certain order, and, if necessary, are positively promoted (through an easing of professional and land taxes, for example) in order to enable the transformation towards the optimum state.

3. Tariff measures and generally new plans of transportation institutions should be similarly directed; the construction of streets, especially, should be managed accordingly.

These are the most important economic-political measures; to them, measures of land and settlement policy should, of course, be added. These measures include land-planning[11] and general settlement plans, annexation policy,[12] and finally, the questions of a new division of Germany which are particularly decisive. An exact theoretical base for a new division in Germany or the division of a state into economic regions (regionalism in France and England, problems of the division of the country in Russia) is still almost entirely missing. These plans and thoughts have been created more or less for this case alone, whereby the feeling or judicious decision (*Taktik*)—geographically speaking—has been substituted for the theoretical foundations. Above all, it often remains indistinct just what the goals of such aspiring measures should be; the total contrasts of the leading principles[13] show this clearly: on the one hand the identity of the type of economic activity, i.e., the prevalence of certain professions, should be directed by these organizing principles;[14] and on the other hand the mutual complementary nature of the economy, i.e., the economic harmony within a certain region, the relative autarky of the region,[15] should be directed by it. Semenow speaks very precisely in the first case of "special districts" and in the other case of "integrated districts."[16] A state action toward making districts of the state region must simultaneously have two goals: first, the attainment of the highest rationality in the economy by means and methods of economic policy, which is a mere task of calculation and is to be solved with the help of economic theory; and second, the strengthening of the state—here, the calculation of the comparison in numbers is more difficult because statecraft does not yet employ many precise theoretical methods. Whether these goals correspond with spatial or with integrated districts can be proved absolutely, whereby the theory as it is developed in this work becomes especially useful. These goals seem to be recognized by the Soviet Union, which has acted accordingly.

Naturally, in colonial or less developed regions, planning might extend to several further measures, for in these regions the systems of central places are still unstable and imperfect. Therefore, in these cases, the knowledge of the theoretical optimum in the distribution of central places is of the greatest practical importance.

9. Business Cycle

A dynamic theory of the economic causes of the development of central places must deal with those facts which, in economics, are combined under the heading of business cycles.[17] Questions of business cycles are highly important to theoretical economics because all of the inter-relationships of individual economic factors and processes are sublimated in the business cycle. The business cycle is therefore a subject of economic theory.[18] The business cycle is not the reason for including economic theory in this work, because our aim is not to describe and explain the processes of economic life. For practical reasons, we shall be able to discuss these processes only after investigating static and dynamic examples.

From the point of view of static economics, the entire economy must be brought into equilibrium, since all individual factors—demand, supply, production, price, investment, wages, etc.,—have fundamental roles according to the laws of economics. If any change expediting or hampering the process occurs, the individual factors will react according to the laws of dynamic theory. The result is an interaction of the economic factors, with its entire complex of consequential effects, until the individual factors have taken new positions in a new equilibrium. These dynamic processes are not always identical with business cycle processes. We may speak of business cycle processes only when the movement or reaction is greater and more complex than usual. This excessive stimulation of activity following some original change is partly due to irrational elements. For example, the change which originally vitalized the economy may make producers and consumers so confident that they engage in even greater activity, increasing their production and consumption by more than was justified by the original stimulating change. In other words, they assumed that the change was permanent, while it was in fact only temporary. The excessive stimulation of activity, however, also occurs partly because factors reacting to the original change in turn cause reactions by other factors. Thus, reaction is cumulative and not merely a summation of actions—and here only social, not physical factors, are considered.

If, for example, one place has more favorable labor conditions, such as higher wages (the reasons are of no interest to us), than elsewhere, the supply of workers seeking employment will increase. The demand for consumer goods (for example, lodging) will be greater and, based on supply, prices will increase. Simultaneously, wages will be decreased as a result of the increased labor supply. Finally, local wages will have decreased so much and prices will have increased so much, that the labor conditions are no longer more favorable than at other places, and the workers will no longer consider migrating. Nevertheless, workers continue to move into the area which had had higher wages, because they had already resolved to move, perhaps weeks before, at a time when the prospects for employment in that place were favorable. But they neglected to investigate at the moment of executing the decision to move, or more precisely, at the moment of arrival at the new place, to see whether their expectations were still valid. Let us trace a typical sequential development: At first, there is equilibrium; then the appearance of a new element (which the favorable working conditions called forth); this creates a strained situation (more favorable working conditions here than elsewhere); then action (immigration); then reaction (declining wages, rising prices); now, there is an excess of action (further migration, in spite of the fact that working conditions are no longer more favorable than elsewhere, resulting in further lowering of wages and raising of prices); and finally, there is a shortage of jobs as a result of the migration of workers to that place at which conditions had been permitted to become unfavorable. As a result of the sharp decline in wages, production costs further decline, the hiring of new workers ceases, etc. In such a case, there is only momentary equilibrium, and this equilibrium is really only theoretical. In this example, brought on by the expiration of the specific crisis, the crisis occurs between the time of the worker's decision to move (because he compares his present work place with the other) and the time of arrival at the new place of work (a decision which was not good because the excess of workers over jobs was already too great).

In this illustration, we see a small and simplified business cycle. Aggregate economic development is a synthesis of a vast number of such cyclical variations. If, in this example, the rising phase of the cycle with a growing labor force had not yet been completed, and there remained an excess of population, the development would have continued in the form of an increase in the labor force, which previously had been increasing (which might have been the case if the duration of the rise was long or if the neighboring region offered competition); and the end result would have been a decline in population and a general downward development. The movement really has two elements working simultaneously: a periodical variation and a clearly continuous progressive or regressive movement (both of which are combined in a single curve).[19] This state of affairs appears to be simple and clear. It would be more complete if there were more such cyclical movements occurring at the same time. Perhaps the periodical curve described is of purely local character, and would be better understood if it represented a longer period of time, or a larger, national, or international economic area; it might also be better understood if it referred to seasonal businesses, such as agriculture, textiles, and coal mining. If the decline of one cyclical curve coincided with the rise of another curve, then the two curves would have diametrically opposed effects on the economy. If the two curves simultaneously rise, then their effects are potentially good. On the other hand, the combination of cyclical influences would be active in a different way in the development of the region.

For the sake of our current investigation, it is of manifold importance to describe the business cycle. We should not permit ourselves, in a monograph on the geography of settlements, to draw false conclusions from the long development of economic growth or decay, especially if this development is based on the details of a small region. Only the long development is of interest to us in economic geography, not the momentary stage of the business cycle.

It is interesting that the importance of central places and the sizes of their hinterlands are influenced positively by a crisis. At the time of the rise in business, local production and profits are increased as each business produces and offers more central goods. Large-scale building construction and income grow as building credit is extended, until the time when plans of construction are either completed or changed (when the cycle passes its peak). The revival which new building brings to a labor market is frequently arrested by the sudden increase in demand for credit and building materials, which raises the rate of interest and prices of materials; this, in turn, raises building costs above the original estimates. Economic theory, less concerned with the essential idea of spatiality, omits any reference to this idea with regard to the central places. With improving business conditions, prices at the central place in question rise, and the ranges of the central goods are reduced. The dispersed places in this region, lying at its periphery, are now satisfactorily supplied by other places, as is evidenced by the decline of the consumption of central goods at the prosperous and expanding place. Central goods accumulate in the warehouses of the merchants as sales decline. The payment of interest and other credit costs force the merchants to reduce their prices as they reduce production and as unemployment increases. This results in the migration of workers from one part of the country to another. At the end of the cycle, we thus find excess production and extensive arrangements for the supply of central goods at this place (e.g., freight, coffee, etc.), still lower prices, and more unemployment. These lower prices bring about an expansion of the complementary region of this place, where production plans are perfected, frequently permitting lower costs of production, and thereby restoring equilibrium. Furthermore, from long observation, we see that in this case, the surrounding region develops; and, last, that the place itself is favorably developed. On the other hand, if during the crisis, firms, on the basis of their calculations, suspend work, with the result that all creditors and tradesmen suffer losses, then the number of types of central goods supplied diminishes and the importance of the central place weakens along with that of its surrounding region.

However, there is something else of importance to us. During the business expansion, a central place may be quickly raised in importance, say from an M-place to an A-place, as the offer of A-goods becomes more profitable. With a sudden change, the M-place may achieve A-importance (a higher ranking place is more profitable than a lower ranking one). Similarly, adjustment to economic decline may, at the moment, be especially damaging and critical to the central place; and, eventually, the decline in this place and its neighboring central place may temporarily be determined by a prevailing principle, say, the traffic principle, which reveals the favorable locations. From observation, we may conclude that the transition from one rank of importance to another is quickly accomplished, while the typical size of the place is more stable and demonstrates an equilibrium condition. An inventory of central places shows that the size of a place remains stable in comparison to the period of transition and adjustment.

NOTES

1. Strakosch determines the turning point as being in the 1880's. He says that "the farmer had just learned to enjoy the luxury of the market economy." The farmer had just found the circle of purchasers who were always ready to buy and to pay well; at that time the change occurred, which was interrupted only by the War for a short time. (Siegfried Strakosch, *Das Agrarproblem im neuen Europa* (Berlin: 1930), p. 30.)

2. Alfred Weber, "Labor Orientation," *Theory of the Location of Industries,* trans. C. J. Friedrich (Chicago: University of Chicago Press, 1957), Chap. iv.

3. Alfred Weber, *ibid.*

4. Oppenheimer places great importance on this and says flatly: Cooperation develops (as a "secondary town") in a place where the benefits of cooperation are lacking and the higher cost of possible profits are an overcompensation of production. (Franz Oppenheimer, *Theorie der reinen und politischen Ökonomie* (Berlin: 1910), p. 513.)

5. Haufe reached the same conclusion (Helmut Haufe, "Die geographische Struktur des deutschen Eisenbahnverkehrs," in *Veröffentlichungen des geographischen Seminars der Universität Leipzig,* 2 (Langensalza: 1931), p. 7) when he used a time unit as the original measure of the traffic distance, e.g., the trip of one day—*die Tagereise.*

6. Kurt Hassert (*Allgemeine Verkehrsgeographie,* 2nd ed. (Berlin and Leipzig: 1931), Vol. I, p. 85) similarly concedes that the region including all those places which can be reached by "lines of a day's journey" may be interpreted in two ways. Hassert understands a day's journey to be a roundtrip in one day, including a stay in town for several hours.

7. Von Richthofen (*Vorlesungen über allgemeine Siedlungs- und Verkehrsgeographie,* version and edition of Otto Schlüter (Berlin: 1908), p. 210) mentions that in China, 100 *li* equals ten hours, e.g., equal to one day's travel on a plain 55 km. wide, and correspondingly less going up mountains and more coming down. The Swiss *ure* has a similar meaning as a measure of distance.

8. Hettner was quite right in saying that the location conditions of the settlements are to be viewed as partly the result of the present and partly the result of the past. (Alfred Hettner, "Die Lage der menschlichen Ansiedelungen," in *Geographische Zeitschrift*, 1 (Leipzig: 1895).)

9. See Robert Gradmann, *Süddeutschland* (Stuttgart: 1931), Vol. I, p. 166.

10. Sven Helander stated in a very academic speech about "the rational fundamentals of economic policy": Economic policy is a "complement to the free market economy which has to go into effect where the free market economy is, for various reasons, not capable of obtaining the optimum economic results." This state adds an "independent principle" to economic policy because a state, in order to be a state, needs a state-region and a state-people through which it gives "a separate value to the land to the human labor, independent of the market conditions." It must be asserted that this noneconomic value of land and human labor is added to the economic values. That the two foundations of the state figure alone according to their pure economic value in the economic processes should be prevented, so to speak, for this is the independent principle of a public economic policy. (Quoted from excerpts reprinted in *Akademische Nachrichten der Studentenschaft der Hochschule für Wirtschaft- und Sozialwissenschaften (Handelshochschule) Nürnberg*, 2nd year, 10 (Nuremberg: 1932), 5.)

11. It is not sufficient to have "a pertinent limitation of certain economic regions against one another," that is, of more or less homogeneous regions, as Pfannschmidt seems to imagine; the more important task for land-planning is the pertinent limitation of the supplying regions, that is, of the market regions and their distribution to the respective existing or still-to-be-developed centers. See Martin Pfannschmidt, "Geographische und volkwirtschaftliche Grundlagen von Landeskunde und Landesplanung," in *Mitteilungen des sächsisch-Thüringer Vereins für Erdkunde*, 52nd year (Halle: 1929), 104.

See also Wolfgang Schmerler's survey which is very fundamental and affords a rich index of literature: "Die Landesplanung in Deutschland," in *Zeitschrift für Kommunalwirtschaft*, 22nd year (Berlin: 1932), 885-984.

12. See Reuscher, "Das Vorortproblem mit besonderer Berücksichtigung der kommunalrechtlichen Stellung der großstädtischen Vorortgemeinden," in *Verwaltungsarchiv, Zeitschrift für Verwaltungsrecht und Verwaltungsgerichtsbarkeit*, 35 (Berlin: 1930), 138ff.

13. Otto Haussleiter discusses this in "Verwaltungsgliederung und Reichsreform," in *Zeitschrift für die gesamten Staatswissenschaften*, 92 (Tübingen: 1932), 212ff.

14. Thus it is for Erwin Scheu with his arrangement of a new administrative province with twenty-two administrative districts in Germany. ("Wirtschaftsprovinzen und Wirtschaftsbezirke," in *Weltpolische Bücherei*, 2 (Berlin: 1928).)

15. This latter principle gives the basis for the new division of the Soviet Union into twenty-one administrative districts. (See Hans von Eckardt, *Rußland* (Leipzig: 1930), pp. 391ff.)

Walter Vogel (*Politische Geographie, Aus Natur und Geisteswelt* (Berlin and Leipzig: 1922), p. 28) calls a region constructed on such principles, "an economic-harmonic landscape."

16. J. Semenow, "Die Revolution und die inneren Grenzen Rußlands," in *Zeitschrift für Geopolitik* (Berlin: 1927), 970.

17. See Rudolf Stucken, *Die Konjunkturen des Wirtschaftslebens* (Jena: 1932) and Gustav Cassel, *Theoretische Sozialökonomie* (Leipzig: 1927).

18. Eugene von Böhm-Bawerk, "Besprechung von E. von Bergmann's

'Geschichte der nationalökonomischen Krisentheorien,' " in *Zeitschrift für Volkswirtschaft, Sozialpolitik und Verwaltung*, 7 (1898).

19. In business cycle theory this line of general development is called *trend*. It is well known and used in higher mathematical methods such as the method of least squares.

D
Results

GENERAL AND SPECIAL ECONOMIC THEORY

In concluding the theoretical part, we shall direct attention to the following:

Economic theory must be divided into a general and a special theory. The general theory concerns itself with those economic relationships and events which exist and are effective in every past and future time period, among all peoples, and in all countries. The rules and laws which are formulated in the general theory must, therefore, be valid at all times and in all places regardless of the concrete time and local distinctions of economic systems. The number of these rules and laws is comparatively small. Because they are generally worded, their value is frequently not very great. The special theory (Alfred Weber calls it "realistic" in contrast to pure, i.e., general theory[1]) is different; it develops the rules and laws which are valid only for a specific economic system, determined with respect to time and culture.[2] Depending upon how narrowly one construes the term *economic system,* one obtains theories of greater or lesser individuality. Perhaps, if one interprets economic system to mean "western," or more particularly, "western-capitalistic," one excludes the economic forms of the feudal Middle Ages.[3]

In this work, such a division into a general theory on the one hand, and a special capitalistic theory on the other, has not been made; such a division would be impracticable within the framework of this work. Here, the theory should not be systematic, but rather preparatory (*propädeutisch*); it is supposed to serve a particular aim, to determine geographic reality at present, that is, to explain the number, sizes, and dis-

tribution of central places in southern Germany. Therefore, the elements
of a general theory—like the principle of highest rationality, the opposition of central and dispersed supply, and the factors of scarcity of goods
and of unlimited demands—have not been distinguished from the elements of the capitalistic theory—such as, freedom of supply, freedom of
consumption, and free mobility.

It might be of interest for us to give a general insight into what the
special theory would look like if, instead of a capitalistic economic system, another, perhaps socialistic, economic system[4] dominated.

No economic system can exist without a regulator which brings the
almost unlimited wants of man into harmony with the scarcity of goods
and the fact that the production of these goods creates costs, which may
consist of labor or of making goods available, and the consumption of
the means of production such as tools, buildings, soil, and raw materials.
This regulator may be instinct, tradition, religious doctrine, state authority, or the will of the ruler. In a capitalistic economy, it is the price
of the goods, of labor, etc., along with free competition, free production,
and free consumption. In a socialistic economy, an institution (which
could not actually be described as the state in the accepted meaning but
rather as economic assembly—*Wirtschaftsgremium*—or economic council), standing above the individual, is looked upon as being such a regulator. This supreme economic council has the task of bringing those
practically unlimited wants of the population into harmony with the
limited amounts of goods which can be produced. This is possible only
if a certain number of wants are left unsatisfied. In the capitalistic economic system the wants of those persons who can no longer pay or do
not want to pay the prices for desired goods which are supposed to satisfy
these wants remain unsatisfied. Therefore, the price determines who acquires a piece of this limited quantity of goods and who foregoes it. In
the hypothetical socialistic economic system, the regulator is supposed
to be not the price of the good but the judgment of the economic council which, according to the contribution of the individual to the community, allots to him a portion of the limited amount of goods according to certain imaginary norms of justice, efficiency, wants, community,
etc., based on scientific foundations and legally established.

If the price, as a regulator of the economy (of production and of
consumption), is eliminated and another regulator, say, the rules and
the organized reason of an economic body, replaces it, it is clear that
there will be no fundamental change in the pattern of the sizes and distribution of the central places because the so-called economic principle
—of obtaining the greatest possible satisfaction of wants with the least
possible expenditure (least cost)—is effective and decisive in the capitalistic as well as in the socialistic economic system. The only difference is

that one regulator with its deficiency—the price—is replaced by another regulator, which most likely also has deficiencies—such as the reasoning of the scientific and political economic leadership. The aim of both systems is the same: to bring unlimited wants into harmony with a scarcity of goods. Whether the one or the other regulator is better and functions more in accord with its purpose, etc., is a question to be discussed practically and scientifically; whether the one or the other regulator is to be preferred, as it effects a more just distribution of the scarce goods, is a question of world philosophy (*Weltanschauung*) and is therefore beyond the realm of scientific discussion.

In individual cases, deviations and shiftings in regard to the size and distribution of the central places will be effected through the transition from one economic system, e.g., capitalism, to another economic system, e.g., socialism. But this will happen not in respect to the scheme itself, but in respect to the concrete mathematical values on which it is based: the number of central places, their distances between them, and their typical sizes. To deal with this question is, however, not the task of this work. Our attention should be directed to the limitations on the application of our theory.

NOTES

1. Alfred Weber, "Die industrielle Standortlehre (allgemeine und kapitalistische Theorie des Standortes)," *Grundriß der Sozialökonomie* (Tübingen: 1914), pp. 10ff.

2. See above all Werner Sombart, *Die drei Nationalökonomien, Geschichte und System der Lehre von der Wirtschaft* (Munich and Leipzig: 1930), pp. 320ff.

3. It is to the scientific merit of Karl Marx, especially in *Das Kapital* (1867) and in "Zur Kritik der politischen Ökonomie" (1859) that he emphasized that several categories of economic theory such as wages, prices, and interest, which were up to that time considered to be categories of general economic theory, are solely historical categories, i.e., elements of a temporal economic system and, like all elements, dependent upon time, perishable. This fundamental view was developed further, especially by Sombart and Cassel.

4. Gustav Cassel always examines his theory as to whether, and to what extent, it also has validity in a socialistic economy.

II

THE CONNECTING PART

Application of the Theory of Location
to the Actual Geography of Settlements

INTRODUCTION: THE PROBLEM

In the theory in the first part, we avoided using examples from actual geography, although such examples would have clarified our considerations. But the theory was derived deductively, obtained only by pure reasoning. A demonstration of concrete examples would have revealed facts and it thus would have seemed that the theory was, at least partly, created by the inductive method. It is the first task of the emprical part (as the special concrete part of a treatise is frequently called in economics) to demonstrate reality and to explain it according to the theory.[1]

But it is not possible, without further consideration, to apply the theory to reality; it is necessary first to put both in the same schematic concept. This schematic concept was only partly developed in the course of the theoretical considerations (wherefore the theory was indeed anticipated); at first, we must prepare our picture of reality so that it will correspond with the theoretical schematic concept. Such will be the purpose of Part II of this book.

First we must answer the question posed in the introduction: What are at present the central places of southern Germany? Our question is quite concrete, namely, whether this town is a central place or that village a dispersed one—or an indeterminate one. But to make matters simpler, we shall inexactly consider a place which is not central as a dispersed place, too. Furthermore, we must answer the equally concrete question of whether such a central place in southern Germany, as we have found it, possesses a higher or only a lower position in the order

137

of central places; that is, to which size-type does it belong? To answer both of these questions is now our task. To do so, we must first find a method to decide whether a given central place is central and to which size-type it belongs; or briefly, to find a method with the help of which we can determine the importance of a place.

A

The Method of
Determination of
Central Places

1. The Importance of a Place

From the definition of *central place* we gave in the first part of the book, one can see that *central place* is not equivalent to *town,* because it refers to only one important characteristic of a settlement, namely, its possession of a central function. It is important in this investigation to find without exception all places which fall under this term in southern Germany, because only then can we determine how far our theoretical scheme of the distribution of the central places might be encountered in reality, which concrete measures form the basis of our scheme, and, as far as might otherwise be possible, to explain deviations from the scheme. We cannot proceed as do statisticians, who schematically call all settlement units with more than 2000 inhabitants *urban settlements;* nor can we proceed as do historians of the geography of settlements who record the geographical development of settlements, although such a study is advantageous for other purposes. According to the former method, all places which are called towns in the terminology of the administration (with the addition of, perhaps, market places) are categorized as urban places and set in contrast to the mere "country places."

First, one must determine which factors contribute to the importance of a place, that is, which factors make it a central place. These factors all involve the exchange of central goods and services. If we collect all these factors which are present at one place, we will have found the importance of the place.

Whether central goods and services are exchanged at a certain central place, may be best determined by considering the institutions which that central place has for the exchange of central goods. One such institution is the market place, which has been almost a symbol of the central place—especially in the Middle Ages. The modern central place, which has only recently become a central place, does not necessarily possess this visible symbol. Semantically, the expression *market* has become common as a definition of the location of an exchange of goods and services; thus, people speak of money markets, labor markets, etc. If—temporarily—we choose the institutions or establishments for the exchange of goods and services as measures of the importance of a central place, then we must notice that, in a proper sense, such factors are not really measures of the importance of the place, but only of the exchange itself.

Let us list the establishments for the exchange of central goods and services. The individual types are compiled into groups in order to give an idea of the factors which form the concrete contents of the importance of the place. They are as follows:

1. Institutions of administration
   a. Lower types: *Standesamt* (marriage, birth, and death office in the Rhineland), town police station, *Bürgermeisterei* (mayor's office), *Steuererhebestelle* (branch office of internal revenue)
   b. Middle types: County offices, lowest courts, county tax offices
   c. Higher types: Provincial government, next higher courts, labor offices
   d. Highest types: Central offices of the state government and the highest court
2. Institutions of cultural and religious importance
   a. Lower (elementary) schools, middle (junior high) schools, public libraries, the seat of the lowest religious administration
   b. High schools, country school administration, and church *Dekanate* (bishop's seat)
   c. & d. Universities, scientific institutes, state libraries, museums, theaters, bishop's seats
3. Institutions of importance in health and sanitation
   a. Physicians, veterinarians, dentists
   b. Apothecaries, country doctors, country hospitals
   c. Specialists, scientific institutes, large hospitals, sanitariums

4. Institutions of social importance
   a. Hotels, cinemas, local newspapers
   b. The above, but of greater importance
   c. Night clubs, stage productions, big newspapers, sports stadia, radio stations
5. Institutions for the organization of economic and social life
   a. Independent artificers, guilds, consumer co-ops, local social clubs
   b. County organizations of the above and also lawyers, notaries public
   c. State organizations of the above and chambers of commerce, of trade, of agriculture, and of artificers
6. Institutions of commerce and finance
   a. Shops of all types, loan offices, warehouses with large inventories (agricultural brokers), weekly markets
   b. Special shops, chain stores, consumer co-ops, savings and loan associations, banks and their branches
   c. Department stores, wholesalers, brokers (not agricultural), foreign trade agents and agencies from other German lands, stock exchanges, branches of the national bank
7. Professional institutions
   a. General carpenters, repair garages, breweries, mills
   b. Special carpenters, large bakeries, slaughterhouses, gas works, electric (steam) plants
   c. The above, but of greater complexity
8. Importance as a labor market
   Each according to the number and size of the economic activities and the strength of the labor force, [*i.e., the demand and supply of labor*]
9. Institutions of transportation and communication
   a. Railroad stations, bus terminals, highway intersections, post offices (or, more important, post agencies)
   b. Stops for express trains, railroad junctions, post offices of middle rank, central telephone offices
   c. Terminals for express trains, offices of the directors of railroad districts and post office districts

In other words, every place at which a central institution exists, is a central place. But here is the first difficulty; for instance, is a grocery a central institution in our sense? And what about a school, a church, etc? We need only consider those institutions which have a certain far-reaching importance for a wider region. What, however, is the minimum standard for a central institution? A bigger grocery shop, a middle or a high school, a church with a larger church district—all definitely should be considered as central institutions. Small shops, elementary schools, and simple village churches should not be considered as central institutions because they have only local importance. We must find a measure with which we can determine when such an institution is to be considered a central one and when only a local one.

Furthermore, we want to be able to compare the centralities of two places and to classify the places in a lower or a higher size-class according to their centralities. For this purpose, we must express centrality in quantities (or in degrees of intensity of concentration). Therefore, let us simply add together all central institutions and establishments; the sum will be the basis, as a measure of size, for comparison and classification. A university has, as a central institution, a weight different from that of a high school, and a high school with 1000 pupils has a weight different from that of a high school with only 100 pupils. Every central institution must be weighted, the school according to both its rank (university, high school, middle school) and its number of pupils; the hospital according to its number of meals served (it is not sufficient to know the number of patients or the number of hospital beds); the store according to its sales; the station according to the number of trains stopping and the number of tickets sold; etc.

But even all that is not sufficient; the values thus obtained must be combined in order somehow if one is to express the entire importance of the place. But should the values be added together, or multiplied together, or combined in some other way? As the importance of a place is a degree of intensity, the simple sum of the sizes of the individual elements which create this importance is a very inexact measure because the importance of a place is thereby undervalued, especially in regard to the larger towns which have a greater number of individual central elements. We have already seen in the theory that adding a new type of central good to the consumption of central goods causes the importance of the central place to increase more than does the consumption of this newly added type. Above all, the values obtained for the single central institutions must be compared with the others if they are to be combined in the entire importance of the central place. They will be determined by a standard measure, similar to money, which will also measure the various values of the different economic, cultural, and health goods and services. That means that if one wishes to find the aggregate importance of a central place, one cannot express the sale of a store in money and the importance of a hospital in meals served. The best method would be to make the economic success of an effective sale of central goods (that is, the net income of those who offer the central goods) the basis of measurement. But this presents a difficulty, for we must determine not only the net income originating economically and expressible in money, but also the ideal net income of an educational institution, administration institution, or entertainment institution, etc.

Thus we see what great difficulties we shall encounter if we wish to determine the central importance of a place so exactly that we will be able to say, "This place is a central place and it belongs to the M-type." The whole problem lies in the quantification of the central importance of a place.[2]

Because the various elements of the concrete contents of the importance of a specific place are not always easily recognizable, and because it is so difficult to quantify the importance precisely, it seems that it would be nearly impossible to find a method for quantifying the central places so that their sizes could be easily compared. It almost seems advisable to return to the usual limitations and quantifications, that is, to the number of inhabitants as an expression of the size of a place and to the limit of 2000 inhabitants for calling a place a town, and to correct as much as possible all the mistakes which result from this method.

But it is not necessary to give up, because there is a perplexingly simple and sufficiently exact method for determining through numbers the importance of a place as a central place: one need only count the telephone connections;* the number corresponds rather exactly to the importance of a place.

First, we shall prove deductively that the telephone connection method is usable. All institutions which serve in the exchange of central goods and services need to come into contact with a larger and mainly dispersedly living circle of persons. It is just this condition which makes them central institutions. And nothing today is as necessary or as characteristic of importance as the telephone. It is almost the symbol of whether an institution has a real central importance or only a local one. The telephone is a kind of common denominator to which all the various factors which make up the importance of a place can be reduced. Thus, the problem of quantifying importance is solved. But in larger towns the intra-urban use of the telephone is stressed, while in smaller places, there are proportionately more long-distance calls per connection.

The usefulness of this method must also be proved inductively. The result of this study will at the same time produce the proof. You need only compare Map 1,† which depicts the distribution of the population

---

* A telephone connection refers to a single telephone installation, excluding other extensions on the same number.

† All maps appear in the Appendix.

(in which 400 inhabitants are equal to one point) with Map 2, which depicts the distribution of the central institutions (corresponding to the number of telephone connections, each ten telephone connections equal to one point). The application of the telephone distribution method of identifying central places (Map 2) produces a far different appearance than does the application of the population distribution method (Map 1); a comparison of the two maps is therefore quite noteworthy.

There is something that should be noticed concerning the techniques of the two maps:* the relationship between the scales of the maps and the values of the points are so chosen that only the dots representing the larger places are disproportionately large on the map. Because of this, the larger settlements often overlap the smaller neighboring settlements on the maps. This could have been avoided either by an increase of the scale of the map or by an increase in the value of a point.[3] However, we want to show how these neighboring settlements beyond the boundaries of the larger towns are bound together. The large town is connected to all the dwellings in the region and beyond; the neighboring places therefore have a relationship with the large town because a large percentage of their residents travel daily to that place to purchase various commodities and to practice their professions. Also, those nearby areas used for gardening by city residents (whereon they may reside while gardening), like the tourist areas to which the region's residents make excursions, are related to the large town. By scaling the population density map at 1:1,000,000, one-quarter of a square millimeter was made to represent 400 inhabitants; thus, with a population density of 1600 inhabitants per sq. km., the space which the point occupies on the map is proportionate, according to the scale, to the area which the houses of the settlement actually cover. With a higher population density, an overflow will exist, and some points will be beyond the limits of the settlements. The number of 400 inhabitants has also another meaning: villages of 400 inhabitants are very common, and this number is typical for the smaller but already independent rural communities. Below 200 or 300 inhabitants, there are hamlet settlements. For cases in which several scattered settlements together totaled 400 inhabitants, the point was put at the specific gravity point of the population total. And two points mark the typical *Gewanndorf* † (600 to 1000 inhabitants), and three or more points mark industrialized villages or market places, towns, or other central places (1000 inhabitants or more). In the case of the large towns, where the number of points covers a proportionately greater area than the area of the actual settlement, the excess points were put at places

---

* Some of the distinctions referred to in Christaller's maps may not be easily discernible because of the reduction in the size of the maps.

† A sort of dwarf town.

where the settlement has influenced the surrounding country most strongly, e.g., politically or economically, in regions used by agricultural and gardening communities.

The map of the distribution of telephone connections was to have the same scale as the population density map; the sum of the points on the two maps was supposed to be as equal as possible, so that the differences in the distribution would be obvious. Thereby, the value of a point was set at ten telephone connections on the second map, because in the whole region,* 40 inhabitants on the average have one telephone connection, which means that 400 inhabitants have ten telephone connections. This number of ten telephone connections is also a characteristic number for the central place of the lowest order. With these lowest numbers (in regions which have six connections as a minimum), places usually become genuinely central. The points were distributed on this map with little deviation. In each district as many points are displayed as correspond to the sum of the telephone connections. Thereby, every place of a district (regularly the size of a district of the lowest court) was given one point for every ten telephone connections, and the remaining points were distributed to those places which had the next lower numbers of telephone connections.

The enumeration of telephone connections, which was performed with the help of telephone directories, involved some technical problems. To settle those problems, we enumerated every connection which had an economically independent character, including auxiliary connections belonging to the same enterprise. Public telephones were not counted because they are frequently only an indication of the degree of dispersion of the rural population.

The number of telephone connections, however, does not, without further qualification, correspond with the importance of a place. Before we obtain usable indices for complex comparisons—which we may call the specific importance†—we must eliminate some sources of mistakes. They consist of the following:

1. The agglomeration as such brings a higher telephone number (in consequence of a relatively higher number of private telephone connections).
2. Regionally, a higher telephone index is obtained where the demand for informing and being informed is higher (for instance, the Rhineland), where people are wealthier (regions with bountiful crops, especially wine regions), and where professions exist

---

* Here Christaller is referring to the whole of southern Germany, meaning that in this area there were, on the average, 40 persons to each telephone.

† This is clarified below.

which are especially dependent on telephones (the small industry
of the Black Forest, the *Fichtel Gebrige*—mountains of the fir
forest, and the Thüringer forests).*

3. There are also local exceptions (spas, main tourist regions in the
Bavarian Alps, at Lake Constance, etc.; distinguished residential
regions and places at the border).

These sources of mistakes will be eliminated. Number 1 is difficult to
eliminate, but on the other hand it is not too necessary that it be eliminated. Although in larger towns, private persons are more likely to have
telephones, the single central institutions are often correspondingly
larger, and yet are counted as having only one telephone connection.
Hence, pluses and minuses tend to balance each other.

The sources of mistakes in Number 2 can be eliminated in the following manner: We determine the average number of connections in a
region per 100 inhabitants. If we find in one region, two connections to
100 inhabitants but in another, four, it can then be assumed that in the
latter region the demand for telephone connections is twice as great; if
we give one telephone in this region the value of one-half, then we can
compare the values of every place of the two regions.

As to Number 3, the local sources of mistakes cannot be eliminated
in the same manner because it is impossible to compute a regional reduction-coefficient as in Number 2; but it is possible to introduce an
estimated special reduction-coefficient.

The relations to be shown are as follows:

$$B_z = T_z$$

in which B_z is the importance of a central place, and T_z is the number
of telephone connections. This is the formula for the general or rough
importance. After elimination of the sources of mistakes we can obtain
the specific importance which offers comparable values:

$$SB_z = T_z \left(\frac{E_g}{40\ T_g} \right)$$

in which SB_z is the specific importance of a central place, T_z is the number of telephone connections in this place, and $E_g/40\ T_g$ is the reduction-
coefficient. This reduction-coefficient can be found by relating the ratio
E_g/T_g (number of inhabitants of the region equals E_g and the number of
telephone connections in the region equals T_g) to the normal ratio of inhabitants to the telephones, which is 40:1 for southern Germany. Thus,
in a normal region in which there are 40 inhabitants to each telephone

---

* These small farms were widely separated and needed intercommunication for
selling.

connection, the specific importance of place Number 1 is equal to the number of telephones, for instance $SB_{z(1)} = 80$. In a region in which there is one telephone connection for every 20 inhabitants and the respective place Number 2 also has 80 telephone connections, then its specific importance is:

$$SB_{z(2)} = 80 \times \frac{20}{40 \times 1} = 40.$$

In this book, we avoid computing the specific importance of a place in this manner because it is meaningless to us; we wish to express the centrality—i.e., the extent to which a place exercises more than the normal amount of influence over the surrounding complementary region—rather than the absolute importance.

2. The Centrality of a Place

The centrality of a place is equal to its surplus of importance, that is, equal to the relative importance of this place in regard to a region belonging to it. If we say that importance equals the number of telephone connections, then we might say: In a region of 4000 inhabitants there are 100 telephone connections (i.e., one connection for every 40 inhabitants); in the central place of a region with 2000 inhabitants, there should therefore be 50 telephone connections for satisfying the local demand of the central population. But if there are 80 connections in the central place, the surplus of importance of the central place will be: $80 - 50 = 30$ connections. The importance of the dispersed places of the region (with 2000 inhabitants living dispersedly) should thus be 50 telephone connections. But if there are only 20 connections in the dispersed places, the importance-deficit will be 30. Hence, importance-deficit of the dispersed places is balanced by the importance-surplus of the central place.

The formula for the centrality of a place is therefore:

$$Z_z = T_z - E_z\left(\frac{T_g}{E_g}\right)$$

in which T_z is the number of telephone connections at the central place; E_z is the number of inhabitants of the central place; T_g is the number of telephone connections in the region; and E_g is the number of inhabitants of the region. We shall define the expression $E_z(T_g/E_g)$ as the *expected importance* and T_z as the *actual importance*. The difference between them is the importance-surplus, or the centrality. The fraction T_g/E_g thus states the telephone density of the entire region based on the number of inhabitants; it will therefore be called the *telephone density*.

In the tables at the end of this book,* the numbers of inhabitants and telephone connections are not shown; only the numbers of points on the maps are shown. There is no change in the formula except that T means ten telephone connections and E means 400 inhabitants.

When we have obtained values for the centrality of a place, we must remember that these values are mere symbols for the expression of the central importance of a place; neither the demonstration of the importance of a place by the number of telephone connections nor the method of computing the centrality is exact in a mathematical sense; but the values obtained in this way correspond in a much higher degree to the central importance of a place than can the number of inhabitants or the number employed in trade, transportation, or free professions.

Our formula for computing the centrality, it should be mentioned, gives disproportionately high values to regions with higher telephone densities, and disproportionately low values to regions with lower telephone densities. The rough measure of centrality conceals the sources of mistakes in the telephone method which we mentioned above. But we set them aside, for it is advantageous to demonstrate the differences between regions with a high telephone density and those of a low telephone density (for instance, between wealthy and poor regions). A specific centrality which allows for comparison of all places would be computed in a manner similar to the foregoing computation of the specific-importance, which is related to the rough centrality, specifically through the telephone density, 40:1. That means that the value of the rough centrality should be multiplied by $E_g/40T_g$. The values obtained in this way for the specific centrality determine exactly in what relation the central place stands to its region.

Up to now, we have spoken of the central place and its region; naturally, there exists such a region belonging to a central place. However, as we found in the theoretical part,† this region is very difficult to determine; first, because, if we are correct, the complementary region for every type of central good is a different one, depending on the range of the central good, and second, because at its periphery the complementary region touches the complementary regions of neighboring central places in such a way that the border is not stable. In other words, the border shifts with every change in a factor determining the range of central goods. Frequently, the border districts belong simultaneously to the regions of two central places. For determining the rough importance of a place (equivalent to the number of telephone connections), it is not necessary to be familiar with the region of this place. However, we must be acquainted with its region if the rough importance is to be

---

* Only Table I is included in this translation.

† See Part I, B. and C.

reduced to the specific importance, because the reduction-coefficient contains the telephone density of the region and we must know the telephone density of the region if the centrality of a place is to be computed.

Because of that difficulty we hesitate to try to determine the region of a central place exactly;[4] it is only important for us to find a measure of the telephone density (number of inhabitants of a region per telephone connection since this telephone density varies only slightly over short distances). By this method, we estimated the region of a central place. Thereby, the region of a central place of the lowest order was found to include only the neighborhood of the central place, and in no case to include another central place, since each one had its respective region. The regions of central places of a middle order were assumed to be identical with the lower administration districts (counties, etc.); if, however, places of equal or higher centrality (industrial places or health resorts) than the seat of the administration districts lay in these administration districts, their telephones and inhabitants were omitted before computing the average telephone density. To compute the centralities of central places of a higher order, we considered the larger regions, including the central places of a lower order (located in those regions) which were economically or administratively dependent on the central places. Generally speaking, the principle is this: That region is to be used which belongs economically to a central place as a complementary region, especially with regard to the central goods of the highest range which are offered in this central place.

If the task of this elaboration is, among other things, to prove that there are certain typical sizes of central places, we must apply special care when computing the sizes of the central places. Because the importance (rough as well as specific) of a central place, as it was determined in Section 1 of this chapter, has not yet been related to a complementary region, we do not yet have a proper formula for recognizing these typical size groups. This importance consists of two elements, namely: (1) the individual importance of a place which might be rather considerable in health resorts, mining towns, border towns, etc., and (2) the surplus of importance, that is, the importance which represents the supplying of the dispersed places with central goods. The typical size of a place which represents its character as the center point of a region can be recognized only by a measure of its importance-surplus.

Is it the rough or the specific centrality which is decisive for putting a central place in a certain size-class? In order to prove the validity of our theoretically developed scheme concerning size and distribution of central places, only the specific centrality may be decisive. On the basis of the theoretical considerations, we stated that there are certain typical types of central places and no other size-types, that the number of central places belonging to such a type is established by some definite order and not by accident, and that the distribution of central places is meaningful and valid and not conditioned alone by accident, history, space, or nature. These facts apply whether the region is wealthy or poor, densely or thinly populated, favorable or unfavorable for transportation, long or recently settled; and also whether the prices of the central goods offered in the region are high or low, stable or unstable, or whether the transportation costs are uniform or varying, or high or low. All of these circumstances influence the size of the measure of rough centrality; the rough centrality is higher, for instance, in wealthy regions than in poorer regions. But in order to recognize whether our scheme, or "law," is valid we must disregard all individual differences in the various land areas and of the population, and consider only the value of the relationship between the central place and its complementary region as it is expressed by the specific centrality.

In "The Regional Part," * we find that the values for the rough centrality according to the formula, and as they are submitted in the tables at the end of the book and in Maps 3 and 4, are perfect enough to demonstrate the great regularity in the distribution of the individual size-types. This is especially true for predominantly agricultural regions; in more industrialized regions all types are more numerous, so that the indices of importance of the individual size-categories correspond closely with the scheme. Incidentally, it is easy to approximately determine the types as they would be shown on the basis of the specific centrality. The types according to rough centrality are overvalued in regions with a low telephone density and undervalued in regions of a high telephone density. The respective telephone densities are shown in Column 6 of the tables. By using rough centrality, however, we save a great amount of work which would have been added by computing the specific centrality; also, the maps are more precise, and, if the indices pertain to the rough centrality, reality will be approached.

NOTES

1. Compare the procedure of Alfred Weber (*Theory of the Location of Industry*) with regard to the location of industries. I am sorry to say that the practical part of Weber's doctrine is, at present, only very imperfectly represented by some dissertations.

2. Here the former attempt is, by way of mentioning, to quantify the importance of a place. In a speech (published in *Geographische Zeitschrift*, 50 (Leipzig: 1899)), Professor Blind sought to express the traffic importance of a town in numerical values. He based his statement on the assumption (which we have shown is inadmissible) that the effect of a town on another dispersed place

* See Part III, which describes the *L*-System of Munich.

is proportional to the number of inhabitants in that town; but because this effect decreases with decreasing distance, it is necessary to divide the number of the population by the average traffic distance. One should establish the importance of the town (which every dispersed place has) and add all numbers, so that one can compute the entire importance of the town. Apart from the immense (and hardly rewarding) job of counting, the components of this calculation are not commensurable nor are they readily additive; furthermore, the premises are in error.

Considerably simpler, and logically not objectionable, is the method of Hans Bobek, who numbers the members of the "typical urban labor branches the sum of which corresponds with the size of the *Verkehrsspannung* economic potential of the region" (similar to that which we called the importance of the central place); but the possibility of error is considerable with this method. (Hans Bobek, *Grundfragen der Stadtgeographie*, p. 220.)

3. I avoided displaying the greater settlements in the form of a sphere (according to the example of Sten de Geer, *Befolkningens Fördelning i Sverige* (Stockholm: 1919)) because it is not logical to display the smaller settlements by one principle (two-dimensional space) and the larger settlements by another (three-dimensional space); not only is the location of the border between the area point and the spatial sphere display chosen arbitrarily, but also the optical picture of the map is distorted by it, and in a certain way is wrong. For the same reasons, the method of Robert Gradmann (e.g., applied in the map of the expansion of the professional enterprises, *Süddeutschland* (Stuttgart: 1931), Vol. I, Picture 25, p. 179) was not applied since it gave the smaller places the points and the larger places a circle with the respective numbers written in. Otherwise, see the paragraphs about logic of the map as well as the population density maps in Max Eckert, *Die Kartenwissenschaft* (Berlin and Leipzig: 1925), Vol. II, and Hermann Lautensach, *Allgemeine Geographie zur Einführung die Landerkunde* (Gotha: 1926), pp. 262ff.

4. For certain single cases the region of a central place might be determined very well by an official inquiry, such as happened in eastern Germany in order to demonstrate the so-called "distortion of natural and economic borders." The result is submitted cartographically by Wilhelm Volz and Hans Schwelm, *Die deutsche Ostgrenze, Unterlagen zur Erfassung der Grenzzerreßungsschäden* (Leipzig: 1929). This procedure is methodical, as well as very interesting in its contents, but because of the great amount of fieldwork necessary, it is practical only for the narrowest regions.

B

Preliminary Results

1. The Central Places

Up to this point, we have developed a theory concerning the economic determination of the distribution, sizes, and number of central places, and we have found a usable method for analyzing reality. Before going on to Part III, which is concrete and analytical and related to a particular region, we should state some preliminary results of the analysis in order to have a clearer conception of the region and, thereby, to avoid repetition.

All places which have a centrality, (the rough measure of which is defined * as $Z_z = T_z - E_z(T_g/E_g)$, in which T_z and T_g are the numbers in units of ten of telephones in the central place and region respectively, and E_g is the number in units of 400 of inhabitants) of about -0.5 to $+0.5$, which will be regarded as indicating neither a great surplus of importance nor a great deficit of importance, may be designated as *auxiliary central places (hilfszentrale Orte)*. They have, on the average, from five to ten telephones. In regions with a high telephone density, or places with a larger number of inhabitants, a place with twenty or more telephones can still easily be an auxiliary central place. Also, in regions with a low telephone density, or places with a smaller number of inhabitants, the place with less than five telephones can still be an auxiliary central place.

The auxiliary central places are purely neither dispersed places with large deficits of importance nor central places with large surpluses of im-

---

* See the list and definitions of terms in note 2, p. 80.

portance. If we look at the auxiliary central place genetically, we can distinguish three groups:

1. Displaced central places of former historical times: market places and little towns, the locations of which are inconvenient from the standpoint of modern economy and modern traffic. Such places include towns in prominent protective locations on tops of mountains and towns on railroad spurs,[1] which are easily displaced in their functions as central places by more favorably situated railroad places. But many of the numerous market places and little towns, especially in the older regions of established settlements and, during the main period of the medieval town development, the environs not a part of greater homogeneous territorial rule,[2] are also displaced in the modern economy of free intercourse and unification of regional administration. They have undergone a slow transformation back to dispersed places, and this transformation is still going on. Furthermore, this group includes those places which lie near larger towns and which thus lose more and more of their economic independence and their own market region; they become suburbs, or even boroughs, of larger towns and their central importance is absorbed by the higher, and thereby expansive, centralities of the larger neighboring towns. Finally, this group includes those places which lose their markets because of an impoverishment of the land, a change in the border, or other reasons; or, such places are also displaced because of an improvement in the transportation conditions.

2. The rising central places, i.e., dispersed places which have locations favorable from the standpoint of modern economy (in the dynamic theory, we found that such places are required if the land is to be supplied with central goods) belong to this group. This group also includes places within neighborhoods which have changed from agricultural to industrial pursuits, and such places which lie in regions with growing population or growing prosperity (especially regions with tourist trade —provided that no other great town lies in the vicinity). Furthermore, the development of the traffic net and transportation facilities are significant. This is seen in the rising centrality of railroad station places, which are for the most part substitutes for the centrality which other places have lost. Also, quite special circumstances such as the foundation of religious communities, new mine developments, promotion of great industrial plants, and changes in borders can make a settlement, which formerly was not assigned any importance, central. At the beginning of its growth, such a place should be considered as an auxiliary central place; its development is positive and tends toward full centrality, while the deposed central places tend toward dispersion. Both the developing and the declining central places pass through the classification of auxiliary central place.

3. A third group of places is different. This group consists of permanent auxiliary central places. They are, and must remain, permanent auxiliary central places. They include the isolated places in mountain valleys, which because of great natural barriers cannot extend their region or expect any great growth in population or wealth. Also included are those unfortunate speculations Gradmann has called the dwarf-towns;[3] they never had a greater importance and had no chance for development (they lacked a hinterland) because they had no possibility of enlarging their boundaries, that is, of shifting from dispersed agricultural production. This group also includes the places of the house-to-house peddlers, often rural Jewish settlements, the regions of which are not the vicinities but rather vague regions which encompass as far as the peddlers can walk.

These auxiliary central places are indicated by crosses on Map 3. It should be noticed that they lie mostly at the borders of the districts surrounding full central places. That means that they lie in theoretically correct positions—at the limits of the ranges for certain central goods of the lowest order, in remote parts of the land, or near larger towns.

The auxiliary central places just described are in a class between dispersed places and central places. We shall call them H-places. According to the scheme in Part I, "The Theoretical Part," a wreath of six H-places lies around every (even the lowest rank) full central place in such a manner that every H-place simultaneously belongs to the regions of three full central places. Thus, there are two auxiliary central places for every full central place. Naturally, these six places are not, as a rule, actually found; there is only the possibility that auxiliary central places might have been developed at these six locations. If there is a concrete example of one, it will have been the result of many circumstances that we have already become acquainted with, especially in the dynamic theory.

The lowest rank among the full central places belongs to those places which are frequently called simply *markets*. We shall continue to use this term, but in order to avoid confusion with the kind of settlement which has historically and administratively been called a market spot (*Marktflecken*) we shall speak of the M-places. This M-place is characterized mainly by its weekly markets, and still further by having other central institutions of the lowest rank: a vital statistics office, a police station, a physician; and sometimes a veterinarian, a dentist, an inn (not just a restaurant); and perhaps a cooperative, a loan office branch, a large variety of artisans, large repair shops, breweries, or mills. The M-places nearly always have a railroad station, a post office, and a telephone exchange, and there are almost always important crossroads or terminals of bus lines. The number of telephones is between ten and twenty in the wealthy regions (of high telephone density); with a higher population in the place, there will be more telephones, and with a lower telephone density or lower population, even a place with less than ten telephones might belong to the M-place. The centrality, according to our formula, is 0.5 to 2.0, and these M-places are also found in wreaths of six around every central place of a higher order.

The next type of central place is characterized by having a lowest court, an elementary school, a public library, a local museum, an apothecary, a veterinarian, a cinema, a local newspaper, local clubs and co-ops, special shops, savings and loan offices, and, frequently, railway crossroads. Because such a place is a seat of offices, we shall call it an *office town (Amtsstädtchen)*.[4] For the expression to have independent meaning, we shall speak of the A-places. The number of telephones is, on the average, twenty to fifty, and the centrality is two to four. These places, too, are distributed in groups of six around every central place higher than A-rank.

The next type includes the main places* of the *Kreise* in Prussia and Hessen, the *Amtsbezirke* in Baden, the *Oberämter* in Württemberg, and the *Bezirksämter* in Bavaria—in other words, the seats of lower administrative authority, the county town (*Kreisstädtchen*), whence comes the designation of K-place. The central institutions consist of the lower administrative offices, county doctors, county veterinaries, county savings offices, county newspapers, county guilds, and all other types of county organizations; internal revenue offices, high schools, consumer cooperatives, bank branches, and slaughter houses. Many of these places are also stops for the express trains. Their telephones number between 50 and 150 and their centralities are between four and twelve. This group of K-places, contrary to the theory, obviously falls into two subgroups, as may be recognized from the graphic illustration:† one subgroup has a centrality of five or six, and the other has a centrality of from eight to ten. Specifically, those K-places which are lower administrative seats have centralities of eight to ten, while places of a similar economic central meaning and population, but without being lower administrative seats, have centralities of five or six. This latter subgroup has, however, a considerably different function from the group of A-places; it resembles more the K-place with the administration seats, which is why we place them in this group. This classification is also correct for the theoretical scheme.

---

* *Kreis(e)* generally corresponds to our county, but in some instances Christaller is referring specifically to administration units (political areas) in Prussia, where the term is used differently than it is in other parts of the Reich. We can take a *Kreisstädtchen* to be equivalent to a county seat in the United States.

† See the graphs of the frequency distributions in the Appendix, given for the L-system of Munich and for all of southern Germany.

The next higher type of central place is one which is not administratively important, but which is economically important. To be sure, administration circles desire to combine the small lower administration districts into larger units (so-called *Großkreise*)* in order to effect savings in administrative costs. Such a general elimination of small lower administration districts was a mistake. It would be much more sensible to leave certain offices, the services of which have relatively small range (police, general internal administration, county school offices, county church offices), at the old seats, the *K*-places, and perhaps even to create additional seats of this kind. On the other hand, those offices the services of which have a greater range (county doctors, county hospitals, county building offices, cultural building offices, etc.) ought to be transferred from the *K*-place to these places of higher importance. This goal is partially achieved today by the combining of two lower administration districts for these special offices and the placing of the seat of the new combined office at the seat of the larger county. In any case, with such an important change as the complete elimination of a lower administration district it means, we should remember, that all of the services of the lower administrative offices do not have the same range in the sense previously expressed (for the *K*-place). We call these larger places *B*-places, main district places (*Bezirkshauptorte*). Aside from the institutions previously mentioned, the labor office, from an administrative standpoint, also belongs at this place. There are always an accredited high school, medical specialists, daily movies, special shops, and special artisans. Frequently, there are also small department stores, daily newspapers, banks, branches of the *Reichsbank,* gasworks, post offices of a higher rank, etc. This *B*-place deserves the full meaning of *town* (*Stadt*), whereas the *K*-places still will be called *small town* (*Städtchen*).[5] The number of telephones in *B*-places is between 150 and 500; the centrality is between twelve and thirty. But the line of demarcation between the *B*-place and the next higher type is not always very distinct.

The next higher type is the *G*-place, named after the *Gau* district (*Gaubezirk*).† We shall speak later about the size of the *Gau* district. It is important here to determine the typical size of a main place in such a regional unit. The *G*-place is the *"Mittelstadt"* of the *Statistical Yearbook of Germany*, (*Statistisches Jahrbuch des Deutschen Reichs*),‡ at least of the lower *Mittelstadt* group up to about 70,000 inhabitants. The *G*-places are characteristically seats of middle administration offices

---

* See pp. 160-161.

† *Gau* was the name of an old German tribe. *Gau* now means a district, province, county, etc.

‡ *The Statistisches Jahrbuch des Deutschen Reichs* is a census report which classifies towns according to population, in the same manner as the U.S. Bureau of the Census.

corresponding to the *Landeskommissariatsbezirke* of Baden and the *Provinzen* of Hesse. As a rule, they have land courts and chambers of industry and commerce. Many have theaters, varied economic and social organizations, manufacturers' regional selling agents, shops of a higher order, and warehouses; there are also railroad crossroads of greater importance. Frequently, they are university towns, garrison towns, or centers of industrial districts. Their telephones number between 500 and 2500 and their centrality between 30 and 150.

In the next category are the provincial capitals (*Provinzialhauptorte*), the *P*-places, those towns which have a high individual importance and which are the large towns of a broader district. In them are all the urban institutions: streetcars, slaughter houses, gasworks, sporting arenas, theaters, seats of the provincial government (in Prussia, they correspond more to capitals of an administrative area (*Regierungsbezirke*) than to capitals of the provinces; in Bavaria they correspond to seats of the newly combined *Kreise*), commercial colleges, special shops of higher importance, banks, small stock exchanges, and regional seats of the post office and of railway administration. Their populations are from 70,000 to perhaps 400,000; their telephones number 2500 to 25,000; and their indices of centrality are 150 to 1200. The class limit between them and *G*-places is as clear as it is between them and the next higher places.

The highest type of central place still belonging to the framework of our study is the land center (*Landeszentrale*), the *L*-place.[6] These land centers stand out very sharply especially in Germany, and also in Italy and Spain. Their populations average about 500,000; their telephones number over 25,000; and their centrality indices are over 1200.

Above these *L*-places there is only one other clearly definable group: the world cities or national capitals (*Reichshauptstädte*), which we shall designate as *R*-places. They have populations of over 2,000,000. In undeveloped parts of the world, with less population, there is theoretically, according to the scheme of central places, still another type between the *L*- and the *R*-places, because for every two places of a certain type there must always be one place of the next higher type.[7] If we have in Germany perhaps twelve *L*-places (and probably more), one of which, Berlin, is an *R*-place, three of these *L*-places must belong to this in-between type (for instance, Hamburg, Cologne, the functions of which are shared by Düsseldorf, Essen, and Munich). These places will be called *RT*-places, because they represent a part of the state (*Reichsteilstädte*).* In other countries, perhaps in France, this *RT*-place has greater independence. The *L*-places, on the other hand, have respectively less importance. To complete the scheme or distribution of places (where Paris is the *R*-place)

---

* Federal reserves, Army co-ops, and district cities.

we could name Bordeaux and Lyon (or Marseille), as RT-places. In Italy, to complement the R-place of Rome, we could name Milan and Naples as RT-places. And we could do likewise for Great Britain, former Austria-Hungary, Japan, etc.

Following is a tabulation of what we have said concerning the real types of central places in southern Germany:

Type	Population (approximate)	Number of Telephones	Centrality
H	800	5-10	−0.5-+0.5
M	1,200	10-20	0.5-2
A	2,000	20-50	2-4
K	4,000	50-150	4-12
B	10,000	150-500	12-30
G	30,000	500-2,500	30-150
P	100,000	2,500-25,000	150-1,200
L	500,000	25,000-60,000	1,200-3,000
RT	1,000,000	60,000	3,000
R	4,000,000	?	?

There is something to be anticipated concerning the L-places in southern Germany because the distribution of places in Part III, "The Regional Part," is based on the systems of these L-places. Which towns are to be designated as L-places?

No doubt, Munich, Stuttgart, and Frankfurt belong to this group. Including their neighboring places which participate in the central functions of the respective towns, we derive the following data:

Town	Population	Telephones	Centrality
Munich	747,200	50,290	2,825
Frankfurt	688,000	42,100	2,060
Stuttgart	415,800	28,530	1,606

The combination of Nuremberg and Fürth could also be considered a central place of L-importance:

Nuremberg-Fürth	486,400	26,230	1,346

There are no other towns or combinations of towns in southern Germany which have a centrality higher than 1200. The next ones are far-distant Mannheim-Ludwigshafen, which has a centrality of 649, and Karlsruhe, with a centrality of 357. But we should not be wholly satisfied with this result. When we consider that (as we shall see in the next section, the radius of the complementary marketing region of an L-place in southern Germany is about 108 km.), we shall see that the Saar and western Rhine Palatine as well as southern Baden lie outside the range of influence of the neighboring L-towns, Frankfurt and Stuttgart. If we consider towns with L-importance outside of Germany, for instance Nancy and Zurich, then we shall see that the Saar lies partly in the range of Nancy, and that southern Baden lies partly in the range of Zurich. As a matter of fact, however, neither does the L-importance of Stuttgart reach to Landau, Neustadt at the Haardt, and Strassburg, the L-importance of Zurich reach to Freiburg and Offenburg, nor the L-importance of Nancy reach to Hamburg in the Pfalz, Strassburg, and Mulhaose. Furthermore, the upper Rhine region—upper Rhineland as Metz calls it[8]—which nature so clearly formed as an individual entity, is a thoroughly independent L-region and is hardly within the actual ranges of the L-places beyond the Vosges Mountains, the Swiss Jura, and the Black Forest. This L-region obviously lacks only a large town of L-importance. It would not be too far wrong to say, as Metz also has done, that Strassburg is the natural center of this region;[9] but it would hardly comply with present reality. Furthermore, we shall postulate a proposition which corresponds with the logic of our theory and which would be fulfilled in reality as soon as hindrances were removed, because of the validity of the geography of settlements. Because this potential L-function of Strassburg is so obvious, we shall designate it as the fifth L-place in southern Germany, in Part III.[10]

2. The Other Elements of the System

After having categorized the types of systems of central places according to size and importance, we now must determine the sizes of the complementary regions which correspond to the typical sizes of the different types of central places. We shall proceed as we did in determining the sizes of the types of central places (i.e., inductively), by starting with the central places in southern Germany, which we have identified with the help of the telephone method. If the central places are drawn on a map, we shall note with surprise that the result is a regular net of central places. Those regions which formerly appeared to be without towns (upper Bavaria, southern Oberpfalz, and Oberschwaben) are now shown to have central places as much as do other regions, and those regions which are especially dense with towns (Neckar regions, upper Rhine plain, Saar, central Main region) are no longer so outstanding.[11] Our surprise continues when we recognize that the average distance between two central places is generally about 7 to 9 km., so that the radius of the complementary region of the lowest order is 4 to 5 km.—a round number not without importance. This distance means that one hour's distance* is the basic measure according to which the size of this lowest

---

* Distance traveled in one hour.

region is established. In other words: If a trip to town takes longer than an hour, the distance will appear relatively too great and will deter a person from making frequent trips to town. Therefore, there is obviously a large number of central goods with a range of one hour; that is why this clear M-type of central place could be formed—its central goods consist mainly of goods which have ranges of less than one hour. Clearly, the pure time-measure has an important geographical effect, for it basically determines the number and distribution of the central places.[12]

This fact holds so generally for the region with which we deal that in the construction of the lowest regions of the central places on Map 3, we were able to start quite simply by drawing a circle with a radius of 5 km. around the central place—a circle with a radius of precisely one trip-hour, whereby we formed a region that is encompassed by a one-hour isochrone.* There were then only minor corrections to be made when neighboring central places were very near. On the other hand, we refrained from including on the map the complementary region beyond the one-hour isochrone. Thus, those parts of regions which were inadequately supplied by the M-places, or which were not supplied at all, became very clear. Most of them were thinly populated and less developed regions in which, very often, H-places had developed as substitutes for the missing M-places; or, they were unpopulated forests, mountains, or swamps. Accordingly, the typical M-region ranges in size from 40 to 60 sq. km. Where the neighboring M-regions are not very dense, the size limit is set at 80 sq. km.; and where the neighboring M-regions are very dense, they are often less than 40 sq. km. Sometimes we find two or three central places so close together that we can speak of a common M-region; if the places lie less densely together, their regions can be connected. The typical population of these regions—if their center is a normal M-place—is 3000 to 4000, including both the rural population and the central professions at the M-place.

The M-region of a central place has an especially high economic importance, while administratively it is almost without importance. (It is about like the Rhenish *Bürgermeisterei,* and also corresponds to some political communities in the Alpine countries.) However, this high economic importance is not the only reason for basing the representation of Map 3 on M-regions of central places; this measure is the basic measure for all larger regions. According to the theoretical scheme, for every two M-places, there is one place of the next higher order, namely the A-place; that is, three M-regions together form an A-region, the size of which is, on the average, 133 sq. km.; three A-regions form the K-region of 400 sq. km.; three K-regions form a B-region of 1200 sq. km.; etc. The radii

---

* See footnote, p. 44.

are also determined by the sizes of these regions. We have been led to these empirically found numerical values by way of the rational scheme of deduction,—then only by way of elucidation—and we may hence simply refer to the compilation of the table on page 67.

These regions of the central places are typical in their character and can be found everywhere in the world.[13] We mentioned previously the relationship between the M-region and the Rhenish *Bürgermeisterei*.[14] Thus, the A-region is similar to the district of an *Amtsgericht* (the Amt —in Württemberg, the next higher unit, which includes several *Ämter*, called an *Oberamt*).[15] The *Amt* is perhaps the continuance of the earlier medieval counties which functioned as court districts. Later they were, according to the demand, distributed or united; but generally, Below was correct in saying of them: "Old court district borders were maintained very frequently." [16] The K-region corresponds to the present lower administration district, a type which, supported by existing units, developed for the most part only at the beginning of the nineteenth century.[17] The B-region is obviously still more recent; it is quite well established with regard to economic organizations and market conditions, and it seems that it will organize and establish itself with regard to administration respects also.[18] This type is represented in France by the *arrondissement*.* The G-region, however, is a very old type which does not fit too well in the present administration system. According to Vogel, the old *Gau* of the Germans had a size of from 5000 to 10,000 sq. km.; and the *civitate* of Gaul, corresponding to the Roman *pagus* was 11,000 sq. km.[19] The *Gau* division has been developed anew in recent times, especially in sport organization, but its area is for the most part considerably larger. The French *département* corresponds to this type. The P-region clearly corresponds to the Prussian *Regierungsbezirk,* while the Prussian provinces, as well as the Russian *gouvernements,* are mostly typical L-regions. The L-region is large enough to become a strong, independent state, as has happened with the Netherlands, Denmark, Belgium, Switzerland, and the Baltic states. The economic importance of this size-type is proved by the fact that during the War, France, in which this type presently is entirely missing, planned to divide the country into twenty regions, so-called "comités consultatifs d'action économique." In connection with this, there emerged "regionalism," a movement for restoring the old land structure.[20] Also, in England there are tendencies, under the motto of "devolution," [21] to form provincial divisions.

From the number and locations of the typical central places, the typical distances between these places are derived. We have already found

---

* See Dickinson, *City, Region and Regionalism* (London, 1947), pp. 264-265, for a discussion of different administrative divisions in Europe.

the average radius of an M-region to be 4 to 5 km. This makes the average distance between an M-place and another M-place or higher ranking place about 7 to 9 km., in a system constructed according to the marketing principle. In a system based on the traffic principle, the average distances between like places are 5 to 6 km. along the traffic routes, but about 10 km. if perpendicular to the traffic line.

It is possible to compute the other distances in accordance with the theoretical system of central places from this basic distance of 7 km. We call this the typical M-distance (in more densely populated regions it might be as much as 9 km.).[22] We always find the next higher distance by multiplying by $\sqrt{3}$ the last distance which we found. Thus, we find that the A-distance is 12 km. (or up to 15 km);[23] the K-distance is 21 km. (or up to 27 km);[24] the B-distance is 36 km. (or up to 45 km.);[25] the G-distance is 62 km. (or up to 81 km.); the P-distance is 108 km. (or up to 135 km.); and the L-distance is 185 km. (or up to 240 km.). The real typical distances of these types will naturally be lower in very densely settled regions.

In order to find a firm norm, the deviations from which, upward and downward, could be found (whereby the cause of the deviation, as a rule, lies in the sparse or dense settlement of the region), Map 4 is based on distances which correspond to a $\sqrt{3}$ progressive series:*

$$4, 4\sqrt{3}, 4 \times 3, 12\sqrt{3}, 12 \times 3, 36\sqrt{3}, 36 \times 3, 108\sqrt{3}$$

Since this refers only to the system of G-places (exception: also to the system of B-places), only those distances which refer to the G-places (or B-places) are shown. Therefore, the following distances which appear in these places are important for the later analysis:†

1. An inner 12 km. A-ring around the G- (and naturally also the higher ranking) places. Theoretically it exists for all K- and B-places, too, and actually it is found everywhere. We omitted the analysis of the K- and also, for the most part, the B-systems in order not to get too involved.
2. The 21 km. K-ring around the G-places (likewise around the B-, P- and L-places).
3. An outer 24 km. A-ring (I) around the G-, P- and L-places and an outer 32 km. A-ring (II) on which the A-places lie along the communication lines between neighboring B-places.
4. The 36 km. B-ring around the G-, P- and L-places, which completes the G-system.

---

* That is: 4, 6.9, 12, 20.7, 36, 62.1, 108, 185.6. See p. 67.
† See Figure 1, p. 61, for illustrations in the following enumerated statements.

The real geographical location of a central place corresponds more or less to the theoretically correct location of the scheme of central places. Deviations from this theoretical location demand an explanation, because they can be caused only by special economic, historic, or natural circumstances. These deviations from the normal location should be investigated with regard to deviations from the normal distance (see above), and deviations from a central place, toward neighboring systems. We can especially recognize, from the deviations of the latter type, whether the marketing or traffic principle is the decisive principle in the development of the systems. Thus, the history of the geography of settlements is provided a new tool of analysis since one or the other principle must have prevailed in a particular time period or in a given country.

We remember from the statements of the marketing and traffic principles—the separation principle is indifferent in this respect—that in a system of central places which is based on the marketing principle, the direction lines of traffic between the central places in the system are always offset.* That is, in a G-system the K-places always lie on the line which bisects the angle BGB, or as we shall express it, they lie on a between-B-direction line. Similarly, the correct location of the B-places in the sense of the marketing principle is on the between-G-direction line, and the correct location of the G-places is on the between-P-direction line, etc. A direction-line which lies in such a way so that the K-places do not lie on the B-directions (the B-places on the G-directions, etc.) should, for reasons of simplicity (even if the grammar seems awkward), be called an "on-B-direction" or an "on-G-direction" in contrast to the "between-B-direction" or the "between-G-direction". The existence of this type of direction demonstrates that here the traffic principle has decisively determined the development of the system.†

These lines—on Map 4 only the L-lines are drawn—are not to be confused with the actual transportation routes. Basically, they have nothing whatever to do with them. The lines are only geometrical auxiliary means, such as the circles which we have also drawn; and they serve to determine the theoretically correct location of a place, i.e., where its site in the net of central places should be found.

According to the norm, there are always six on-directions lines and six between-directions lines starting at every central place. Sometimes, however, because of the number of neighboring central places or because

---

* See Figure 3, p. 73. (Otherwise, some important higher order central places are bypassed.)

† Here we may see the connection of Lösch's "sector-type" analysis. See A. Lösch, "Kapital, das System von Netzen," in *Die räumliche Ordnung der Wirtschaft* (Jena, 1944), **II**.

of especially massive or extensive land irregularities there are only five (but seldom four); or, there may be as many as seven or eight lines. We know that, normally, a wreath of six central places of a lower rank lies around every central place. If the places of a lower rank lie too far from the center of the system, then there are often more places; if they lie too near, then there are often fewer. The arc of the circle on which they lie is usually subdivided into sections by the typical distance (normal radius), so that the larger circular arc consists of more, and the smaller arc consists of fewer than the normal six sections. Our analysis must find an explanation for this.

3. The Systems

We understand the system of central places to be a number of central places grouped around a central place (that is, the system-forming central place) according to certain rules. These rules may be determined either by economic laws or by sociopolitical propositions or by both. Economic determination of the rule occurs when the central places are distributed according to the marketing or the traffic principle. The economic principle expressed in each case is that the individual economic factors are related to one another in such a way that the least economic expenditures result in the highest degree of effectiveness; and from the point of view of pure economics, the result should be the most favorable. Sociopolitical determination of the order upon which a system is built occurs when the separation principle is expressed in the formation of the system, and chiefly in the manner that certain points in the marketing scheme are taken by several places, i.e., that these places are split up.

The elements of the systems of central places as we have seen are: (1) the system-forming central places; (2) the central places grouped around them; (3) the distances; and (4) the positions in which the central places lie with regard to the system-forming central places and other central places of the system. The area occupied by a system is the region of the system-forming central place (that is, particularly, in regarding its typical central goods).

We speak of a B-system when the system-forming central place forms a system with only typical B-size conditions, i.e., when a place is itself a B-place and when its system ranges up to the central places of the typical 21 km. rings. In the same manner, we speak of G-systems, P-systems, L-systems, and K-systems, etc.

These systems can be either isolated, if the places on the ring which bounds the system belong only to that system and not simultaneously to another system, or normal, if the places on the boundary ring of the system are all simultaneously places on the boundary rings of neighboring systems or if they are subjoined or connected to another system, etc. (in short, if the system is only partially independent).

Normally, a *B*-system with a 21 km. *K*-ring has a system-forming *B*-place and six *K*-places as border-ring places, etc. If, however, the system-forming place of the *B*-system is a *G*-place and the bordering places are *B*-places, then the whole system, in regard to the typical sizes of its central places, will rise to the next higher level. And, vice-versa, if all places of the system belong to a lower size-type, the entire system will then lie on the next lower level. The former can happen in very densely populated, wealthy parts of the country, the latter in very thinly populated, poorer parts.

The systems of central places are not eternal. Changes in location of the capital, decided changes in the transportation system, and similar radical events can disturb or even destroy the old system. Then, a new system will—very gradually—crystallize around the new preferred center. Thus, we can recognize traces of a system of a historically earlier type beside the system of a more recent date which has been superimposed over the old one; we can recognize the up-and-coming and dying systems, etc. Also, a system may expand at the expense of neighboring systems, or an isolated system can join itself to a neighboring system.

According to the degree of association of a system with the systems of the next higher order, we should distribute (add) this system to the systems of a higher order. According to the theoretically normal scheme, the addition is impossible or arbitrary; but in concrete reality, not only natural geographical conditions but also the sociopolitical separation principle governs in the sense of causing deviations from the normal system, whereby a necessary addition of this system to a next higher system results. (In the first case it is an addition caused more by geographical logic; in the second it is caused by deliberate political action.)

All the arrangements formed up to now will be demonstrated in the course of our analysis of the distribution of central places in southern Germany. This analysis will have to solve the following questions after the system-forming central places have been determined:

1. What are the boundaries of the system? According to the theory, the boundaries must run through the central places of the next lower type: What deviations exist and how can they be explained?
2. In regard to contiguous systems: Are they isolated, normal, attached, or a single common system?
3. In regard to the basic distances of the system: Is the system narrow, normal, or wide?

4. Are there between-directions lines or on-directions lines? In the first case, the marketing principle prevails and, in the latter case, the traffic principle prevails.

5. Are the sites which, in a normal system, are taken by a central place of a certain size-type taken by one, two, or three central places—as a rule, of a lower size-type? If they are taken by more than one central place, it is mainly the result of the separation principle.

6. Is the system normal, or is it higher, or is it lower?

7. In which system of a higher order should we place the system being analyzed?

8. What deviations from the normal scheme of a local nature should be noticed?

Now, having made all preparations, we are ready to analyze the geographical facts of the distribution, number, and sizes of the central places in southern Germany, and to determine what determined these geographical data.

NOTES

1. In the provinces of the secondary mountains, towns in spur locations are especially frequent. See Robert Gradmann, "Die städtischen Siedlungen, des Königreichs Württemberg," in *Forschungen zur deutschen Landes- und Volkskunde,* 21, Part II (Stuttgart: 1926), 147f.

2. See Robert Gradmann, *Süddeutschland* (Stuttgart: 1931), Vol. I, p. 166.

3. Robert Gradmann, "Die städtischen Siedlungen . . . ," 168.

4. Kötzschke calls such *A*-places of the Middle Ages and partly includes the *K*-places too, which then had no more than 2000 inhabitants, not literally "un-town-like towns" (*"uneigentliche Städte"*). (Rudolf Kötzschke, "Allgemeine Wirtschaftsgeschichte des Mittelalters," in *Handbuch der Wirtschaftsgeschichte,* ed. Georg Brodnitz (Jena: 1924), p. 574.)

5. Hermann Wagner ("Allgemeine Länderkunde von Europa," in *Lehrbuch der Geographie* (Hannover and Leipzig: 1915), Vol. I, Part I) has the opinion (p. 125) that there are no evident typical differences between the *Kleinstädte* of 5000 to 20,000 inhabitants and the *Landstädte* of 2000 to 5000 in most European states. However, if people speak of them as *Städte* (but only from about 10,000 population on) and *Städtchen,* then there must be an obvious typical difference.

6. They correspond approximately to the *Großstädte* of 50,000 inhabitants of the Middle Ages, cited by Kötzschke: Florence, Milan, Genoa, Barcelona, Cologne, London. The medieval world cities with over 100,000 inhabitants— Constantinople, Venice, Palermo, and Paris—can be called "*R*-places." (Rudolf Kötzschke, *loc. cit.*)

7. The table on page 67 continued for an *R*-region would be: one *R*-place, two *R T*-places, six *L*-places, etc.

8. Fredrich Metz, *Die Oberrheinlande* (Breslau: 1925). He says in the fore-

word: "The upper Rhineland remains the most exclusive natural, cultural, and national unity on the grounds of central Europe."

9. Metz, *ibid.,* pp. 269-272.

10. See "The Regional Part."

11. Compare our Map 4 (Appendix) with Map-Table 8 in Robert Gradmann's *Süddeutschland.*

12. Hassinger proves that the one-hour measure, even under quite different transportation conditions and time evaluations, as in a normal rural *M*-region, has basic importance. He has empirically found that a maximum of about one hour is used by the city population of Vienna to get to their places of work or pleasure; beyond this one-hour isochrone, the city of Vienna and her narrow region ceases. This one-hour isochrone was also valid for London although the corresponding radius is 24 km. for London because of the greater speed of the transportation facilities. (Hugo Hassinger, "Beiträge zur Siedlungs- und Verkehrsgeographie von Wien," in *Mitteilungen der geographischen Gesellschaft,* 53 (Vienna: 1910), 34-51, note 1.)

13. Hettner says: It is desirable to agree on the use of the different expressions for the various sizes of the geographical regions. (Alfred Hettner, *Die Geographie, ihre Geschichte, ihr Wesen und ihre Methoden* (Breslau: 1927), p. 281.) That is difficult to do for regions limited purely geographically because it is rather arbitrary. But for other anthropogeographical aspects, the size of the region is still determined by the character; therefore, every size-type must have a special expression, which the vernacular has produced fourfold. For scientific purposes we choose more precise, rationally developed expressions here.

14. Hermann Wagner (*op. cit.,* p. 833) gives the size-value of political communities insofar as they approach the *M*-region: Italy 34 sq. km.; Münsterland and the Netherlands mostly more than 30 sq. km.; the American townships, on the average, 93 sq. km. The age of this *M*-region is very important; there is, as Otto Maull (*Politische Geographie* (Berlin: 1925), p. 579) mentions, usually a connection between the borders of a Germanic *Hundertschaften* [a company of men with their families—Editor] and the later *Parrish* which approximately corresponds to the *M*-region of the present.

15. It is interesting that in Württemberg there is an average of one town (in the historic meaning) for each 132 sq. km. (Robert Gradmann, "Die städtischen Siedlungen . . . ," p. 13); hence, the Oberamt corresponds exactly with our 133 sq. km. *A*-region.

16. Georg von Below, "Vom Mittelalter zur Neuzeit," in *Wissenschaft und Bildung,* 198 (Leipzig: 1924), 35.

17. See Herman Gruber, *Kreise und Kreisgrenzen Preußens, vornehmlich die Ostpreußens, geographische betrachtet* (Königsberg: 1912), and Fredrich Nüssle, *Die administrative Einteilung des unteren und mittleren württembergischen Neckargebiets. Ein Beitrag zur wirtschafts- und politisch-geographischen Landeskunde von Württemberg* (Stuttgart: 1930). Hermann Wagner calls these districts, not very appropriately, "home districts" (*Heimatsbezirke*). (*Loc. cit.*)

18. See Hermann Losch, "Über die Neueinteilung Württembergs," in *Mitteilungen des württembergischen statistischen Landesamts* (Stuttgart: 1927), 192, or Reuscher, "Das Vorortproblem mit besonderer Berüchsichtigung der kommunalrechtlichen Stellung der großstädtischen Vorortgemeinden," in *Verwaltungsarchiv, Zeitschrift für Verwaltungsrecht und Verwaltungsgerichtsbarkeit,* 35 (Berlin: 1930), 138.

See also "Bericht über die Vorstandssitzung des preußischen Städtetages" [report about the Council Meeting of the Prussian *Städtetages* (organization of Prussian towns—Editor)] on February 9, 1929, in *Der Städtetag*, 23rd year (Berlin: 1929), 144ff. It is said that "through the combination of counties if necessary," sufficient room for the sound development and efficiency of the county (*landkreise*) will be created. Finally, see "Vorschläge zur Abgrenzung der Zuständigkeiten zwischen Reich, Ländern und Gemeinden," in *ibid.*, 1119ff.

19. Walther Vogel, *Politische Geographie, Aus Natur und Geisteswelt* (Berlin and Leipzig: 1922), p. 60.

20. Arnold Bergsträsser, *Staat und Wirtschaft Frankreichs* (Berlin and Leipzig: 1930), Vol. II, pp. 62f.

21. Wilhelm Dibelius, *England* (Berlin and Leipzig: 1929), Vol. I, p. 366.

22. M. Sidaritsch, "Die steirischen Städte und Märkte in vergleichend geographischer Darstellung," in *Sieger-Festschrift* (Vienna: 1924). Sidaritsch found a distance of 8 km. for the markets of the middle country of the Steiermark, the Austrian province.

23. In Württemberg, the average distance between two towns is (according to Robert Gradmann, "Die städtischen Siedlungen . . . ," p. 13) 11.5 km.

24. Friedrich Ratzel (*Anthropogeographie oder Grundzüge der Anwendung der Geographie auf die Geschichte*, 2nd.ed. (Stuttgart: 1912), Vol. II, p. 280) states that small towns and large villages on the mail routes always lie at a distance of 2 to 3 leagues [1 league = 7.42 km., therefore, 14.8 to 22.3 km.] from each other. Erich Schrader ("Die Städte Hessens," in *Jahresbericht des Frankfurter Vereins für Geographie und Statistik* (Frankfurt: 1922), 19) states that 21 km. is the distance of the *Etappenorte* [posts on the lines of communication—formerly the stopping stations of soldiers on the march—Editor]. Both statements are obviously congruent with our determination of the typical K-distance.

25. In connection with the B-distance, the interesting writings of Kuske concerning the city of Cologne should be mentioned. It is remarkable and obvious that this large town prevented others from developing within 30 to 40 km., partly unintentionally and partly through purposeful political and military action; otherwise the neighborhoods of most older German towns have extensions of about 20 to 25 km. (Bruno Kuske, *Die Großstadt Köln als wirtschaftlicher und sozialer Körper* (Köln: 1928), p. 13.)

III

THE REGIONAL PART

The Number, Sizes, and Distribution of the Central Places in Southern Germany

A

The L-System of Munich

I. THE BASIC FACTS

1. The L-Center

We begin our analysis of the central places in southern Germany with the L-system of Munich.* According to our table, Munich has a centrality of 2825 and stands first among the southern German towns. The nearest to it is Frankfurt with 2060, which means that Munich is quite prominent. The reason is that Munich, in a manner similar to Berlin and Prague, concentrates in itself all the higher ranking central functions of an L-region. Consequently, although its neighbor, Augsburg, has almost twice as great a population as Würzburg, Darmstadt, Heidelberg, or Freiburg, it has a smaller centrality—only 224.

If we look for the causes of the high centrality of Munich, we must first consider, besides the consequent concentration of all the central institutions in Munich which we have already mentioned, the size of its region of influence, which exceeds the region of influence of every other town in southern Germany. In a larger sense, it consists not only of the whole state of Bavaria together with the more remote Rhine Palatinate, but also part of Württemberg, and, above all, Tyrol and Salzburg. Thus, we can explain why the centrality of Nuremberg is strikingly small (1346) and that of Stuttgart is relatively small (1606), even though, like Munich, they concentrate in themselves to a high degree the central func-

---

* Although southern Germany includes the L-system of Munich, Nuremberg, Stuttgart, Strassburg, and Frankfurt, only that of Munich is included in this book.

170

tions of their regions. Furthermore, we should note that Munich has the greatest population of the four southern German towns with *L*-center importance, and that, in its population structure, there are relatively few persons engaged in highly industrial work. These are two factors which help produce Munich's high value of centrality. Finally, it should be mentioned that the town itself, and the nearby Alps as well, are popular as tourist and living regions.

In consideration of its unusually high centrality for an *L*-place and of its political, social, and economic regional influences, exceeding by far those of the normal *L*-regions, we shall deem Munich an *RT*-place —for a more complete *RT*-type region of southern Germany (consisting approximately of Bavaria, Württemberg, the two Tyrols, and Salzburg). The region of influence of Munich as an *L*-place naturally does not include, in a proper sense, all of the region mentioned above. Its boundaries will be stated in the course of the analysis.

2. The *L*-Directions Lines

As *L*-systems bordering on the *L*-system of Munich, the systems of Stuttgart and Nuremberg should be considered. Nuremberg, as an *L*-place located approximately north of Munich, will be the L_1 of our scheme.[1] L_2 will be Prague; L_3, Vienna; L_4, Venice; L_5, Zurich; and L_6, Stuttgart. According to our scheme of established distance-values, the neighboring *L*-places should lie on a ring 186 km. from Munich. Only Stuttgart does so, but it does so very exactly. Nuremburg lies at a distance of only 150 km.[2] The traffic distance of Nuremburg is 199 km. by rail and 178 km. by highway, which is normal. The four other *L*-places are, however, considerably farther away than would normally be the case: Zurich is 240 km.; Prague, 300 km.; Venice, 310 km.; and Vienna, 360 km. The explanation can easily be found in the topography and the small population densities.

The *L*-directions lines from Munich are determined by these six *L*-places. They correspond rather well to the scheme because the angles Stuttgart–Munich–Nuremberg, Nuremberg–Munich–Prague, Prague–Munich–Vienna, and Venice–Munich–Zurich are all almost exactly sixty degrees. Only the angle Zurich–Munich–Stuttgart is very acute, and the area in these directions from the *L*-system of Munich is the most densely populated—a fact which possibly causes the conditions of the others. The angle Vienna–Munich–Venice is almost a right angle, and this relatively obtuse angle embraces a region of small population density. Both deviations are conditioned chiefly by the influence of the Alps.

3. The *P*-Places

According to our scheme, the *P*-places lie on a circle of 108 km. radius around the *L*-places. Thus, we find Regensburg (217)[3] as P_1 in the middle of the *L*-triangle Munich–Prague–Nuremberg; it lies exactly on the 108 km. circle. The place P_2 in the middle of Munich–Prague–Vienna lies geometrically in the southern part of the Bohemian Forests; it lies almost exactly at the point where Bavaria, Bohemia, and Austria meet. It is understandable that no central place of *P*-importance can exist at that location. Therefore, its importance must have been distributed according to the separation principle. Thus, we find very beautifully the three representatives of the *P*-position: the Bavarian Passau (62), the Bohemian Budweis with only *G*-importance, and Linz in Austria. The chief part of the *P*-function is acquired by Linz, the importance of which is still further strengthened by the fact that in the triangle Munich–Vienna–Venice, there is no prominent *P*-place. Because Linz lies on the line between Munich and Vienna, it supplies both triangles with central goods of *P*-rank. Passau and Linz both lie 150 km. from their respective *L*-places, Munich and Vienna; Budweis lies 125 km. from Prague; all the distances are somewhat greater than the normal 108 km.

The geometrical place of P_3 should lie at the intersection of Salzburg, Steiermark, and Kärnten, namely in the middle of the triangle Munich–Vienna–Venice. This *P*-area is divided by the peaks of the Alps and is occupied by Salzburg (only a more developed *G*-place), which belongs to the *L*-system of Munich and lies exactly on the 108 km. ring. In the *L*-system of Vienna, the *P*-position falls upon Villach and Klagenfurt, the capitals of Kärnten. In the *L*-system of Venice, it falls upon Udine, the capital of Friuli. P_4, in the middle of Venice–Munich–Zurich, is represented by only two *P*-places: north of the peaks of the Alps by the well developed *P*-place, Innsbruck, and south of the peaks by the *P*-place, Verona, which even competes with the *L*-place of Venice because it has the same importance in land traffic that Munich has north of the Alps. Innsbruck has the advantage of lying exactly on the 108 km. ring around Munich, and Verona lies almost exactly on the 108 km. ring around Venice.

Corresponding to the scheme, that is, to distances of 108 km. from neighboring *P*- and *L*-places, Kempten should be P_5; but it has only a *G*-function. Perhaps, because of the natural and traffic advantages, P_5 should lie on Lake Constance. It might be said that the fifth *P*-position, using the traffic principle (on-*L*-direction), is split up according to the separation principle between five places on Lake Constance: Konstanz (67) in Baden, Friedrichshafen (19) in Württemberg, Lindau (29) in

Bavaria, Bregenz in Austria, and Rorschach in Switzerland (together a centrality of 165). Such an explanation, however, is only partially justified, for a well-developed P-place lies to one side instead of on Lake Constance. This place, St. Gallen, avoids a location at a natural thoroughfare and clearly follows the marketing principle of our scheme. The sixth P-place, which, according to the scheme, should lie on the between-direction of Stuttgart and Nuremberg, is transferred to an on-L-direction of Stuttgart. Thus, it lies more favorably in the middle of the pentagon Munich–Innsbruck–St. Gallen–Stuttgart–Nuremberg. Remarkably, this P-position is, despite the normal distance between Munich and Stuttgart, divided between Ulm and Augsburg. Obviously, the medieval L-system of Augsburg still plays its role, and is somehow responsible for the double-occupation of the sixth P-place. This double occupation is clearly vital since it is distributed according to the separation principle between one place in Bavaria and one place in Württemberg. Ulm lies almost exactly on the 108 km. ring around Munich, while Augsburg is on the 62 km. ring (on which the G-places lie according to the scheme) and represents in a proper sense only a G-place. The locations of the two places in the L-systems correspond more to the traffic principle. The correct locations, according to the marketing principle, would be the locations of Biberach and Nördlingen.

Which of these P-places are to be included in the L-system of Munich and which in other systems? It is clear in the case of the divided P-places: Passau, Salzburg, Innsbruck, Kempten, and Augsburg belong to the system of Munich; Linz and Villach-Klagenfurt belong to Vienna; Udine and Verona to Venice; St. Gallen to Zurich; and Ulm to Stuttgart. There is doubt only in regard to Regensburg. When only one P-place is established, the theoretical boundary between the two L-systems runs through the middle of the P-place common to both systems. But the shorter distance (90 km., as against 105 km. from Munich), as well as the smaller hinterland which chiefly spreads northward, support our inclusion of Regensburg in the L-system of Nuremburg. Consequently, we have two full P-places, Augsburg and Innsbruck, in the Munich system, while Passau, Salzburg, and Kempten are only P-places with G-importance.

4. The G-Places

We now begin the determination of the G-places. According to the scheme, six of them should lie on the 62 km. rings around every place of a higher order, that is, around every P- and L-place. They lie on the between-P-lines (the on-L-lines).

First, we shall look for the G-places on the 62 km. ring around

Munich: G_1, on between-P-direction line Augsburg–Regensburg, is Ingolstadt (34). G_2, on between-P-direction line Regensburg–Passau, is Landshut (51). There is no G_3 on between-P-direction line Passau–Salzburg, but its place is taken by the B-place Mühldorf (17), which, with the nearby K-places Altötting and Neuötting (combined centrality of eleven), has a centrality of twenty-eight—that is, the three combined very nearly approach the G-function (especially if one considers the strongly agrarian character of this region eastward from Munich). G_4, on an indefinite line, is Rosenheim (31); G_5, on the between-P-direction line Innsbruck–Kempten, is missing, for neither Landsberg (11) nor Weilheim (14) exceed the B-function and Garmisch–Partenkirchen (26) lies too isolated and at the periphery. And, finally, G_6 is represented by the P-place Augsburg. Thus, three places are fully developed as G-places (one even as a P-place); one closely approaches G-importance; and one is missing. All lie either exactly (Landshut, Augsburg) or approximately (Ingolstadt, Mühldorf, Rosenheim) on the 62 km. ring. Considering the strong concentration of central functions in Munich, it is not surprising that, with the exceptions of Augsburg and Landshut, all of these places either lie at the lower limit of the G-type, or else do not reach this limit at all. All G-systems formed by these places, with the exception of the P-place of Augsburg, doubtless belong to the P-system of Munich, because the influence of the L-center on the surrounding G-system is always dominant. Therefore, Ingolstadt, lying out of the way, also should be counted in the P-system of Munich.

The wreath of G-places around the P-system of Augsburg includes: (1) G, Ingolstadt; (2) L, Munich; (3) (missing as a G-place); (4) G, Kempten (62); (5) the sister P-place Ulm; and (6) a further undeveloped G-system on the between-P-direction line Ulm–Nuremberg, for example, Nördlingen (19), is considered over any other place as the midpoint. (In former times, Nördlingen had, without a doubt, a G-function.) Of these G-systems, the system of Kempten is the only one without some justification for being counted in the P-system of Augsburg. All of the previously mentioned places, with the exception of Kempten, lie exactly on the 62 km. ring around Augsburg.

A wreath of G-places around Innsbruck is only imperfectly evident because of the natural geographical features as well as the small population density of Tyrol. Between the P-sisters, Innsbruck and Verona, lie two places which have B-importance: Bozen and Trient. Bozen belongs to the P-system of Innsbruck and lies on its 62 km. ring, while Trient lies approximately on the 62 km. ring of Verona. Bozen should also be counted in the L-system of Munich because it belongs to the P-system of Innsbruck, while Trient is nearer to the L-system of Venice.

Thus, we have found the southern border of the L-system of Munich to be at Salurn, the location of the German-Italian language border.[4]

Salzburg, the P-importance of which is questionable, lies 62 km. from Rosenheim, as well as from Mühldorf and Gmunden (G- or B-place?). The former two places should be counted in the P-system of Munich, and the latter in the P-system of Linz.

Passau (62), which lies exactly 62 km. from the P-place of Linz, forms no system of its own; it has only an isolated G-system.

The systems of the G-places of Ingolstadt (34), Landshut (51), and Straubing (46); the isolated B-system of Cham (17); and the G-system of Weiden-Anberg (a combination) all belong to the P-system of Regensburg. Two of them, Ingolstadt and Landshut, should doubtless be included in the L-system of Munich; it is questionable where to place Straubing. Most of the other G-systems lying around Regensburg belong, however, to the L-system of Nuremberg. Insofar as the distances are concerned, Ingolstadt lies exactly on the 62 km. ring around Regensburg. Straubing, however, is considerably nearer; it is approximately on the 36 km. ring. The latter town seems to take the place of Regensburg in the upper Bavarian region. The best place geometrically is Deggendorf, which, with a centrality of eighteen, is a well-developed B-place. The location of Ingolstadt is determined mainly according to the marketing principle. The location of Straubing is determined more according to the traffic principle (in the direction of Passau).

II. AN ANALYSIS OF THE INDIVIDUAL G-SYSTEMS

1. The P-System of Munich

The scheme of the central places, with its modifications which theoretically are to be expected, is demonstrated clearly in an analysis of the individual G-systems. The typical central goods of the G-places are those with a range of 36 to 62 km. The distances of the G-places from one another are, therefore, 62 km. Thus, all places within a 36 km. radius belong to the complementary region of a G-place; that is, in terms of the time-cost measure of passenger traffic, all places which lie within an hour's journey by rail from the G-place (or a total of one and one-half hours round trip) require a cash expenditure of three marks for a round trip. The next lower central places in the G-system are the B-places (six in number) which should lie on the 36 km. ring on the between-G-directions lines.

The ring of the G-system of Munich on which the B-places lie is rather exactly at a distance of 36 km. from Munich. Only to the south is it as high as 45 km., which is about halfway to the barriers of the Alps. B_1, on the between-G-direction line of Ingolstadt–Landshut, is Freising (17); it is located very correctly according to the scheme, and is well developed. B_2, on the between-G-direction line of Landshut–Mühl- dorf, is Erding (12); it is not so well developed because of its remoteness from the traffic and close proximity to Freising. B_3, on the between-G- direction line of Mühldorf–Rosenheim, is Marktgrafing–Ebersberg. They have, together with nearby Kirchseeon, a centrality of eleven, that is, about B-function. B_4, on the G-direction line of Innsbruck, is also strongly represented, by Bad Tölz. B_5, on the between-G-direction line of Innsbruck–Kempten, is Weilheim (14); it forms a rather independent B-system attached to the G-system of Munich. Finally, B_6 is missing; the great nearness of the two high ranking central places, Munich and Augs- burg, which lie only 62 km. away, prevents the existence of a B-place at B_6.

A review will now be made of the other central places of the G-sys- tem of Munich (for particulars, look at the remarks in the table). The places on the K-ring (radius: 21 km.) will be mentioned first: Dachau (11), Marktschwaben (4), and Fürstenfeldbruck (11) are developed as K-places. Starnberg (17), which was able to develop so well because it was the center of a distinguished residential region on Lake Starnberg, is de- veloped as a B-place. The K-places of Wolfratshausen (7) and Holzkirchen (6) lie a little farther away from Munich because of the large forest region south of Munich. Four of these places are on between-G-directions lines and only two of them are on on-G-directions lines. Besides these six K-places on the K-ring, two other K-places belong to the G-system of Munich: Herrsching (5) and Diessen (5); both are located on Lake Ammer. A-places of an inner 12 km. ring have not developed at all, which is understandable because of the great power of absorption of Munich. A-places (theoretically six in number) on the first (I) outer 24 km. A-ring include: Markt-Indersdorf, Glonn and Tutzing, and K-Herr- sching. On the second (II) outer 32 km. A-ring (theoretically with twelve A-places) there are only A-Isen and A-Penzberg; the others have developed only partly, as M-places (for instance, Allershausen, Seeshaupt, and Odelzhausen); and there are no A-places at all in the large forest and swamp districts. Especially noteworthy is the frequency of central places in the lake region between the valley of the Isar River and Lake Ammer; the explanation—higher demand for central goods in a beautiful district which is preferred as a residential area—is near at hand. On the contrary, the evident lack of development of central places in the northwestern part of the system is the result of the purely agricultural, and also poorer, population there.

The G-system of Ingolstadt, which follows in our discussion, is spatially very small. The ring on which the B-places, or at least well-developed K-places, develop as a rule, lies on an average of 29 km. from Ingolstadt. This phenomenon is frequently found where G-places have smaller G-systems than do neighboring P- and L-places. Accordingly, there are only two B-places which belong to this small G-system: Eichstätt (12), located on the between-G-direction line Nuremberg–Nördlingen, and Neuburg-on-Danube (13), located on the between-G-direction line Nördlingen–Augsburg. More numerous on this B-ring are K-places, which are likewise mainly market-oriented: Beilingries (5); Riedenburg (4); and Abenberg (6), together with the nearby A-places of Neustadt and Siegenburg, has a centrality of twelve, and thus clearly represents a B-place. The fifth B-position, lying in the center of the triangle Ingolstadt–Landshut–Munich, and favored by Freising, is represented within the system of Ingolstadt by Au-Hallertau. Finally, the sixth B-position is divided and lies on a between-G-direction line: Pfaffenhofen (9) and Schrobenhausen (9); consequently, both places together do not reach more than a well-developed K-importance.

It is understandable that in the G-system of Ingolstadt, because of its tightness, no K-wreath can develop on a 21 km. ring; it has only K-Wolnzach (5) and the B-places of Neuburg and Eichstätt. Greater density of central places, especially of A- and K-places, is evident in the Hallertau, because of the intensive hop culture. The nearness of the B-place of Neuburg-on-Danube to Ingolstadt is remarkable; the B-place which is determined by the G-triangle Ingolstadt–Augsburg–Nördlingen is represented by Donauwörth and Neuburg, both B-places. That both have B-importance rather than K-importance, as might have been expected as the result of splitting a B-place, could only happen because of the importance of the nearby G-places. Thus, the importance of Ingolstadt is diminished by Neuburg; and the importance of Nördlingen (even in the B-importance) is diminished by Donauwörth.

The G-system of Landshut is looser, but is not fully expanded; the B-ring is an average of 30 km. instead of 36 km. from the G-place; and the southeastern sector is indistinctly developed. B_1, on between-direction line Ingolstadt–Regensburg, is represented by K-Abensberg. B_2 is not developed because of the nearness of Regensburg and Straubing, though its rudiments are evident in the M-Mallersdorf and the A-Neufahrn. B_3 is divided because of the great distance from Landshut to Passau, and is represented by Dingolfing (6) and Landau-on-Isar (8). B_4 is also divided, for the same reason, among Massing-Gangkofen, Eggenfelden, and Pfarrkirchen. Incidentally, B_5 (Erding) has an offshoot in K-Dorfen (5). Finally, B_6 is Freising. The K-ring around Landshut is clearly evident (and rather exactly) at the normal 21 km. distance. It is marked by the two K-places of Moosburg (8) and Vilsbiburg (7). The other four K-places are represented by the *A*-combination of Rottenburg–Pfaffenhausen, the *A*-place of Ergoldsbach, the *M*-combination of Wörth-on-Isar–Postau-Niederviehbach and the *M*-place of Taufkirchen. The inner *A*-ring is marked only by Geisenhausen; and the outer 24 km. ring is marked by the *A*-places of Neufahrn, Frontenhausen, and Velden, and the *K*-place of Mainburg (7).

In the undeveloped *G*-system of Mühldorf, the nucleus is missing; Mühldorf is only a *B*-place with a centrality of seventeen and, even after adding the values for Altötting and Neuötting, has a centrality of only twenty-eight. Therefore, we have before us only an isolated *B*-system, the *K*-ring of which is very clearly developed at a distance of 26 km. from the center. It is determined by the *K*-places of Vilsbiburg (7), Eggenfelden (10), Burghausen (6), Trostberg (6), Wasserburg (8), Haag (4), and Dorfen (5)—altogether seven *K*-places (the *K*-ring is too far from the center), most of which are situated in the directions of the neighboring *G*-places (for *K*-place market-orientation). A 36 km. *B*-ring appears only towards more distant Passau and is strictly adhered to by the *B*-places of Pfarrkirchen and Braunau-Sinnbach. *A*-places to be noted on the inner 12 km. *A*-ring are Neumarkt; the *K*-places of Altötting, Neuötting, and Kraiburg; and the *M*-places of Garching and Ampfing.

Why has no *G*-place so far developed in this area to the east of Munich? The reason is partly that up to the present, the character of the population has been almost exclusively agricultural; thus, the demand for the delivery of central goods from *G*-places has not been so strong. The absence of a *G*-place is also partly due to the existence of a plurality of important places: Mühldorf (the place of pilgrimage), Altötting, the old Salzach River town of Burghausen, and Braunau in Austria. The increasing industrialization of the Inn and Salzach River areas, as a result of cheap electricity from the exceptionally abundant supply of water power, will, without a doubt, increase considerably the demand of central goods of the *G*-order. One of the places mentioned above could finally become the *G*-place of the area.

The next *G*-system, Rosenheim, is quite well developed. The *B*-ring has an average radius of about 33 km.; towards Munich, it is less; but towards Salzburg, it is greater, as is to be expected from the distances of these two towns from Rosenheim. Four of the six corner points of the system are clearly represented by the three *B*-places of Tegernsee (13), Kufstein, and Traunstein (18), and the substitute for *B*, Marktgrafing–Ebersberg; the two other corner points are occupied by the *K*-places of Wasserburg (8) and Trostberg (6). The *K*-ring is marked by the *K*-places of Schliersee (with a centrality of five, or only a weak *K*-significance), Miesbach (5), and Prien (10). All cases are not oriented according to the marketing principle, which is conditioned by the fact that the central places develop better at the edges of mountains than in narrow valleys. It should be pointed out that the village of Tegernsee has a *B*-function because it is a preferred living place in the center of the tourist trade; otherwise another *B*-place in addition to nearby Bad Tölz would be unnecessary. An extraordinary position is taken by the *K*-place of Bad Aibling (8), since it is very close to the *G*-place of Rosenheim. This circumstance is explained only in part by the fact that Aibling is both a spa and a county seat. The *A*-places of the system—Gmund, Bruckmühl, Brannenburg, Oberaudorf, Niederaschau, Endorf, Obing, and Ruhpolding—are not very characteristically situated. Their locations are, in part, strongly determined by the topography. However, the typical 12 km. distances are generally observed. The accumulation of important central places around Lake Schlier and Lake Tegern (also, Bayrischzell already has almost an *A*-function) occurs because of the tourist trade and the large number of retired people, both of which increase the demand for central goods.

Southwest of Munich, among the *G*-systems of Munich, Kempten, and Innsbruck, is an area which is large enough to support an independent *G*-system. But, in spite of its favorable structure for the consumption of central goods, the number of inhabitants is hardly enough to support a *G*-place—the district of Garmisch, for example, has a population density of only 29.02 and the district of Tölz a density of 29.29 inhabitants per sq. km., with the populations of the main cities included. In addition, quite a substantial part of the rural population (only recently emigrated from the cities, especially from Munich) has obtained a certain level of prosperity and can now afford the central goods of Munich, even though these goods are more expensive than locally-available goods because of the greater distance they must be transported. Here we find an incomplete system: four strictly-developed *B*-corner points of Landsberg, Bad Tölz, Garmisch–Partenkirchen, and Kaufbeuren, perhaps a fifth corner point of Füssen (7), which remained a *K*-place because of nearby Reutte in Austria, and a sixth corner point by either Weilheim or Starnberg (as you choose). The center of this system could be Schongau (5), which, even after adding Peiting, has a centrality of only eight; *K*-Murnau with a centrality of nine, but most likely Weilheim which has a centrality of fourteen. The most important place of the area is Garmisch–Partenkirchen with the considerable centrality of twenty-six. It will hardly develop into an independent *G*-place, because of its remote situation in the very thinly populated high mountain district; its partial lack, insufficiency, or expensiveness of traffic connections with the East and West, and the higher prices for central goods in a center of tourist trade. Among the other central places of this area, the *A*-places with the characteristic 12 km. distances are on the between-directions lines of

Steingaden–Schongau, Oberammergau–Murnau–Garmisch, Mittenwald–Garmisch, Kochel–Penzberg–Murnau, and Penzberg–Kochel–Bad Tölz. The apparent absence of central places, even those with M-functions, in the area between Schongau and Kaufbeuren as well as between Weilheim and Landsberg is, for the most part, conditioned by the existence of extensive, unpopulated forest areas. Peissenberg has, in spite of its high number of inhabitants, only M-significance, because its population consists mostly of miners of bituminous coal (*Pechkohle*) and because of its proximity to the B-place of Weilheim.

2. The P-System of Augsburg

We begin with the G-system of the P-place of Augsburg. We should expect this system to be very large, because a more important central place naturally has a larger complementary region. This expectation is entirely confirmed. On the 36 km. ring of the B-places, there are situated, as B_1 (on the between-line of Nördlingen and Ingolstadt) the two B-places of Donauwörth (13) and Neuburg-on-Danube (13). The K-place of Schrobenhausen (9) should be considered as B_2. On the between-direction line of Munich and Kempten, Landsberg-on-Lech (11) is clearly developed as B_3. Today, its centrality is rather small; formerly, it was probably larger, but its location on a secondary line (the neighboring Buchloe was more favored by traffic) and the extension of the area of Munich as far as Lake Ammer have decreased its importance. Close to the on-direction line of Kempten, there is Mindelheim (13) as B_4. On the between-direction line of Kempten and Ulm, is K-Krumbach (10) as B_5, which, together with neighboring K-Thannhausen (4), has a centrality of fourteen. On the between-direction line of Ulm and Nördlingen, are, finally, the three K-places of Dillingen (8), Lauingen (6), and Gundelfingen (5). They are so close to each other that they must be regarded as B_6, with a centrality of nineteen. We include them in the Ulm system. Also, the 21 km. K-ring around Augsburg is quite nicely developed. On the theoretically correct between-B-direction line, are the K-places of Mering (with a centrality of only four, because it is a little too close to Augsburg), Schwabmünchen (7), and Wertingen (4), as well as Zusmarshausen (its district office has now been dissolved) which has remained an A-place; furthermore, K-Aichach (8), which is shifted to the B-direction line. A-Meitingen and M-Biberbach, with a combined centrality of three, should also be enumerated here. On the inner 12 km. A-ring, there are the A-places of Fischbach, Bobingen, and Friedberg. On the first (I) outer 24 km. A-ring, there are the aforesaid Wertingen, and also Pöttmes and Altmünster. On the second (II) 32 km. A-ring (according to the pattern, two A-places always lie on a line connecting two neighboring B-places) lie Rain and Burgheim (the former with a centrality of six which is even a K-importance), between Bonnawörth and Neuburg; Buchloe (with a centrality of six, as an important railroad junction of K-importance) and Türkheim between Landsberg and Mindelheim; Pfaffenhausen and Kirchheim between Mindelheim and Krumbach-Thannhausen; one A-place, Burgau, between Krumbach and Dillingen; and finally, only one, Höchstätt, between Dillingen and Donauwörth.

Thus, we find that the G-system of Augsburg conforms to the rule to a surprising degree. The only deviations are the division (which probably can be explained only historically) of the sixth B-position among the three K-places of Dillingen, Lauingen, and Gundelfingen; and the accumulation of three B-places of Landsberg, Mindelheim, and Kaufbeuren, in the South; two K-places of Buchloe and Bad Wörrishofen (with a centrality of five, as a spa enjoying a special position); and one A-place, Türkheim. This accumulation may probably be considered either a substitution for, or a cause of, the absence of a G-system southwest of Munich.

The first G-system, no longer belonging to the P-system of Munich, is Kempten. It belongs, instead, to the P-systems of Augsburg and Ulm (approximately) rather than to the P-system of St. Gallen because the area of the Bregenzer Mountains is inserted into the framework of the system. The G-area of Kempten is quite densely populated and very favorably developed from an economic point of view (the dairy economy of Algau), in spite of its mountains and poor communication facilities; for this reason, the intervals are often small on the B-ring towards the east and the west. On the B-ring, there are the following B-places: As B_1, on the G-direction line of Augsburg, is Mindelheim (13). As B_2 (besides Landsberg which belongs to the system of Augsburg, on the between-direction line of Augsburg–Munich), there is Kaufbeuren (14). As B_3, on the G-direction line of Innsbruck, is the K-place of Füssen (7), which, together with Reutte in Austria, fills the B-position. As B_4, on the between-direction line of Innsbruck–St. Gallen, there should be, geometrically, K-Oberstdorf (7); actually, the two K-places of Immenstadt (7) and Sonthofen (7)—a combined centrality of fourteen—have significant B-importance and, because of the remoteness of Oberstdorf, take its place. K-Isny (8) should actually be considered as B_5 in an indefinite direction, but its position is taken in reality by B-Leutkirch (14). Finally, as B_6, in the direction of Ulm, there is surprisingly very strongly developed (almost of G-importance) Memmingen, which is developed to a surprising degree, with a centrality of thirty-one. The development of an independent G-system alongside or in place of the G-system of Kempten was impossible, probably because of the proximity of Ulm and Augsburg. A *B*-circle is, however, clearly evident, with *B*-places of Biberach, Leutkirch, Kempten, Kaufbeuren, Mindelheim, and Illertisser —though one cannot say that these *B*-places are dependent on Memmingen.

Approximately on the 21 km. *K*-ring around Kempten there are the *K*-places of Obergünzberg (5); Markt Oberdorf (5); the aforesaid places of Sonthofen, Immenstadt, Isny (8); *A*-Grönenbach, or *A*-Legau; and, finally, Ottobeuren (6), all on the between-direction lines toward the places of the *B*-rings. A sixth *K*-position is established by the two *A*-places of Nesselwang and Pfronten. The *K*-ring is also quite regular, though less so with respect to the *A*-places.

The Algau is a typical area of the isolated (*Einöd*) settlements. We find here considerable accumulations of *A*- and *K*-places (in the Bavarian part as well as in the Württemberg part), a smaller number of *M*-places, and, perhaps, only fifteen *H*-places as compared with the thirty-five *H*-places in the Augsburg system. Therefore, the thesis, already developed in theory, is here proved by the fact that a relationship exists between the degree of diversity of agricultural settlements and the number and sizes of urban settlements.

3. The Alpine System

The *G*-systems of Augsburg and Kempten determine the westward extent of the *L*-system of Munich. South of Munich is situated the *G*-system of Innsbruck. Without a doubt, it must be counted as part of the *L*-system of Munich, although, politically, it belongs to Austria. However, its direct connection with the system situated north of it is interrupted by the chain of the northern Kalkalpen. Innsbruck, with 70,000 inhabitants, is of course a *P*-place; it is also in north Tyrol, which forms a *G*-system. If the whole of north Tyrol had to be supplied with central goods of *G*-range (36 to 62 km.), there would be two *G*-places, probably Imst and Jenbach. Because the fixed point, Innsbruck, was determined by nature and history, and at the same time satisfied the traffic and market principles, and because the thin population of north Tyrol could not support three places of *G*-importance, the entire higher centralized function was embodied by Innsbruck.

Because of the dominant influence of the natural conditions of high mountains and their valleys, Innsbruck does not have a *G*-system, in the strict sense. We are, therefore, satisfied to state that in the system of Innsbruck, the normal intervals between *B*-, *G*-, or *P*-places, respectively, are mostly 36 km.—e.g., Innsbruck–Schwaz (somewhat shorter because this area is heavily populated), Schwaz–Kufstein, Kufstein–Rosenheim, and Kufstein–Kitzbühel. Towards the west, the distance from

Innsbruck to Landeck is twice 36 km. The *B*-place theoretically expected at the entrance to the Ötz valley is missing. As far as the valley system is concerned, a 21 km. ring around Innsbruck, marked by Telfs and Matrei, can be distinguished.

Although it actually does not belong within the scope of the present inquiry, the situation south of the Brenner Pass will be mentioned briefly. Here, the *G*-place of Bozen, considered as a part of the *P*-system of Innsbruck, possesses its own *G*-system, although the *G*-system is not so clearly developed because of the mountainous character of the area. On its 36 km. *B*-ring, we find the *B*-places of Meran and Brixen, and also the typical *B*-distances between Brixen and Sterzing, Brixen and Bruneck, Bruneck and Innichen, and Innichen and Linz.

In analyzing the *G*-system of Salzburg, it should again be borne in mind that the non-German parts are dealt with only cursorily. On the 36 km. *B*-ring, we find, in the German area, only the *B*-place of Traunstein (18) and to the south, in Austrian territory, *B*-Bischofshofen; in the north, *B*-Braunau can still be considered as situated on the *B*-ring of Salzburg. To the east, the *B*-place of Bad Ischl can hardly be considered as part of the Salzburg system. Here, the connection obviously breaks with the neighboring *G*-system because Gmunden, evaluated as a *B*-place (as probably is also Vöcklabruck), is no longer touched by the *B*-system of Salzburg. The *B*-ring of Salzburg is marked by the four *B*-places and perhaps by the *K*-places of Burghausen, Lofer, and Sallfelden. The 21 km. *K*-ring is quite nicely developed by Berchtesgaden (17), a place which obtained *B*-importance by being a preferred tourist attraction; by *K*-Bad Reichenhall (10); by the *A*-sister-places of Laufen (4) and Oberndorf, which together exercise *K*-functions; and in the east, by Neumarkt and St. Gilgen, which should be considered as *K*-places. A sixth *K*-position is occupied by *B*-Hallein and *A*-Golling, the positions of which vary somewhat from the 21 km. ring. The *K*-place of Freilassing-Salzburghofen (6) can be considered a German representative of the *G*- and *P*-places of Salzburg. It is significant for the whole *G*-system of Salzburg that its development has ignored completely the borders of Germany. The system is developed on both sides of the border equally, as much as the high mountains permit.

South of the *G*-system of Salzburg, there is no actual *G*-system. This is explainable by the low density of population and the obstacles of the mountains. But we find the characteristic 36 km. distances preserved between *B*-places in the following sets of *B*-places: Kitzbühel–Zell-am-See, Zell-am-See–Bischofshofen, Zell-am-See–Bad and Hof Gastein, Zell-am-See–Berchtesgaden, and Bischofshofen–Schladming. In any case, the whole area belongs to the system of Salzburg in the wider sense and, consequently, to the *L*-system of Munich.

4. The Eastern G-Systems

There are two more systems to be discussed, Passau and Straubing, which are, to a lesser extent in respect to traffic, connected to Munich, and from which they are separated by the G-systems of Landshut and Mühldorf-Ötting. Therefore, their position in the L-system of Munich is rather isolated.

As far as the G-system of Passau is concerned, the more distant B-ring is striking. Its average radius is 47 km. instead of 36 km. but if we take into account the geographical position of the two most important B-places on this ring, Deggendorf (18) and Braunau, and also the position of Passau itself—all three situated on the mouths of rivers, then this deviation will be understandable. Other places on the B-ring are: Pfarrkirchen (10), hardly having a B-function, the importance of which is diminished by the proximity of Eggenfelden, which has nearly equal importance; Landau-on-Isar–Eichendorf (Landau, however, is situated completely outside the system of Passau): Ried, in Austrian territory, which probably deserves B-importance; and Haslach, which should be counted as part of the B-system of Linz. North of Passau, the B-position is represented by only one K-place, Grafenau (5), because this mountainous area is covered with forests and is developed very little. Market orientation is predominant.

Because the B-ring of the Passau system is developed at irregular distances, the K-ring, to the contrary, is developed with greater consistency at a 21 km. distance. On it we find: K-Vilshofen (10) and K-Griesbach (4) on between-directions lines; A-Pocking (3) which, combined with M-Ruhstorf, fulfills K-functions on the Braunau direction line (the between-direction line of Braunau and Ried is unoccupied); Engelhartszell in Austria (probably only an A-place, next to A-Wegscheid in Germany), again on a between-direction line; K-Waldkirchen (5) on a between-direction line; and, finally, A-Tittling (combined with Fürstenstein, a centrality of four) in the direction of Grafenau. An inner 12 km. A-ring is occupied by Shärding, with Neuhaus-Sulzbach lying close by; Fürstenzell; Haunzenberg; and M-Hutthurm. There follow also the places of the outer A-ring.

We now turn to the last G-system, which we considered as a part of the L-system of Munich, that of Straubing. It has the character of a branch-system, and, indeed, is connected with the larger system of Regensburg. Accordingly, it is only partly developed to the south and east. As a result of the prosperity of the country, we find, on the B-ring at an average distance of 30 km., the following places on the between-directions lines of Landshut and Passau: a B-position represented by two K-places,

Dingelfing and Landau; and in the next sector, north of Passau, well developed Deggendorf (18). Another B-position should be found where K-Viechtach (6) is situated, but here a different distribution of B-places is conditioned partly by the natural circumstances of the mountains and the river system, and partly by the neighboring Bohemian border of another distribution of B-places. These areas are situated outside of the G-systems, the centers of which are located on the Donau; this is the reason that they have their own centers which can have only B-importance because of the limited possibilities of the extension of the areas. This explains the existence of the B-place, Cham, and the K-place Zwiesel (8), which occupies a second isolated B-position. Were Zwiesel, in accordance with its central location, the county seat of the county, instead of Regen, Zwiesel could well obtain B-importance. Around this B-system of Zwiesel, there lies a 12 km. A-ring, occupied by K-Regen (6), A-Bodenmais, A-Bayrisch Eisenstein, K-Böhmisch Eisenstein, M-Spiegelau, and M-Kirchberg. A 12 km. K-ring is occupied by K-Grafenau and A-Ruhmannsfelden. Returning to the G-system of Straubing, let us describe the other rings: On the 21 km. K-ring, K-places are missing altogether because Straubing was highly successful in concentrating the middle and higher central functions within its own walls. Therefore, the K-ring is actually marked by few A-places. On the 12 km. A-ring, there is a county seat, Bogen, which has A-importance only because of its nearness to Straubing. K-Plattling (7) should be considered as a branch of B-Deggendorf on the main traffic line.

III. RESULTS

A short summary of the results will follow. Four fully developed P-systems—Munich, Augsburg, Innsbruck, and Regensburg—together comprise the L-system of Munich. The L-place of Munich has a centrality of 2800, and each of the three P-places has a centrality of about 220 (estimated for Innsbruck). Furthermore, there are three participating, isolated G-systems which must exercise P-functions, partly in consequence of their isolation: Salzburg, Passau, and Kempten; Passau and Kempten each have a centrality of about sixty, while Salzburg has a centrality of about ninety. The G-system of Bozen, the centrality of which is also about ninety, is also rather isolated. The G-systems of the places mentioned are all fully developed and the regularity of their locations is greatly disturbed only by the mountain ranges. Three other G-systems in the wreath around Munich are not so well developed, partly because of the high mountains (Rosenheim) and partly because they are in the neighborhoods of G-systems of more important places (Ingolstadt, Landshut). The same holds for Straubing in the P-system of Regensburg.

The centrality of these four G-places averages forty (thirty-one to fifty-one, to be exact). Finally, there are five large regions which do not belong to any G-system: first, the area east of Munich, with centers at Mühldorf, Altötting, and Neuötting; second, the area southwest of Munich, with its most important place at Garmisch-Partenkirchen; third, the area south of the province of Salzburg; fourth, the eastern and western regions of north Tyrol; and fifth, the Bavarian Forests, with a center at Zwiesel. Of all these regions, the one around Mühldorf will soon develop its own G-system; this is not to be expected of the others. Consequently, the L-system of Munich may be divided into sixteen regions with regard to places which properly supply urban goods, that is, with central goods offered only in G-places or in places of a higher type. Eleven of them do supply such goods; five, however, do not. All G-places in the L-system of Munich form their own G-systems, in contrast to the L-systems which will be discussed later. The order of the eleven G-regions according to their size and importance is: (1) Munich, (2) Augsburg, (3) Passau, (4) Innsbruck, (5) Salzburg, (6) Bozen, (7) Kempten, (8) Rosenheim, (9) Landshut, (10) Straubing, and (11) Ingolstadt. Then follow five regions without G-centers. The order of importance of the central places corresponds almost exactly with the order of the regions just given, which demonstrates clearly that the size of the central place and the size and development of the region mutually determine one another. The correctness of the theoretical scheme is thus very well proved. The chief deviations, anticipated by the theory, result from the poor traffic conditions and the thin population of the Alps area on the one hand, and from the high power of attraction of the L-place, Munich, on the other hand.

Altogether, as far as the region within the German borders is concerned, twenty B-places lie in the ranges of the individual G-systems; there are also three others, which dissolve into closely lying neighboring K-places (Immenstadt–Sonthofen, Dillingen–Lauingen–Gundelfingen, and Abensberg–Neustadt–Siegenburg). But we must then subtract from this number of twenty-three three places which we include in the L-systems of Stuttgart or Nuremberg. (The three are Leutkirch, Dillingen, and Eichstätt). Thus, the L-system of Munich possesses twenty places with B-functions. Three more—Starnberg, Berchtesgaden, and Tegernsee—must also be subtracted because they derive their B-importance as a consequence of certain circumstances. Finally, there are two others—Landsberg and Pfarrkirchen—which, because their centrality is under twelve, have doubtful B-functions.) Thus, we arrive at fifteen normal B-places—a number which is still within the scheme of the theory and conforms to the higher number of eighteen in an L-system, taking into consideration that there must still be added to the G-system a set of B-places for Tyrol and Salzburg. The centrality of these *B*-places, if we disregard the exceptional cases of Memmingen (31) and Garmisch-Partenkirchen (26), is between twelve and eighteen—the typical sizes are thirteen and seventeen. Eighteen of the twenty-three *B*-places lie on the *B*-rings of the *G*-systems (exceptions: Starnberg, Berchtesgaden, Immenstadt, Sonthofen, and Neuburg-on-Danube—all only 21 km., and Mühldorf). There are sixteen *B*-places on the 36 km. rings of the five fully developed *B*-systems of Munich, Augsburg, Kempten, Passau, and Regensburg. Seven are in the center and at the southwest margin of Munich and Mühldorf, two regions which did not develop into *G*-systems at all. Only eight are in the four *G*-systems of Ingolstadt, Landshut, Straubing, and Rosenheim, all of which are restricted to within the 36 km. radius, or are otherwise hampered. Only one (Tegernsee) should not be counted in the aforesaid groups. Consequently, the most favorable possibilities for the development of *B*-places are either at a distance of 36 km. from the *L*-, *P*-, and the more important *G*-places; or, in regions which lie quite outside the *G*-system. The market principle is the dominant influence in the location of fifteen of the *B*-places, and the traffic principle is dominant in only four cases. In four cases, it is doubtful which is the dominant influence, partly because of compromise between the two principles and partly because of topographical factors.

In the *L*-system of Munich, bordered by the crossline on Map 4, there lie in the area within the German national borders (which will be elaborated in more detail) fifty-nine *K*-places with a centrality from four to eleven. If we look at the first frequency distribution of the graph (page 204), we find two typical frequency values with centralities of six and ten. Of these fifty-nine *K*-places, thirty-two lie on the typical *K*-rings around the system-forming *G*- or *B*-places; the other twenty-seven lie partly on *B*-rings as undeveloped or divided *B*-places. (Some of these *B*-places are strongly developed *A*-places, and some are shifted *K*-places.) Some thirty-eight are oriented according to the market principle and fourteen according to the traffic principle; seven have an indistinct location.[*]

Furthermore, there are 81 *A*-places with a typical centrality of three (partly also two and four), 180 *M*-places with a centrality of one (partly also two), and finally, 192 *H*-places. The progression from the *L*- down to the *H*-places—counted only for the region within German borders—is consequently:

$$1 : 1 : 6 : 18 : 59 : 81 : 180 : 192.$$

The normal progression for two-thirds of an *L*-system is:

$$1 : 1 : 4 : 12 : 36 : 108 : 324.$$

---

[*] See Map 5.

Accordingly, the G-, B-, and K-places are represented about one-and-one-half times as strongly as would correspond with our scheme. On the other hand, the number of A-places is smaller, and the M- and H-places together correspond approximately with the normal number of M-places in the scheme.

The G-places, strikingly, are equally distributed over the whole system. The B-places, very frequently, are found on a line from Memmingen to Tegernsee, that is, in central Swabia and in that part of the northern marginal region of the Alps where no G-place has developed. The K-places are also rather equally distributed; but there are none in the triangle made by Regensburg, Straubing, and Landshut. The A-places in Swabia (in Algau) and in lower Bavaria occur much more frequently than in upper Bavaria, where they are missing, especially around Munich. The M-places lie prevalently in the more densely populated regions, above all, in the northern marginal region of the Alps (tourist trade).

The locations of the central places in the L-system of Munich are mostly oriented according to the market principle. The traffic principle is dominant in the large valleys of the Alps, above all in the Inn and Salzach River valleys, at the northern edge of the Salzburg Alps, in the area adjoining Innsbruck–Kempten–Ulm, and with some lines radiating from Munich and other large towns; otherwise, the traffic principle is dominant only in individual locations. The partition of theoretically expected central places, conditioned mostly by the separation principle, is found mainly in the border districts (Salzburg, Mühldorf–Ötting–Simbach, Füssen, Dillingen, Abensberg, Straubling), as well as with regard to the divided P-places.

NOTES

1. We number: beginning in the North with No. 1 and continuing in a clockwise direction, N.E., No. 2, S.E., No. 3, S., No. 4, S.W., No. 5, and N.W., No. 6.

2. The air distance is always given for the distances because we do not deal with lines or routes but with elements of a real distribution. The real transportation distances modify these geometrical distances and may be referred to in order to explain distances not corresponding with the norm.

3. The numbers in the parentheses following the names of the places refer to the centralities according to the table at the end of the book.

4. Johann Sölch ("Die Brennergrenze eine 'natürliche' Grenze?" in *Tiroler Heimat,* 4 (Innsbruck: 1924), 58) and Rudolph Sieger ("Die neuen Grenzen in den Alpen," in *Zeitschrift des deutsch-österreichischen Alpenvereins* (1923), 89) come to the same conclusion, but from different points of view; our system border corresponds approximately with the "organic" border of these two authors.

IV
CONCLUSION

A

Verification of the Theory

1. Laws of Distribution

The regional part of our investigation has shown with clarity to what a great degree the market, the traffic, and the separation principles determine the distribution, sizes, and number of central places. We may call these principles *laws of distribution of central places,* or *laws of settlement,* which fundamentally and often determine, with astonishing exactness, the locations of central places.

If the central places lie at certain equal distances and in the proper orientation with respect to central places of a higher order; and if they can be grouped so that there is a certain number of places belonging to each group; then it can be concluded that almost without exception the location of central places conforms to the principle of marketing. It is chiefly and uncontestedly valid for the largely agricultural provinces, which are less densely populated and relatively poor, regardless of whether they were originally unforested and long-settled; or originally forested and settled only in recent times. These areas include nearly all of Bavaria east of the Rhine, parts of Lorraine, the high plateaus of medium-sized mountains such as the Swabian and Frankish Alps, and the Hunsrück Mountains and the Taunus Range, all of which have little or no industrialization. The principle of marketing, even in the valleys of mountain regions, is often a stronger determinant than the orographical conditions; this is true in, for example, the Bavarian and Oberpfälzer forests and the western part of the Hessian Mountains of central Germany.

If central places lie along lines running from a central place of a higher order to another central place of a higher order; and if the distances between places lying on these lines are less than for those places lying off these lines, the number of places of which, furthermore, is higher than usual; and if the size-groups are less typically formed into natural groups; then it can be concluded that the locations of central places conform to the traffic principle and are determined either by that principle (especially for the plains and far regions where there are no natural barriers) or by orographical conditions (especially for rivers, valleys and mountainsides). The origin, however, is a different one. Where orographical conditions are determining, we may say that a pseudo-traffic principle is at work. Although the routes of traffic are forced to follow river valleys or mountainsides, we cannot say, in these cases, that the advantages of traffic determined the system of distribution of central places. The natural conditions determine the traffic routes, as well as the location of the central places. The distribution of central places may be determined by the traffic principle even where real traffic does not develop in clear opposition to the rational principles of the marketing of goods. This is the case, for example, in the northern and southern parts and the margins of the Rhine plain and in the Saar. The distribution may also be determined by the traffic principle where strong long-distance traffic has resulted from the existence of a large town with P- or L-importance. The traffic-oriented locations of the central places in the neighborhoods of such large towns on the lines radiating from them are thus to be explained. In rare cases, such a long-distance line, of modern or medieval origin, has determined the location of central places far from the large towns. This has happened in such places as upper Swabia, the Algau district of southwest Bavaria, and Oberpfalz. In almost every other case, locations that seem to have been determined by the traffic principle, were in fact determined by nature, or by a pseudo-traffic principle. These locations include places in the valleys of the upper Neckar, the lower Main, the Hessian Kinzig and environs, the Odenwald forest region, the Alps, the Thuringian Forests, the Fichtel Gebrige (fir mountains), and at the northern edge of the Bavarian Alps.

It is most difficult to trace the effectiveness of the separation principle from the picture of the present distribution of the central places; its effectiveness can be clearly proved only by historical studies. When any site, which, contrary to the scheme of the marketing principle, is occupied not by a central place of the expected size, but instead by two or several central places of a lower rank lying closely together, it is probable that the separation principle was responsible. As soon as the existing complex of central places is split by boundaries, so that at least one of these central places belongs to a politically independent region, the evidence indicates that the separation principle was responsible. Generally, in this work, we have waived such historical statements and have been satisfied with considering the present border arrangements. Thus, we could demonstrate that the split of P- and G-places, especially, was conditioned by the separation principle. Basel–Freiburg–Mulhouse, Linz–Passau–Budweis, Ulm–Augsburg, and Plauen–Hof–Eger are especially fine examples. The points of the scheme may, without being influenced by the separation principle, be distributed among several central places of lower order; such certainly will be the case if the triangle which is formed by three higher ranking central places and in the middle of which lies the point is larger than normal. The marketing principle then will be better satisfied by a plurality of places than by only one place.

In those cases in which the traffic or the separation principle rules, the marketing principle perhaps also rules simultaneously, as for instance in the distribution of central places of a lower order, especially, clearly, around Strassburg.

Since the marketing principle is clearly dominant in determining the distribution of the central places in southern Germany, we may say, generally, then, that the marketing principle is the primary and chief law of distribution of the central places. The traffic and the separation principles are only secondary laws causing deviations; these laws are effective in practice only under certain conditions. These conditions, with respect to the traffic principle, include: (1) when there is ample demand for central goods of a lower or higher order, with reference to central places of a lower or a higher order, respectively; (2) if the traffic route had in former, or has in modern, times an outstanding importance; (3) if the natural conditions favored or permitted it; and (4) if, at the time of the consolidation of the net of the central places, traffic played an outstanding role in the economic and social life. The conditions relevant to the separation principle are: (1) if the noneconomic, sociopolitical determinants are stronger than the rational economic determinants; (2) if, especially at the time of the consolidation of the net of central places, this state of affairs existed; (3) if the natural conditions favored or admitted this situation. Thus, if we consider the interplay of all the three principles, we shall have a general explanation for the distribution, sizes, and number of the central places.

2. Tertiary Deviations Explainable by Economics

There are many other deviations from our theoretical scheme of the distribution, sizes, and number of central places; that is, deviations should be expected in accordance with the main law of distribution and the laws of deviation. All deviations must be explainable by economic theory, whether they are special local or general regional deviations. Also, the deviations which are caused by natural factors of topography, etc., must be included in economic explanations: A highly important natural factor, then, has a high economic importance (causing a location to be favorable), and will, therefore, in time, prevail over a less important natural factor with less economic importance (and a less favorable location).

These tertiary deviations can be regional ones and they can refer to:

(1) The sizes of the central places, in cases in which the whole system, or perhaps only a sector or a ring of the system, is raised to a higher level (with general wealth and a dense population) or is reduced to a lower level (with general poverty and a thin population). Examples of the first type are the G-systems of Stuttgart, Karlsruhe, almost all of Mannheim, most of Saarbrücken, Eger, Hof, and Koburg. Examples of the latter type are the G-systems of Bamberg and Regensburg, and the B-systems of Ansbach, Weiden, and Bayreuth.

(2) The distances from the system-building central places in cases in which the whole system, despite correct typical sizes of central places, is widely or narrowly spaced. This state of being narrowly spaced can be caused by the relative smallness of the central places (e.g., Landshut, Ingolstadt, Bayreuth, and Saarburg) or through being narrowed by neighboring, stronger systems (e.g., Pforzheim, Freiburg, and Darmstadt). The state of being broadly spaced can be caused by the relative size of the central places (in the G-systems of Munich, Augsburg, Nuremburg, and Strassburg, and in the B-systems of Straubing) or by the lack of neighboring systems, which causes a lessened demand for central goods of a higher order (e.g., Passau, Salzburg, and Innsbruck).

(3) The number of the central places: There is a greater number of G- and P-places in regions which are especially densely populated, wealthy, or industrial, or which are vineyard regions. Such regions include the entire upper Rhine plain including the marginal zones, the central region of Württemberg, the northeastern part of Bavaria on the right bank of the Rhine, and the region around Lake Constance. There are more B-places in wealthy regions in which the G-places are missing (Baar, northeastern Württemberg, and the marginal regions of the Alps); there are fewer in wealthier or more industrialized regions (middle Germany, Lake Constance region, vicinities of Stuttgart, Frankfurt, Mannheim, and Karlsruhe), and in regions of heavy industry with fewer G-places (Saar). There are more K- and A-places in the regions just mentioned; there are fewer in regions lying favorably for traffic, above all, those regions which surround the upper Rhine plain (Black Forest, Odenwald (forests), Vogelsberg (mountain), and Vosges Mountains), or in regions of isolated settlements (upper Swabia, Algau, and the Bavarian

Forests). In addition to the greater number of central places of middle and higher order (Pfalz, Rhenish Hesse, Wetterau, Kaiserstuhl, and the whole Gau region from the upper Gau to Schweinfurt), there is a greater number of M-places in the especially wealthy regions, and in the especially poor regions, as substitutes for the missing middle-ranking central places (e.g., in some parts of the Keuper region, in Westrich, or in Oberpfalz), or in the wealthy regions of unfavorable transportation (Alps, southeastern Black Forest). However, there are only a very few central places: (a) in the case of the G-places in agricultural regions in a limited area around a large town (such as, south of Nuremburg and east of Munich); (b) in the case of the more common B-places (such as to the northeast and southwest of the L-systems of Stuttgart, at the northern edge of the Alps, and in regions strongly limited by natural and political boundaries, which permit only isolated B-systems—e.g., the Bohemian Forests and the Alps); B-places (such as in the poorer regions of Oberpfalz and the Bohemian Forests), the influences of which cause the partition of B-positions (such as in the area around Regensburg, in the narrow valley of the Rhine and its vicinity), and if there is a comparatively great density of G-places in purely agricultural areas, such as lower Bavaria and Oberpfalz; (c) in the cases of K- and A-places in especially poor areas, such as Nordgau, the Oberpfalz Forests, and Körperhohen; in thickly wooded and thinly populated areas such as Spessart, Kardt, and the area around Bamberg and Bayreuth; in the vicinity of large towns such as Munich, Regensburg and Würzburg; and, (d) in the case of M-places, such as in the isolated regions of the Black Forest, upper Swabia, Algau, and, to some extent in the Bohemian Forests; in the heavily industrialized areas of the Saar and the large industrial regions of Frankfurt, Mannheim, and Hof; in especially poor regions like the Münsinger Alps; in the Nordgau; and in the Hessian mountains of central Germany (Rhön).

The tertiary deviations also can be of a local nature. With regard to the sizes of the central places, the centrality of a place is higher than would correspond to its position in the system of central places. This is especially evident in the case of spas, such as Wiesbaden, Baden-Baden, Kissingen, Bad Nauheim, and Badenweiler, which are places bound to absolute points on the surface of the globe; and, for the same reasons, in the case of mining towns, the clearest example of which is Oberstein-Idar (even though today it processes mainly imported stones). A transition from local to regional ranks of central places is evident in rural areas which are preferred as residences, especially in the vicinities of large towns (such as on the southeastern slope of Taunus, in the neighborhood of Heidelberg, the lake area southwest of Munich), but also farther away from the larger cities (such as the Alps, the Tegernsee, Garmisch-

Partenkirchen, Berchtesgaden, and their surroundings; and the shores of Lake Constance).

Local deviations with regard to the distances between central places are, for one thing, determined through the permanent differences in prices at neighboring central places for central goods. Spas with high prices are no competition for nearby central places with low prices (e.g., Baden-Baden–Rastatt and Bad Nauheim–Freidberg). Also, the intervention of borders causes higher prices (through customs duties)—at least the distance between places on opposite sides of a border is subjectively valued higher, so that an actual distance which is smaller than normal has a subjective value which corresponds to the normal economic distance. This occurs, for example, with the distances between Lörrach and Basel on the Eger, and between Freilassing and Salzburg. A similar effect can result from mountain barriers, such as between Tegernsee and Schliersee.

Local deviations with regard to the number of central places are mainly caused in the same way as the deviations with regard to size: an additional central place is created because of the special economic significance of a certain point on the surface of the globe. In this category belong shrines, such as Altötting and Walldürn.

3. Deviations Not Explainable by Economics

Deviations from the rational pattern of central places not explainable by economics will be only enumerated here, for they are not a direct subject of the present inquiry. These deviations are primarily those which can be explained by completely different causes, which we group together as historical. Here belong places founded by the sovereign nobility (residences, the locations of which strongly deviate from our pattern—e.g., Ludwigsburg, Erlangen, Darmstadt, and to a lesser extent Zweibrücken, Pirasens, Bayreuth, Koburg, and Karlsruhe); places founded by immigrants or religious sects and communities (e.g., Hanau, Heuendettelsau, and (Königsfeld); or industrial towns, which owe their prosperity to the spirit of enterprise of an individual or to some other historical circumstance (e.g., Pirmassens, Kelkheim, Büsselsheim, Gaggenau, Rheinfelden, Schramberg, Gmünd, Schwabach, Lauscha, Schweinfurt, Pforzheim, and Mülhausen).

Physiographical deviations occur mainly in small areas: The theoretical point for a central place is only a general estimate. Which locality in particular—that is, which topographical position—is actually chosen, whether valley or valley spur, etc., is dependent both on the usual valuation of the position at the time of the founding of the town (e.g., its suitability for defense), and on the geographical existence of such a preferred location. But these questions are not of major concern in this discussion, for we are more interested in the geographical,[1] or, from the point of view of valuation, the economic situation of the town. In larger areas, these deviations are positive; that is, the geographical circumstances attract the central places. This especially occurs with regard to river valleys (particularly small valleys); mouths of rivers; fords; great plains in mountain areas; sides of mountains (as along the narrow valleys of the Rhine, Main, and Neckar Rivers, along the Alpine valleys of Inn, Salzach, and along the sides of the mountains limiting the lowland of the upper Rhine); the edges of the Alps, and the edges of the Bavarian Forests towards the Danube. This category includes all those cases which we spoke of as being pseudo-traffic-oriented. There are negative deviations where positions which theoretically should be filled within a network of central places are in fact not occupied because they are in impassable or thinly populated areas. Such positions include the three B-positions around Mülhausen, which are in fact situated on the roundtop Sulzer summit, on Black Forest Mountains, and on the Mont Terri Mountains; or, as in the P-system of Kassel, where two G-places are situated in the Knüll Mountains, or on the Kahler Asten Mountain.

In the high mountains, there are, of course, quite considerable physiographically conditioned deviations from the pattern. Here, the natural circumstances are so dominant that, in many cases, it is hardly any longer possible to speak of an actual system of central places. Still, it should be noted that, as a general rule, the typical distances are nevertheless observed; in other words, economic principles determine the distribution of central places to the extent that natural circumstances permit. Because of the absence of the L-places in the high mountain areas, adjacent L-systems are deformed, as for example that of Stuttgart in the southeast, and that of Munich, especially in the southwest. Similarly, an outstanding natural landscape which approximately corresponds with the boundaries of a tract of land [2] (*Zwecklandschaft*) can determine the distribution of a network of central places, as in Bohemia, where the center is occupied by Prague; in such a case, there can be no second L-place. As a further result, the adjacent L-system is also deformed.

Among the deviations which are not explainable economically, historically, or physiographically, those caused by people should be mentioned. These deviations include ones caused by inclinations toward centralization or toward federalism. That is why, in France, the L-type of central places is very weakly developed, while the R-type (Paris) and apparently the G-type also (*département* capitals) strongly dominate. In Germany, on the other hand, the L-type is strongly developed, and the P-type is correspondingly weaker. In Bavaria and Württemberg, no P-place has a centrality of more than 250, while the L-places have centralities of 1400 or more, a centrality six to twelve times as much as the highest P-places.

Besides these deviations explainable by the character of people, we shall mention those caused militarily. For example, the position of border fortresses is anything but a pure market (that is, a supply) position; it coincides, instead, with an ideal traffic position. In a country with the free communications of a modern economy, these deviations have been eliminated to a large extent, but they have not been in non-European areas, such as the Asiatic countries in which considerations of security still predominate in the selection of a position for a town.

NOTES

1. Marcel Poëte speaks very significantly in this connection of a "geographical framework" (*cadre géographique*), in contrast to "site," which he defines as "the portion occupied by the village." ("Introduction à l'Urbanisme," *L'évolution des villes* (Paris: 1929)), pp. 31ff., 78ff.

2. According to Walther Vogel, *Politische Geographie, Aus Natur und Geisteswelt* (Berlin and Leipzig: 1922), pp. 25ff.

B

Methodological Results
for the Geography
of Settlements

1. The Economic Method in the Geography of Settlements

We have dealt, purely according to an economic method, with town geography, and have, likewise, considered also one characteristic of a town, namely its function as a central place. Thus, we have disregarded, above all, the entire complex of the determination of urban development through industrialization, which falls more in the scope of the theory of the location of industry as it is discussed by Alfred Weber, Creutzburg, and others. We have been satisfied with developing the primary net of central places, on which the phenomena of industrialization may be superimposed. It should be observed, therefore, that industry affects the relative importance—the centrality—of the places relatively little. This fact had been veiled, up to now, because we had become accustomed to demonstrate the size and importance of a town solely by the schematic method of looking at the total population.

The economic method, in the pure form in which we have applied it here, had not, up to now, been applied in the geography of settlements or, incidentally, in economic geography. Bobek went further in his investigation of Innsbruck,[1] yet he had to be satisfied, in respect to the spatial conditions, with the tools which were then only scarcely and imperfectly offered by economic science. Bobek could not forge for himself those tools which were necessary for delving into the really important facts in an investigation in the geography of settlement. The works of Hassinger on Vienna,[2] and the new one by him on Basel,[3] are of no small fundamental importance. He used the economic distance (the time-cost distance) of the places surrounding a town in order to determine the range of influence of a town, and thus to determine a factor which itself considerably determines the size of the town and also enables one to recognize the size of the entire complex of the town. Finally, the procedure of Schlüter should be mentioned. He considered the value of the land—only in respect to rural settlements, however—which he determined from the land valuation for tax purposes, and combined that with the development of the settlements.[4] Otherwise, there was no real economic method applied in the geography of settlements. That the economic determination of the number, location, and sizes of towns was occasionally stressed, does not mean that the economic method was also employed; perhaps only the historical method (Gradmann),[5] the statistical method (Olbricht,[6] Schott,[7] Hasse[8]), or even the usual descriptive methods of most of the "investigations" in the geography of settlements was used. The geography of settlements has been limited, for the most part, to economic types; it has been satisfied with a largely systematic treatment of the phenomena, without properly stating (*aufzurollen*) the economic-geographical problems, not to mention solving them (above all, Hettner's composition concerning the economic types of settlements should be mentioned,[9] which threw this whole question into discussion for the first time; furthermore, Marinelli[10] and Aurousseau[11] should also be mentioned). If that systematic method of considering only the visible form of the appearance of the settlements remains the ruling point of view, then its scientific value will often be very small (in regard to this, see Geisler).[12] We must at last go beyond the *Linné* stage of mere systematizing!

2. Other Methods of the Geography of Settlements

Because, in this investigation, we have employed almost exclusively the economic method—under which we subsume the more sociological "understanding," as well as the more objective mathematical methods. The form has been auxiliarily mathematical (that is, reckoning of sizes), but the content has concerned the comprehension of the psychological relationships. We have by no means thereby denied the justification of the existence of other geography-of-settlements methods. On the contrary, they are very necessary in order to prove the correctness of results obtained by the economic method, and in order to explain the noneconomic reasons for the determination of the number, distribution, and sizes of the towns.

Thus, we cannot disregard the historical method, either for special investigations of monographical character, or for general investigations in which the historical method only enables us to understand the ideas of an economy and the concrete economic system born out of it, as a rule, at the time of the creation of the towns. In this investigation, the historical method was employed, although only secondarily. In either sort, the work by Gradmann on the settlement of Württemberg[13] will always remain outstanding, as the results obtained therein by the historical method correspond in a high degree to those obtained here by the economic method, as, for example, with respect to the significance for their development of the market function of towns, or with respect to the overestimation of the influence of traffic on the development of settlements. It should be understood that there can be only one scientific perception of truth, regardless of the method one uses.

The statistical method is indispensable, for one thing, in order to determine whether the theoretically expected circumstances actually exist; and for another, to reveal problems which our method can solve better than any other method. In the present inquiry, extensive use has been made of the statistical method; the method of the telephone connections, for instance, is completely statistical.

The geographical method, that is, setting into relationship one series of observations with others made in the same area or at the same place, on the surface of the globe, can naturally never be displaced by the economic method. We also made extensive use of the geographical method when we laid out the theoretical pattern of central places over the surface of the globe, and then compared the actual circumstances with these ideal circumstances (the "ideal types" of Max Weber). We made this comparison by drawing maps. By the way, it should be mentioned that great caution is necessary when the concrete network of the distribution of central places is compared with the natural facts of the earth's surface. For example, with regard to the fertility of the soil, the two series of facts to be compared first must be reduced to the same terms; that is, they must be made as comparable as possible. Because the distribution of central places is an economically conditioned phenomenon, one can base the comparison only on the economic value judgment of the people concerning the fertility of the soil—inaccessible fertile soil is valueless, and relatively infertile soil near large cities has high value, but not because of its objective, natural degree of fertility. Many mistakes are still made in this respect. The results of a study of the geography of settlements with such mistakes are either meaningless, and evoke smiles from the nongeographer; or are directly false, if series of facts which cannot be compared are brought into causal relationships. Because of such mistakes, the so-called geographical method of the geography of settlements (Ratzel, von Richthofen, Hassert) has been firmly discredited. This does not, however, discredit a logically correct use of the geographical method.

3. National Economy of Economic Geography

Is what we have offered in the present study economic geography or national economics? This question will be posed by many a reader. The geographer will tend to call it national economics; the economist will tend to call it geography. The author is not interested in this question at all, because the terminology and classification is irrelevant for the special result we sought to achieve. The main matter is the posing of the question, and the question is, without a doubt, geographical. The problems which are to be solved are geographical. They can be solved, however, only with the help of economic theory and economic methods.

It is generally acknowledged that the morphologist needs fundamental geological knowledge, and that the geographical botanist needs botanical knowledge. But the economic geographer thinks in general that he is able to do without theoretical economic knowledge; he is satisfied with statistics, applied economics, and economic history. When economic geography, with its subdivisions, raises itself "from an essentially descriptive discipline" (which explains the facts only in single cases) to a discipline which strives fundamentally to find laws, "it steps up alongside of the disciplines of physical geography." [14] It is because laws of economic geography are of an economic nature, just as those of geographical botany are of a physiological nature and those of morphology are of a chemical-physical nature, that only economic theory can point the way to finding these laws. If economic theory now takes little interest in spatial conditions and distribution of economic phenomena and activities, then it is the unavoidable task of the science of economic geography to search itself for the economic-geographical laws. Economic geography is enabled to perform this task because it is a part of the chorological science of geography, and therefore possesses, to a much greater extent, a conception of spatial factors. This conception often is lacking in national economics, so that the rational schemes of national economists—as for example those offered by Alfred Weber in relationship to the *Theory of Location of Industries*—often lack the necessary conception of space and therefore are too denaturalized, as a result of which the value of economic-geographical knowledge is diminished. But it is irrelevant for economic geography where its laws come from; all that matters is that the laws are applicable, and therefore really explain complicated economic-geographical phenomena—and activities, which should, in my opinion, also be taken into the sphere of economic geography—and finally, as a consequence, are useful in economic and political practice.

NOTES

1. Hans Bobek, "Innsbruck. Eine Gebirgsstadt, ihr Lebensraum und ihre Erscheinung," in *Forschungen zur deutschen Landes- und Volkskunde,* 25 (Stuttgart: 1928).

2. Hugo Hassinger, "Beiträge zur Siedlungs- und Verkehrsgeographie von Wien," in *Mitteilungen der geographischen Gesellschaft,* 53 (Vienna: 1910).

3. Hugo Hassinger, "Basel," in *Beiträge zur Oberrheinischen Landeskunde,* ed. Fredrich Metz (Breslau: 1927).

4. Otto Schlüter, *Die Siedlungen im nordöstlichen Thüringen* (Berlin: 1903).

5. Robert Gradmann, "Die städtischen Siedlungen des Königreichs Württemberg," in *Forschungen zur deutschen Landes- und Volkskunde,* 21, Part II (Stuttgart: 1926).

6. Karl Olbricht, "Die deutschen Großstädte," in *Petermanns Mitteilungen* (1913).

7. Sigmund Schott, "Die großstädtischen Agglomerationen des Deutschen Reichs, 1871-1910," in *Die Schriften des Verbands deutscher Städtestatistiker,* Part I (Breslau: 1912).

8. Ernst Hasse, "Die Intensität großstädtischer Menschenanhäufungen," in *Allgemeines staatliches Archiv,* 2nd year (Tübingen: 1892).

9. Alfred Hettner, "Die wirtschaftlichen Typen der Ansiedelungen," in *Geographische Zeitschrift,* 8th year (Leipzig: 1902), 98.

10. Olinto Marinelli, "Dei tipi economici dei centri abitati, a proposito di alcune citta italiane ed americane," in *Rivista Geografica Italiana,* 22, 23 (Florence: 1916), 413ff.

11. M. Aurousseau, "The Arrangement of Rural Population," in *Geographical Review* (New York: 1920), 223ff.

12. W. Geisler, "Die deutsche Stadt—ein Beitrag zur Morphologie der Kulturlandschaft," in *Forschungen zur deutschen Landes- und Volkskunde,* 22 (Stuttgart: 1924), 5.

13. Robert Gradmann, *op. cit.*

14. Alfred Hettner, "Der gegenwärtige Stand der Verkehrsgeographie," in *Geographische Zeitschrift,* 3rd year (Leipzig: 1895), 629.

APPENDIX

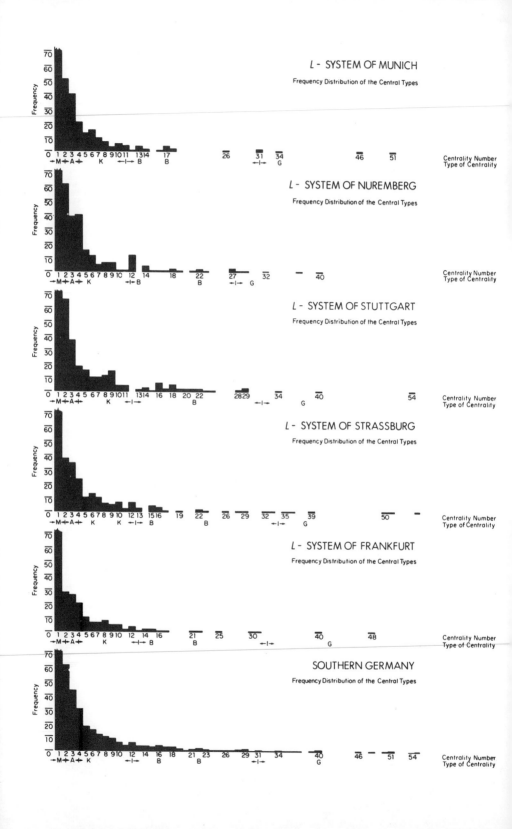

Table I

THE *L*-SYSTEM OF MUNICH

Column number	*Description*
1	Numerical order.
2	Names of places.

3   The political designations of the places. Abbreviations:

U. St.	Unmitteilbare Stadt, or Stadtkreis	= independent city
St.	Stadt	= city
Mf.	Marktflecken	= market spot
Df.	Dorf (gemeinde)	= village
F. Df.	Filial-dorf (keine eigene Gemeinde bildend)	= less than a village

4   Number of inhabitants, 1 = 400 inhabitants; consequently the numbers correspond with the number of points on Map 1. The results of the census of June 16, 1925 are the basis for Germany, the census of July 10, 1927 are for the Saar region.

5   Number of telephone connections, 1 = 10 telephone connections; consequently the numbers correspond with the number of points on Map 2. The bases for the numbers are the official telephone directories edited for Germany between the end of March and August, 1931, and for the Saar region, November, 1930.

6   Telephone density; 1 means the normal relationship of 10 telephone connections to 400 inhabitants. Numbers under 1 mean a lesser, and numbers over 1 mean a higher, telephone density.

7   The rounded numbers of the centrality.

8   Central types; they are drawn up on Maps 3 and 4.

9   Remarks.

For other information look at the discussion of Part II.

1	2	3	4	5	6	7	8	9
1 München	U.St.	1868	5029	1,18	2825	L	
2 Augsburg..........	U.St.	461	648	0,92	224	P	
3 Innsbruck	?	?	?	?	?	P	
4 Kempten	U.St.	69	131	1,0	62	G	
5 Passau	U.St.	73	103	0,55	62	G	
6 Landshut..........	U.St.	76	89	0,5	51	G	
7 Straubing	U.St.	59	78	0,55	46	G	
8 Ingolstadt	U.St.	67	66	0,48	34	G	
9 Rosenheim	U.St.	48	65	0,7	31	G	
10 Salzburg	?	?	?	?	?	G	
11 Bozen.............	?	?	?	?	?	G	
12 Memmingen	U.St.	37	63	0,86	31	B	
13 Garmisch-Partenk. ..	Mf.	30	86	2,0	26	B	

1	2	3	4	5	6	7	8	9
14 Deggendorf	U.St.	24	30	0,5	18	B	
15 Traunstein	U.St.	24	37	0,8	18	B	
16 Freising	U.St.	39	33	0,42	17	B	
17 Starnberg	St.	13	43	2,0	17	B	
18 Mühldorf	St.	15	25	0,5	17	B	1
19 Berchtesgaden	Mf.	9	35	2,0	17	B	
20 Bad Tölz	St.	17	41	1,45	16	B	
21 Weilheim	St.	15	24	0,7	14	B	
22 Kaufbeuren........	U.St.	25	30	0,65	14	B	
23 Mindelheim........	St.	12	21	0,7	13	B	
24 Donauwörth	U.St.	12	19	0,45	13	B	
25 Neuburg a. D.	U.St.	19	22	0,46	13	B	
26 Tegernsee	Df.	8	41	3,5	13	B	2
27 Erding	St.	11	16	0,35	12	B	
28 Landsberg a. L.	U.St.	19	20	0,46	11	B	
29 Pfarrkirchen	St.	9	14	0,46	10	B	3
30 Alt- und Neuötting ..	St.	22	22	0,5	11	K	
31 Fürstenfeldbruck ...	Mf.	13	18	0,55	11	K	
32 Dachau	Mf.	20	20	0,44	11	K	
33 Bad Reichenhall.....	St.	22	54	2,0	10	K	4
34 Prien-Stock........	Mf.	5	16	1,2	10	K	5
35 Vilshofen...........	St.	10	15	0,46	10	K	
36 Eggenfelden	St.	8	13	0,37	10	K	
37 Murnau	Mf.	6	16	1,2	9	K	
38 Schrobenhausen	St.	10	13	0,35	9	K	
39 Pfaffenhofen........	St.	11	14	0,43	9	K	
40 Moosburg	St.	10	12	0,4	8	K	
41 Aichach	St.	9	11	0,33	8	K	
42 Landau a. I.	St.	8	12	0,47	8	K	
43 Wasserburg	St.	12	13	0,4	8	K	
44 Bad Aibling	Mf.	11	18	0,9	8	K	
45 Zwiesel............	St.	12	15	0,57	8	K	6
46 Marktgrafing	Mf.	4	9	0,6	7	K	7
47 Sonthofen	St.	11	18	1,0	7	K	8
48 Immenstadt	St.	14	20	0,9	7	K	
49 Oberstdorf..........	Mf.	10	26	1,9	7	K	
50 Wolfratshausen	Mf.	6	12	0,8	7	K	
51 Schwabmünchen	Mf.	9	12	0,54	7	K	
52 Mainburg...........	Mf.	7	11	0,55	7	K	
53 Plattling	St.	14	13	0,4	7	K	
54 Vilsbiburg	Mf.	8	11	0,42	7	K	

[1] With Alt- and Neuötting together a centrality of 28.
[2] Extraordinarily high number.
[3] On the whole, barely B-function.
[4] As a bath place, it is in an exceptional position.
[5] Unusually high number.
[6] Important as the main district place of Regen, it should be a B-place.
[7] With Ebersberg, a centrality of 10.
[8] With Immenstadt a centrality of 10 and B-functions.

1	2	3	4	5	6	7	8	9
55	Füssen	St.	16	21	0,9	7	K	
56	Holzkirchen	Mf.	7	10	0,5	6	K	
57	Buchloe	Mf.	6	9	0,5	6	K	
58	Ottobeuren	Mf.	6	10	0,63	6	K	
59	Abensberg	St.	7	9	0,5	6	K	1
60	Rain	St.	4	8	0,4	6	K	
61	Dingolfing	St.	8	10	0,44	6	K	
62	Viechtach	Mf.	5	8	0,4	6	K	
63	Regen	Mf.	8	11	0,57	6	K	
64	Burghausen	St.	13	12	0,5	6	K	
65	Trostberg	St.	7	10	0,6	6	K	
66	Freilassing	Df.	5	9	0,6	6	K	2
67	Herrsching	Df.	3	11	1,9	5	K	3
68	Dorfen	Mf.	6	7	0,3	5	K	
69	Miesbach	St.	11	14	0,8	5	K	
70	Schongau	St.	8	10	0,6	5	K	4
71	Marktoberdorf	Mf.	6	9	0,6	5	K	
72	Obergünzburg	Mf.	4	7	0,55	5	K	
73	Bad Wörishofen	Df.	7	17	1,7	5	K	5
74	Diessen -St. Georgen	Mf.	6	12	1,1	5	K	
75	Wolnzach	Mf.	7	8	0,4	5	K	
76	Grafenau	St.	4	7	0,35	5	K	
77	Waldkirchen	Mf.	4	7	0,4	5	K	6
78	Osterhofen	St.	8	8	0,4	5	K	
79	Simbach a. Inn	Df.	12	10	0,44	5	K	7
80	Markt Schwaben	Mf.	5	6	0,4	4	K	
81	Schliersee	Mf.	4	12	2,0	4	K	
82	Oberstaufen	Mf.	4	8	0,9	4	K	
83	Mering	Mf.	7	7	0,4	4	K	8
84	Wertingen	St.	5	6	0,4	4	K	
85	Au Hallertau	Mf.	3	6	0,45	4	K	
86	Griesbach	Mf.	3	6	0,5	4	K	
87	Haag	Mf.	3	5	0,35	4	K	
88	Thannhausen	Mf.	4	6	0,4	4	K	

Jurisdiction of Munich:

| 89 | Höhenkirchen | Df. | 2 | 2 | 0,5 | 1 | M | 9 |

H-places: the town Pasing; and villages Planegg, Allach, Schleißheim, Garching, Ismaning, Feldkirchen, Haar, Unterhaching, Deisenhofen, Grünwald, Pullach, altogether absorbed by Munich; and the village Aying.

---

[1] With Neustadt a centrality of 9 and represents a *B*-position.
[2] In addition to Salzburghofen.
[3] Excursion and living place.
[4] With Peiting a centrality of 8.
[5] As a bath place, it is in an exceptional position.
[6] Important as the main district place of Freyung–Wolfstein.
[7] Participator in the *B*-function of Braunau.
[8] Important as the main district place of Friedberg.
[9] With Siegertsbrunn.

1	2	3	4	5	6	7	8	9

Jurisdiction of Starnberg:

90	Tutzing	Df.	5	13	2,0	3	A	
91	Gauting	Df.	7	16	2,1	1	M	
92	Feldafing	Df.	3	10	3,0	1	M	1
93	Weßling	Df.	1	3	1,8	1	M	

H-places: villages Oberalfing-Seefeld, Inning, and Gilching.

Jurisdiction of Wolfratshausen:

94	Schäftlarn-Ebenhsn. .	Df.	5	7	1,2	1	M	
95	Sauerlach	Df.	2	2	0,7	1	M	
96	Beuerberg	Df.	1	1	0,5	1	M	
97	Dietramszell	Df.	2	1	0,3	1	M	2

H-places: villages Leoni-Allmannshöhe, Ammerland–Münsing, Baierbrunn, Ascholding, and Großdingharting.

Jurisdiction of Fürstenfeldbruck:

98	Olching	Df.	7	3	0,35	1	M	
99	Maisach	Df.	4	2	0,35	1	M	
100	Moorenweis	Df.	2	1	0,2	1	M	
101	Althegnenberg	Df.	1	1	0,3	1	M	

H-places: villages Türkenfeld, Wildenroth, Germering, and Mammendorf–Nannhofen.

Jurisdiction of Dachau:

102	Markt Indersdorf	Mf.	2	4	0,3	3	A	
103	Petershausen	Df.	2	2	0,3	1	M	
104	Haimhausen	Df.	2	1	0,3	1	M	
105	Odelzhausen	Df.	1	2	0,3	1	M	

H-places: villages Hohenkammer, Röhrmoos, Schwabhausen, and Sulzemoos.

Jurisdiction of Freising:

106	Nandlstadt	Mf.	3	3	0,3	2	M	
107	Allershausen	Df.	1	1	0,25	1	M	
108	Kranzberg	Df.	1	1	0,25	1	M	
109	Neufahrn	Df.	2	1	0,3	1	M	
110	Attenkirchen	Df.	1	1	0,2	1	M	
111	Mauern	Df.	1	1	0,2	1	M	
112	Bruckberg	Df.	1	1	0,3	1	M	

H-places: villages Unterzolling, Langenbach, and Hallbergmoos.

Jurisdiction of Erding:

113	Taufkirchen	Df.	2	3	0,25	2	M	
114	Wartenberg	Mf.	3	2	0,2	1	M	

H-places: village Lengsdorf.

Jurisdiction of Ebersberg:

115	Ebersberg	Mf.	5	6	0,5	3	A	3
116	Glonn	Mf.	2	3	0,4	2	A	

[1] With Possenhofen.
[2] With Schönegg.
[3] As a train stop, Marktgrafing is more important.

1	2	3	4	5	6	7	8	9
117	Kirchseeon	F.Df.	2	2	0,5	1	M	
118	Zorneding	Df.	2	2	0,6	1	M	
119	Steinhöring	Df.	2	1	0,3	1	M	

H-places: villages Moosach, Aßling, and Hohenlinden.

Jurisdiction of Miesbach:

120	Gmund	F.Df.	2	6	2,0	2	A	
121	Bad Wiessee	Df.	3	12	3,5	2	M	1
122	Bayrischzell	Df.	1	4	2,0	2	M	
123	Schaftlach	Df.	1	2	0,8	1	M	
124	Fischbachau	Df.	1	2	0,8	1	M	
125	Kreuth	Df.	1	2	1,0	1	M	

H-places: villages Wörnsmühle and Thalham.

Jurisdiction of Tölz:

126	Kochel	Df.	4	6	1,0	2	A	
127	Lenggries	Df.	4	5	1,0	1	M	
128	Benediktbeuern	Df.	2	3	0,8	1	M	
129	Bichl	Df.	1	2	0,8	1	M	
130	Walchensee	F.Df.	1	2	0,9	1	M	

H-places: villages Jachenau and Bad Heilbrunn.

Jurisdiction of Garmisch:

131	Oberammergau	Df.	6	15	2,0	3	A	
132	Mittenwald	Mf.	7	11	1,3	2	A	
133	Bad Kohlgrub	F.Df.	1	3	1,7	1	M	
134	Oberau	Df.	1	2	1,3	1	M	
135	Wallgau	Df.	1	2	1,0	1	M	

H-places: villages Unter- and Obergrainau, and Ohlstadt.

Jurisdiction of Weilheim:

136	Penzberg	St.	12	7	0,5	2	A	
137	Unterpeißenberg	Mf.	12	7	0,5	1	M	
138	Seeshaupt	Df.	2	5	1,8	1	M	
139	Uffing	Df.	2	2	0,6	1	M	
140	Huglfing	Df.	2	1	0,5	1	M	
141	Pähl	Df.	1	1	0,5	1	M	

H-places: villages Obersöchering and Wessobrunn.

Jurisdiction of Schongau:

142	Peiting	Df.	6	6	0,45	3	A	2
143	Steingaden	F.Df.	1	3	0,5	2	A	
144	Rottenbuch	Df.	1	1	0,4	1	M	
145	Kinsau	Df.	1	1	0,4	1	M	

H-places: villages Bernbeuern, Hohenpeißenberg, Schwabsoien, and Bayersoien.

Jurisdiction of Füssen:

146	Nesselwang	Mf.	3	6	1,0	3	A	
147	Pfronten	Df.	7	9	1,0	2	A	

---

[1] With Abwinkl, a spa.

[2] Together with Schongau.

1	2	3	4	5	6	7	8	9
148	Lechbruck	Df.	3	2	0,5	1	M	
149	Seeg	Df.	2	2	0,5	1	M	
150	Trauchgau..........	Df.	1	1	0,5	1	M	

H-place: village Roßhaupten.

Jurisdiction of Sonthofen:

151	Hindelang	Mf.	4	9	1,5	3	A	1
152	Wertach	Mf.	2	4	1,0	2	M	
153	Fischen	Df.	2	4	1,5	1	M	

H-places: villages Voderburg, Thalkirchdorf, Rettenberg, and Missen.

Jurisdiction of Kempten:

154	Dietmannsried	Mf.	3	4	0,7	2	A	
155	Altusried	Mf.	2	4	0,7	2	A	
156	Oberdorf	F.Df.	1	1	0,6	1	M	
157	Weitnau	Mf.	2	2	0,6	1	M	
158	Oy-Mittelberg	Df.	2	3	1,0	1	M	
159	Wildpoldsried	Df.	1	2	0,6	1	M	
160	Wiggensbach	Df.	1	2	0,6	1	M	
161	Kimratshofen	Df.	1	2	0,6	1	M	

H-places: marketspot Waltenhofen, Sulzberg, and villages Buchenberg and Kreuztal.

Jurisdiction of Marktoberdorf:

162	Unterthingau	Mf.	2	3	0,5	2	A	
163	Aitrang	Df.	2	3	0,5	2	M	
164	Ronsberg	Mf.	1	1	0,4	1	M	
165	Görisried	Df.	1	1	0,5	1	M	
166	Stötten	Df.	1	1	0,4	1	M	

H-places: villages Bidingen, Freisenried. (Bidingen should be an M-place.)

Jurisdiction of Kaufbeuren:

167	Waal	Mf.	2	2	0,3	1	M	
168	Westendorf	Df.	1	1	0,3	1	M	
169	Asch	Df.	1	1	0,35	1	M	
170	Denklingen	Df.	2	2	0,35	1	M	

H-places: villages Baisweil (should be an M-place), Pforzen, Aufkrich, and marketspot Blonhofen, Leeder, and Irsee.

Jurisdiction of Mindelheim:

171	Türkheim	Mf.	6	6	0,45	3	A	
172	Pfaffenhausen.......	Mf.	3	4	0,4	3	A	
173	Kirchheim	Mf.	3	4	0,4	3	A	
174	Dirlewang	Mf.	2	2	0,35	1	M	
175	Markt Wald	Mf.	2	1	0,3	1	M	

H-places: villages Loppenhausen and Ettringen.

Jurisdiction of Memmingen:

176	Grönenbach	Mf.	2	4	0,7	3	A	
177	Legau..............	Mf.	2	4	0,7	2	A	

---

[1] With the spa, Oberdorf.

1	2	3	4	5	6	7	8	9
178	Markt Rettenbach .. Mf.	2	3	0,4	2	A		
179	Erkheim .... Df.	3	3	0,5	1	M		
180	Fellheim .... Df.	1	2	0,5	1	M		

H-places: Lautrach and Böhen.

Eastern district of Leutkirch (eastern part):

181	Aitrach .... Df.	2	2	0,5	1	M	1
182	Tannheim .... Df.	2	2	0,5	1	M	

H-places: missing.

Jurisdiction of Krumbach (eastern half) and Günzburg (eastern half):

183	Burgau .... St.	7	6	0,4	3	A	
184	Ziemetshausen ...... Mf.	3	2	0,35	1	M	2
185	Jettingen.......... Mf.	4	3	0,4	1	M	
186	Burtenbach .... Mf.	3	2	0,3	1	M	

H-place: Münsterhausen.

Jurisdiction of Zusmarshausen (district without K-place presently developing).

187	Fischach .... Df.	2	5	0,4	4	A
188	Zusmarshausen...... Mf.	3	4	0,4	3	A
189	Dinkelscherben...... Mf.	3	2	0,4	1	M
190	Welden .... Mf.	2	2	0,3	1	M

H-places: villages Altenmünster and Horgau.

Jurisdiction of Augsburg:

191	Gessertshausen ..... Df.	1	2	0,3	1	M

H-places: village Gablingen. Absorbed: St. Göggingen.

Jurisdiction of Schwabmünchen:

192	Bobingen .... Df.	7	5	0,4	3	A	
193	Lechfeld .... Df.	2	2	0,3	1	M	3
194	Mickhausen .... Df.	1	1	0,4	1	M	

H-places: villages Langenneufnach, Großaitingen, and Mittelneufnach.

Jurisdiction of Landsberg on-the-Lahn:

195	Utting .... Df.	3	6	1,3	2	M
196	Unterschondorf ..... Df.	3	5	1,2	1	M
197	Schwabhausen ...... Df.	1	1	0,3	1	M
198	Egling .... Df.	2	1	0,25	1	M

H-places: villages Kaufering, Issing, and Prittriching.

Jurisdiction of Friedberg:

199	Friedberg .... St.	10	8	0,4	4	A	4

H-places: villages Eurasburg and Dasing.

---

[1] With Marstetten.
[2] With Thannhausen, a combined district.
[3] Lechfeld includes outlying warehouses and monasteries.
[4] Already within the city limits of Augsburg.

1	2	3	4	5	6	7	8	9

Jurisdiction of Aichach:

1	2	3	4	5	6	7	8	9
200	Pöttmes .... Mf.	3	4	0,2	3	A		
201	Altomünster .... Mf.	3	3	0,2	2	A		
202	Aindling .... Mf.	2	2	0,2	1	M		

H-places: villages Sielenbach, Schiltberg, Affing, and Hilgartshausen, and marketspots Kühbach and Inchenhofen (very strongly transformed).

Jurisdiction of Wertingen:

203	Meitingen .... Df.	2	3	0,35	2	A		
204	Uttenwiesen .... Df.	2	2	0,3	1	M		
205	Biberbach .... Mf.	1	1	0,3	1	M		

H-places: villages Villenbach and Emersacker.

Jurisdiction of Donauwörth (partially) and Dillingen (partially):

206	Marxheim .... Df.	1	1	0,2	1	M		
207	Nordendorf .... Df.	1	2	0,3	1	M		
208	Harburg .... St.	4	2	0,3	1	M		
209	Bissingen .... Mf.	1	1	0,2	1	M		

H-places: villages Tapfheim, Schwenningen, Mertingen, Kaisheim, and Amerdingen.

Jurisdiction of Neuburg a. D.:

210	Burgheim .... Mf.	3	3	0,4	2	A		
211	Rennertshofen ...... Mf.	2	2	0,3	1	M		
212	Ehekirchen .... Df.	1	1	0,2	1	M		
213	Karlshuld .... Df.	3	2	0,25	1	M		
214	Ludwigsmoos .... Df.	1	1	0,2	1	M		

H-place: village Thierhaupten (here a falling *M*-place).

Jurisdiction of Schrobenhausen:

215	Hohenwart .... Mf.	3	2	0,2	1	M		
216	Niederarnbach ...... F.Df.	1	1	0,2	1	M		

H-places: villages Sandizell and Gerolsbach.

Jurisdiction of Ingolstadt:

217	Reichertshofen ..... Mf.	3	2	0,2	1	M		
218	Eitensheim .... Df.	2	1	0,2	1	M		
219	Pförring .... Mf.	3	2	0,3	1	M		
220	Kösching .... Mf.	6	3	0,3	1	M		

H-places: villages Manching, Stammham, and Oberdolling, and marketspot Gaimersheim.

Jurisdiction of Pfaffenhofen:

221	Geisenfeld .... Mf.	5	5	0,4	3	A		
222	Vohburg .... Mf.	4	3	0,3	2	M		
223	Münchsmünster ..... Df.	2	1	0,3	1	M		
224	Schweitenkirchen.... Df.	1	1	0,2	1	M		

H-places: villages Pörnbach, Reichertshausen, and Jetzendorf.

Jurisdiction of Mainburg (district without A- and M-places):

H-places: villages Elsendorf and Volkenschwand.

---

[1] More important as the marketspot Gaimersheim.

1	2	3	4	5	6	7	8	9

Jurisdiction of Rottenburg (district without K-places, but with three A-places):

225	Rottenburg . . . . Mf.	3	4	0,45	3	A	
226	Pfeffenhausen . . . . . . Mf.	3	4	0,4	3	A	
227	Langquaid . . . . Mf.	3	4	0,4	3	A	
228	Wildenberg . . . . Df.	2	1	0,35	1	M	1

H-place: village Hohenthann.

Jurisdiction of Kelheim (southern part):

229	Neustadt a. d. D. . . . St.	5	5	0,45	3	A	2
230	Siegenburg . . . . Mf.	4	5	0,4	3	A	
231	Rohr . . . . Mf.	3	2	0,35	1	M	

H-place: village Herrnwahltann.

Jurisdiction of Mallersdorf (district without K-places):

232	Geiselhöring . . . . Mf.	6	6	0,45	3	A	
233	Neufahrn . . . . Df.	2	3	0,45	2	A	
234	Ergoldsbach . . . . Mf.	5	4	0,45	2	A	
235	Mallersdorf . . . . Df.	3	3	0,5	2	M	3
236	Pfaffenberg . . . . Mf.	2	2	0,5	1	M	
237	Schierling . . . . Df.	4	2	0,4	1	M	4

H-places: villages Bayerbach and Eggmühl.

Jurisdiction of Landshut:

238	Essenbach . . . . Df.	3	2	0,3	1	M	
239	Wörth a. I. . . . . Df.	1	1	0,3	1	M	
240	Postau . . . . Df.	1	1	0,3	1	M	5

H-places: villages Pfettrach, Furth, Unterneuhausen, Kronwinkl, and Buch a. E.

Jurisdiction of Dingolfing:

241	Reisbach . . . . Mf.	2	3	0,3	2	M	
242	Loiching . . . . Df.	1	1	0,3	1	M	
243	Niederviehbach . . . . . Df.	2	2	0,3	1	M	
244	Mengkofen . . . . Df.	2	2	0,3	1	M	

H-place: village Mamming.

Jurisdiction of Landau a. I.:

245	Eichendorf . . . . Mf.	3	4	0,35	3	A	
246	Wallersdorf . . . . Df.	4	4	0,4	2	A	
247	Pilsting . . . . Mf.	3	2	0,4	1	M	6

H-place: village Haunersdorf.

Jurisdiction of Straubing (strongly centralized in Straubing):

248	Leiblfing . . . . Df.	1	2	0,45	2	M	
249	Straßkirchen . . . . Df.	3	3	0,5	2	M	
250	Oberschneiding . . . . . Df.	1	1	0,45	1	M	

H-places: villages Rain and Kirchroth (of the jurisdiction of Regensburg).

---

1 With Pürkwang.
2 With Abensberg takes a *B*-position.
3 With Pfaffenberg still not *K*-function.
4 Could still through the rail station place, Eggmühl, be displaced.
5 With Wörth a combined region.
6 Belongs to the region of Landau.

Jurisdiction of Bogen (district without a K-place):

251	Bogen	Mf.	4	5	0,3	3	A	1
252	Mitterfels	Df.	2	3	0,3	2	A	
253	Schwarzach	Df.	2	3	0,3	2	A	
254	Englmar	Df.	2	1	0,2	1	M	
255	Wiesenfelden	Df.	2	1	0,15	1	M	
256	Stallwang	Df.	1	1	0,15	1	M	

H-places: villages Rattenberg, Konzell, Neukirchen, and Bernried.

Jurisdiction of Deggendorf:

257	Hengersberg	Mf.	4	5	0,35	4	A	
258	Metten	Df.	4	3	0,4	1	M	2
259	Schöllnach	Df.	2	2	0,35	1	M	
260	Stephansposching	Df.	1	1	0,4	1	M	

H-places: villages Lalling and marketspot Winzer.

Jurisdiction of Viechtach:

261	Teisnach	Df.	2	4	0,3	3	A	
262	Ruhmannsfelden	Mf.	3	4	0,35	3	A	3
263	Gotteszell	Df.	1	1	0,35	1	M	

H-places: none

Jurisdiction of Regen:

264	Bodenmais	Df.	5	5	0,4	3	A	
265	Bayr. Eisenstein	Df.	2	3	0,6	2	A	4
266	Kirchberg	Df.	1	1	0,3	1	M	
267	Frauenau	Df.	2	2	0,4	1	M	

H-places: villages Rinchnach, Kirchdorf, and Bischofsmais.

Jurisdiction of Gratenau:

268	Spiegelau	F.Df.	2	3	0,35	2	M	
269	Schönberg	Mf.	2	2	0,25	2	M	

H-places: villages Zenting, and Sohöfweg.

Jurisdiction of Freyung–Wolfstein:

270	Freyung-Wolfstein	Mf.	3	5	0,4	4	A	5
271	Perlesreuth	Mf.	1	2	0,25	2	M	
272	Haidmühle	F.Df.	1	1	0,4	1	M	6
273	Neureichenau	F.Df.	1	1	0,3	1	M	
274	Röhrnbach	Mf.	1	1	0,3	1	M	
275	Mauth	Df.	1	1	0,3	1	M	

H-places: villages Bischofsreuth. Untergrainet, Herzogsreuth, Karlsberg, and Hohenau.

---

[1] Because of the neighboring Straubing is strongly retarded.
[2] Belongs to the region of Deggendorf.
[3] With Gotteszell a combined region.
[4] Border place separated from Böhmisch–Eisenstein.
[5] Waldkirchen is more important as the main district place.
[6] Border place.

1	2	3	4	5	6	7	8	9

Jurisdiction of Wegscheid (district without K-places):

276	Wegscheid	Mf.	3	4	0,45	3	A	
277	Hauzenberg	Mf.	4	5	0,4	3	A	
278	Untergriesbach	Mf.	3	3	0,45	2	M	
279	Obernzell	Mf.	3	3	0,4	2	M	
280	Breitenberg	Df.	1	1	0,3	1	M	

H-places: none.

Jurisdiction of Passau:

281	Fürstenzell	Df.	2	4	0,55	3	A	
282	Tittling	Mf.	3	5	0,45	3	A	
283	Neuhaus	Df.	2	3	0,5	2	M	1
284	Sulzbach	Df.	1	2	0,5	1	M	
285	Fürstenstein	Df.	2	2	0,4	1	M	
286	Hutthurn	Mf.	2	2	0,5	1	M	

H-places: villages Sandbach, Bad Höhenstadt, Thyrnau, and Dommelstadt.

Jurisdiction of Vilshofen:

287	Ortenburg	Mf.	3	5	0,5	3	A	
288	Aidenbach	Mf.	3	4	0,4	3	A	
289	Eging	Df.	2	2	0,35	1	M	

H-places: villages Otterskirchen, Gergweis, Moos, Oberpöring (better as an *M*-place), and marketspot Hofkirchen (should rightly be an *M*-place).

Jurisdiction of Griesbach:

290	Pocking	Df.	3	5	0,5	3	A	2
291	Rotthalmünster	Mf.	4	5	0,5	3	A	
292	Birnbach	Df.	2	2	0,4	1	M	
293	Kößlarn	Mf.	2	2	0,4	1	M	
294	Ruhstorf	Df.	2	2	0,5	1	M	
295	Tettenweis	Df.	2	2	0,5	1	M	

H-places: villages Aigen and Haarbach, and marketspot Hartkirchen.

Jurisdiction of Pfarrkirchen:

296	Tann	Mf.	3	5	0,3	4	A	
297	Triftern	Mf.	3	3	0,3	2	M	
298	Ering	Df.	2	2	0,4	1	M	

H-places: villages Anzenkirchen, Egglham, Dietersburg, and Wittibreuth.

Jurisdiction of Eggenfelden:

299	Arnstorf	Mf.	4	5	0,35	4	A	
300	Gangkofen	Mf.	4	4	0,35	3	A	
301	Massing	Mf.	2	3	0,35	2	A	
302	Simbach b. E.	Mf.	2	2	0,3	1	M	

H-places: villages Kollbach, Schönau, Falkenberg, and Wurmannsquick.

Jurisdiction of Vilsbiburg:

| 303 | Velden | Mf. | 4 | 5 | 0,35 | 4 | A | |
| 304 | Frontenhausen | Mf. | 4 | 5 | 0,3 | 4 | A | |

---

[1] With Sulzbach a combined region and with *A*-importance.

[2] With Ruhstorf a combined region and with *K*-importance.

1	2	3	4	5	6	7	8	9
305	Geisenhausen .... Mf.		4	4	0,35	3	A	
306	Gerzen .... Df.		2	1	0,3	1	M	
	H-place: Altfraunhofen.							

Jurisdiction of Mühldorf:

1	2	3	4	5	6	7	8	9
307	Neumarkt .... Mf.		4	5	0,3	4	A	
308	Kraiburg .... Mf.		3	4	0,3	3	A	
309	Ampfing .... Df.		2	2	0,4	1	M	
310	Buchbach .... Mf.		1	2	0,3	1	M	1
	H-places: villages Schwindegg, Peterskirchen, and Oberneukirchen.							

Jurisdiction of Altötting:

1	2	3	4	5	6	7	8	9
311	Garching-Hart ...... Df.		2	2	0,3	1	M	
312	Marktl .... Mf.		2	2	0,4	1	M	
313	Reischach .... Df.		1	1	0,3	1	M	
314	Tüßling .... Mf.		2	1	0,4	1	M	
	H-places: villages Pleiskirchen, Burgkirchen, Töging, and Kirchweidach.							

Jurisdiction of Wasserburg:

1	2	3	4	5	6	7	8	9
315	Isen .... Mf.		3	4	0,4	3	A	
316	Gars .... Mf.		1	3	0,4	2	A	
317	Rott a. Inn .... Df.		3	2	0,35	1	M	
	H-places: villages Amerang, Schonstett, and Albaching.							

Jurisdiction of Aibling:

1	2	3	4	5	6	7	8	9
318	Bruckmühl .... Df.		1	4	0,5	3	A	
319	Feldkirchen b. W. ... Df.		1	3	0,5	2	M	
320	Au b. Aibling .... Df.		1	2	0,6	1	M	
321	Feilnbach .... Df.		1	2	0,6	1	M	
322	Ostermünchen ...... Df.		1	1	0,4	1	M	
	H-places: villages Kolbermoor and Schönau.							

Jurisdiction of Rosenheim:

1	2	3	4	5	6	7	8	9
323	Endorf .... Df.		3	6	0,8	4	A	
324	Brannenburg .... Df.		4	5	0,8	2	A	
325	Oberaudorf .... Df.		2	4	0,7	2	A	
326	Nd.- u. Hohenaschau. Df.		3	6	1,0	2	A	
327	Kiefersfelden .... Df.		3	3	0,7	1	M	
328	Halfing .... Df.		2	2	0,5	1	M	
	H-places: villages Vogtareuth, Eggstädt, Breitbrunn, Bernau, Frasdorf, Sachrang, Törwang, and Nußdorf, and marketspot Neubeuern.							

Jurisdiction of Traunstein:

1	2	3	4	5	6	7	8	9
329	Ruhpolding .... Df.		3	6	1,0	3	A	
330	Obing .... Df.		2	3	0,3	2	A	
331	Siegsdorf .... F.Df.		2	4	0,8	2	M	
332	Inzell .... Df.		1	2	1,0	1	M	
333	Übersee .... Df.		2	3	1,0	1	M	

[1] Close by the rail place of Schwindegg.
[2] Properly important as an A-place.

1	2	3	4	5	6	7	8	9
334	Grassau	Df.	2	3	1,0	1	M	
335	Marquartstein.......	F.Df.	2	3	1,0	1	M	[1]
336	Schnaitsee	Df.	2	2	0,3	1	M	
337	Reit i. Winkl	Df.	2	3	0,9	1	M	
338	Matzing	Df.	1	1	0,4	1	M	
339	Altenmarkt........	Df.	3	2	0,5	1	M	

H-places: villages Bergen, Grabenstätt, Niederseeon, Schleching, Seebruck, and Kienberg.

Jurisdiction of Laufen:

340	Laufen............	St.	7	7	0,45	4	A	[2]
341	Tittmoning........	St.	4	3	0,4	2	A	
342	Waging	Mf.	3	3	0,45	2	A	
343	Teisendorf........	Mf.	4	4	0,6	2	M	
344	Kirchanschöring.....	Df.	1	1	0,4	1	M	
345	Palling............	Df.	2	2	0,3	1	M	

H-places: villages Friedolfing, Tengling, and Tyrlaching.

Jurisdiction of Berchtesgaden:

346	Königsee	Df.	1	3	1,6	1	M	
347	Ramsau	Df.	1	3	1,6	1	M	
348	Schellenberg.......	Mf.	1	2	1,4	1	M	
349	Piding	Df.	1	1	0,7	1	M	

H-place: village Anger.

---

[1] With Grassau a combined region and of *A*-function.
[2] Freilassing is more important as the main district place.

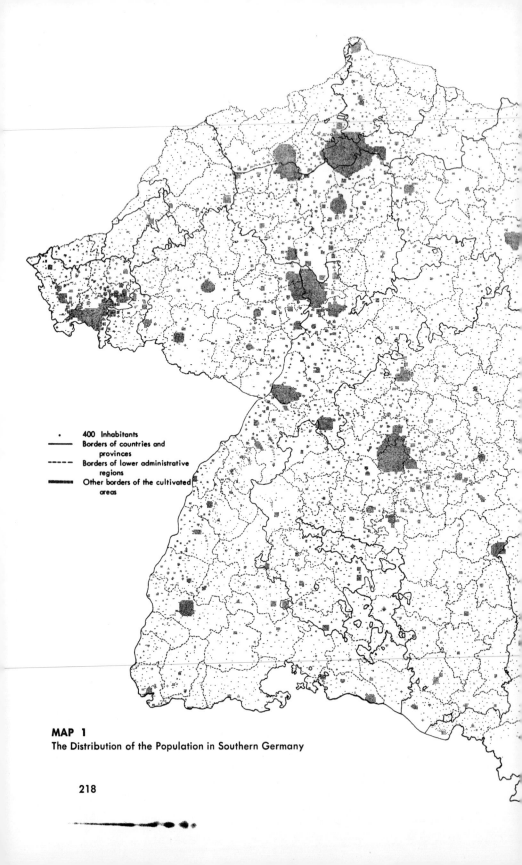

MAP 1
The Distribution of the Population in Southern Germany

Legend:
- • 400 Inhabitants
- —— Borders of countries and provinces
- ---- Borders of lower administrative regions
- ▪▪▪▪ Other borders of the cultivated areas

218

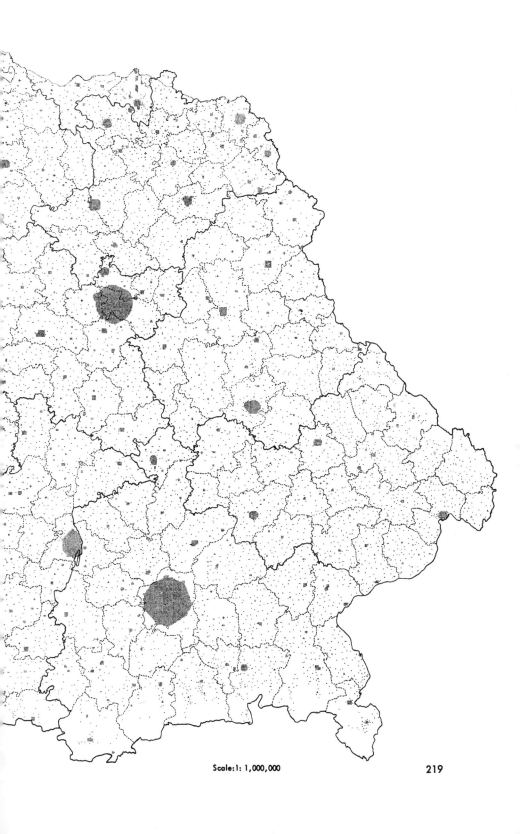

Scale: 1: 1,000,000

· 10 telephone connections

MAP 2
The Distribution of the Central Institutions in Southern Germany

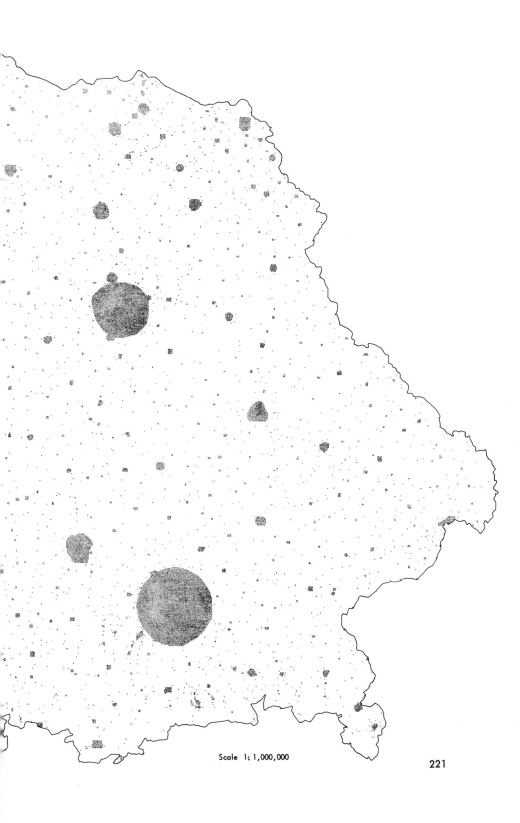

Scale 1: 1,000,000

MAP 3
The Central Places in Southern Germany and Their M-Regions

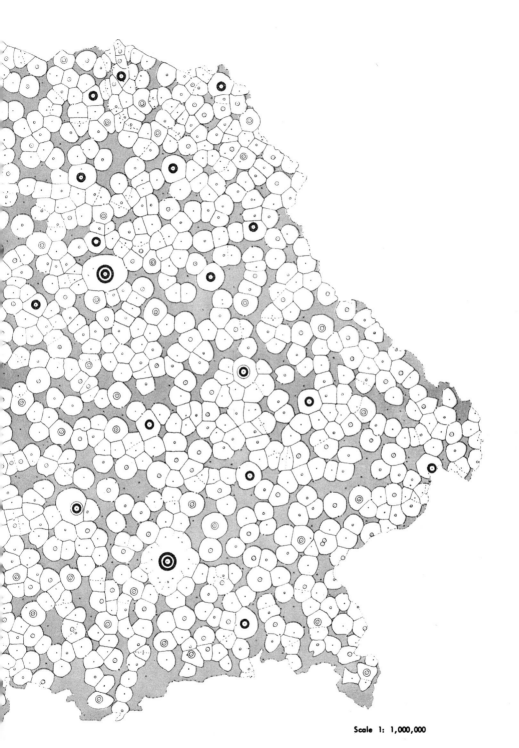

Scale 1: 1,000,000

223

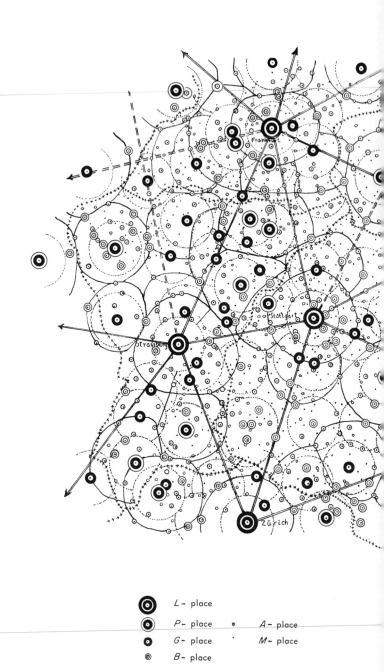

◉	L – place
◉	P – place
◉	G – place
◉	B – place

∘	A – place
·	M – place

MAP 4
The Distribution of Towns as Central Places in Southern Germany

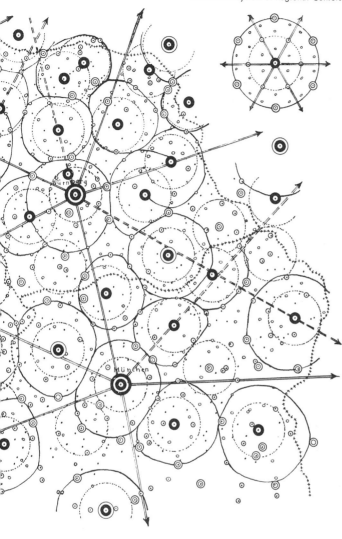

•••••••   21 km. K– ring (schematic)

————   Ring of B – places (average 36 km.)

+++++++   Borders of L–systems

═══   Principal interconnections of L – centers

══ ══   Secondary interconnections of L – centers

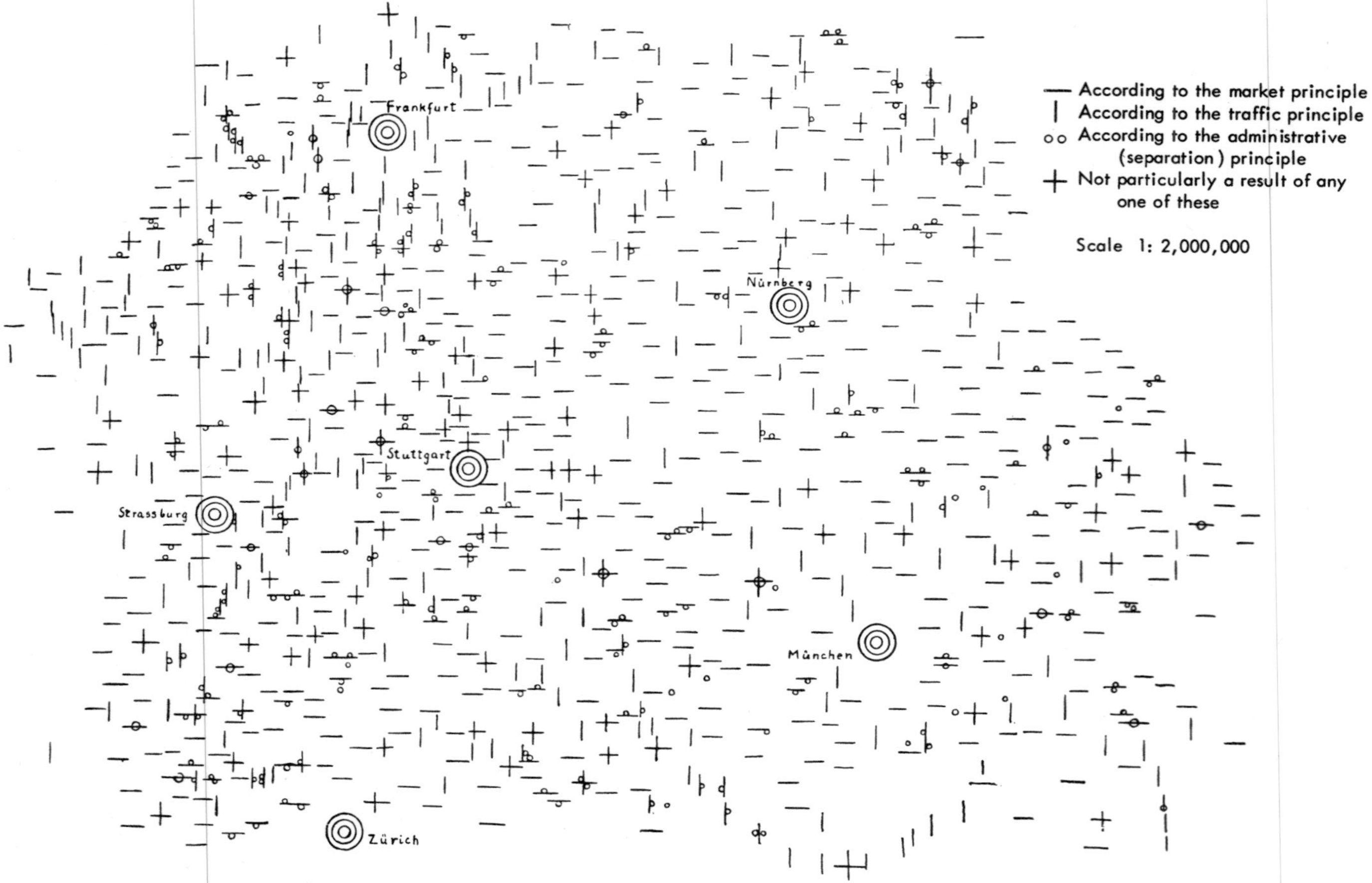
Frankfurt
Nürnberg
Stuttgart
Strassburg
München
Zürich
According to the market principle
According to the traffic principle
According to the administrative (separation) principle
Not particularly a result of any one of these
Scale 1: 2,000,000

MAP 5
The Three Principles of Location of the Central Places

BIBLIOGRAPHY

BOOKS

1. Baskin, Carlisle W., "A Critique and Translation of Walter Christaller's *Die zentralen Orte in Süddeutschland.*" Doctoral dissertation, University of Virginia, 1957.

2. Berry, B. T. L., and Allen Pred, *Central Place Studies: A Bibliography of Theory and Applications (Bibliography Series, No. 1)*, Philadelphia: 1961. Begins with a review of central place theory and of Christaller's *Die zentralen Orte in Süddeutschland.*

3. Christaller, Walter, *Die Ländliche Siedlungsweise im Deutschen Reich und ihre Beziehungen zur Gemeinde organization.* Stuttgart and Berlin: W. Kohlhammer, 1937. A descriptive list of different types of settlements and their population sizes in Germany, and a discussion of the factors determining them. Finally, a discussion of the "ideal scheme of market sites."

4. Daggett, Stuart, *Principles of Inland Transportation.* New York and London: Harper & Row, Publishers, 1941. See Chap. xxi, "Theories of Location," pp. 452-479.

5. Dickinson, F. G., *Distribution of Physicians by Medical Service Areas.* Chicago: Bureau of Medical Economic Research, AMA, 1954.

6. Dickinson, R. E., *City, Region and Regionalism.* London: Routledge & Kegan Paul, Ltd., 1947.

7. Duncan, Otis D., et al., *Metropolis and Region.* Baltimore: Johns Hopkins Press, 1960.

8. Fuchs, Victor R., *Changes in the Location of Manufacturing in the United States since 1929.* New Haven: Yale University Press, 1962. Contains maps, tables.

9. Hoover, E. M., *Location Theory and the Shoe and Leather Industries.* Cambridge: Harvard University Press, 1937.

10. *Interregional Highways,* House Report No. 379, 78th Cong., 2nd sess., 1944. Washington, D.C.: Government Printing Office, 1944.

11. Isard, Walter, *Location and Space-Economy.* Cambridge: Massachusetts Institute of Technology, 1956.

12. Lösch, August, *Economics of Location*. (2nd Rev. ed.), trans. Wolfgang F. Stolper. New Haven: Yale University Press, 1954. Contains maps.

13. House Committee on National Resources, *Our Cities, Their Role in the National Economy*. 75th Cong., 1st sess., Washington, D.C.: Government Printing Office, 1937. Included are many maps depicting growth of cities, which censuses they originated in, and other population characteristics. A list of other studies is given on page 71.

14. Madden, Carl H., "The Growth of the Cities in the United States: An Aspect of the Development of an Economic System." Doctoral dissertation, University of Virginia, 1954.

15. House Committee on National Resources, *The Structure of the American Economy, Part I: Basic Characteristics*. 76th Cong., 1st sess., 1939. Washington, D.C.: Government Printing Office, 1939.

16. Thünen, Johann Heinrich von, *Der isolierte Staat in Beziehung auf Landwirtschaft und Nationalökonomie* (2nd rev. ed.). Jena: 1910.

17. Vaile, R. S., *The Small City and Town*. Minneapolis: University of Minnesota Press, 1930.

18. Weber, Alfred, *Theory of the Location of Industries*. trans. C. J. Friedrich. Chicago: University of Chicago Press, 1957.

ARTICLES

1. Berry, B. J. L., and William L. Garrison, "The Functional Bases of the Central Place Hierarchy," *Economic Geography*, 34 (1958), 145-154. A listing of better-known geographical studies based on Christaller's work.

2. Berry, B. J. L., H. G. Barnum, and Robert J. Tennant, "Comparative Studies of Central Place Systems," (Final Report, NONR 2121-18, NR 389-126). Chicago: United States Office of Naval Research, Geography Branch, University of Chicago Department of Geography, 1962.

3. Brush, John E., "The Hierarchy of Central Places in Southwestern Wisconsin," *Geographical Review*, 43 (July, 1953), 380-402.

4. Christaller, Walter, "Allgemeine geographische Veraussetzungen der deutschen Verwaltungsgliederung," *Jahrbuch für Kommunalwissenschaft*, 1 (Stuttgart and Berlin: 1934), 2.

5. ———, "Rapports Functionnels Entre les Agglomerations Urbaines et les Campagnes," *Comptes Rendus du Congrès International de Géographie*, (Amsterdam: 1938), 123-137. An analysis of the function and relationship between the town and surrounding land, the types of settlements and their distribution sizes and locations. It is generally an updated discussion of *Die zentralen Orte in Süddeutschland*.

6. ———, "Raumtheorie und Raumordnung," *Archiv fur Wirtshaftsplanung*, 1 (1941), 122-126, 131-133. A discussion of the advantages of "agglomeration" of locations at centers with regard to plans and traffic routes.

7. ———, "Das Grundgerüst der räumlichen Ordnung in Europa: Die Systeme

der europäschen zentralen Orte," *Frankfurter Geographische Hefte,* 24, No. 1 (1950). Pages 5-14 give a new statement of general principles of Christaller's system of central places. The balance of the paper describes certain sections and areas of Europe in the terms of the principles.

8. ———, "Beiträge zu einer Geographie des Fremdenverkehrs," *Erdkunde,* 9 (1955), 1-19.

9. ———, "Some Considerations of Tourism Location in Europe," Paper, Third European Congress, Regional Science Association, Lund, Sweden: 1963.

10. ———, "Wandlungen des Fremdenverkehrs und der Bergstrasse, im Odenwald und im Neckartal," *Geographische Rundshau,* 15 (1963), 216-222.

11. Clark, Colin, "The Economic Functions of a City in Relation to its Size," *Econometrica,* 13, No. 2 (April, 1945), 97.

12. Cooley, Charles H., "The Theory of Transportation," *Publications of the American Economic Association* (May, 1894).

13. Dean, W. H., "The Theory of the Geographic Location of Economic Activities" (selections from Harvard doctoral dissertation—processed), Ann Arbor, Mich.: Edwards Brothers, Inc, 1938.

14. Deasy, G. F., "Sales and Service Industries in Luce County, Michigan," *Economic Journal,* 26 (1950). A sociological and historical account of development of Newberry and environs, which discusses the early establishments found there and the relationship of surrounding communities to Newberry. Included are maps of sales areas of selected retail stores and service establishments in Newberry; a map of the location of Newberry with respect to other similar and larger cities which are equally spaced; maps of smaller towns, mostly in the southern half of a circle; U.S. maps of purchase areas of wholesale supplies; and U.S. maps of sales areas of products produced in Newberry which have from local to nationwide distribution.

15. Fleming, J. B., and F. H. Green, "Some Relations Between Country and Town in Scotland," *The Scottish Geographical Magazine,* 68 (Edinburgh: April, 1952), 2-12.

16. Grigsby, S. E., and H. Hoffsommer, "Rural Social Organization of Frederick County, Maryland," *University of Maryland AES Bulletin* No. A-51 (College Park, Maryland: March, 1949). A system of classifying cities, towns, villages, and other identified places in Frederick County by the number of kinds of services and service classifications. Symbols are used. There are many good tables and clear descriptions.

17. Harris, C., "The Functional Classification of Cities in the United States," *Geographical Review,* 33 (1943), 86-99. Topics include:
    The Method: Table I—Criteria Used in Classifying Cities

    The Functional Classification
      Manufacturing cities
      Retail centers
      Diversified cities

Wholesale centers
Transportation centers
Mining towns
University towns
Resort and retirement towns
Other types of cities
Location of cities

18. Kolb, J. H., and L. J. Day, "A Study of Trends in Walworth County, Wisconsin, 1911-13 to 1947-48," *Interdependence in Town and County Relations in Rural Society*. Research Bulletin 172, Agricultural Experiment Station, Madison: University of Wisconsin, December, 1950. Deals with the classification of service centers by service institutions. There are tables, maps, charts, and graphs illustrating much statistical data.

19. Krzyzanowski, Witold, "Literature of Location of Industries," *Journal of Political Economy*, 35 (1927), 278ff.

20. Kneedler, Grace, "An Economic Classification of Cities," *Municipal Year Book*. Chicago: The International City Managers Association, 1945.

21. McCarty, H. H., "A Functional Analysis of Population Distribution," *Geographical Review*, 32 (1942), 282-293.

22. Pred, Allan, "Industrialization, Initial Advantages, and American Metropolitan Growth," *Geographical Review*, 55 (April, 1965), 158-185.

23. Predöhl, Andreas, "The Theory of Location in its Relation to General Economics," *Journal of Political Economy*, 36 (1928). Predöhl bases his argument—that "there is no logical difference between the labor factor and any other local factor"—on Alfred Marshall.

24. Thomas, Edwin N., "Toward an Expanded Central-Place Model," *Geographical Review*, 51 (1961), 400-411.

25. Tobler, Waldo R., "Geographic Area and Map Projection," *Geographical Review*, 52 (1963), 59-78, esp. 74-75.

26. Ullman, E., "Theory of Location of Cities," *American Journal of Sociology*, 46 (1940-41), 853-864. A short criticism of Christaller's explanation of the development of a system of central places.

27. Vining, R., "A Description of Certain Spatial Aspects of an Economic System," *Economic Development and Cultural Change*, 3, No. 2 (January, 1955), 147-195.

28. ———, "Delimitation of Economic Areas: Statistical Conceptions in the Study of the Spatial Structure of an Economic System," *Journal of the American Statistical Association*, 48 (March, 1953), 44-64. Vining reviews Don J. Bogue's, *State Economic Areas—A Description of the Procedure Used in Making a Functional Grouping of Counties of the United States*. Washington: 1951.

74
75
76
77
79
81
83
87
88